Learning Logic

A Practical Guide to Critical Thinking

CUSTOM EDITION

Onzième Edition
PUBLISHING COMPANY

Learning Logic

A Practical Guide to Critical Thinking

A TEXTBOOK

WILLIAM SMITH

SIMONE RUSSELL

Onzième Edition

PUBLISHING COMPANY

Onzième Edition
PUBLISHING COMPANY

Copyright © 2017 by William Smith and Simone Russell
Cover designed by Adel Shafik

Published by Onzième Edition.
http://www.onzieme11edition.com

ISBN 978-0-9995740-4-1

Onzième Edition is a registered trademark of Onzième Edition Publishing Company.

Inquiries: http://www.onzieme11edition.com

Printing number: 9 8 7 6 5 4 3 2 1

Printed in the United States of America

TABLE OF CONTENTS

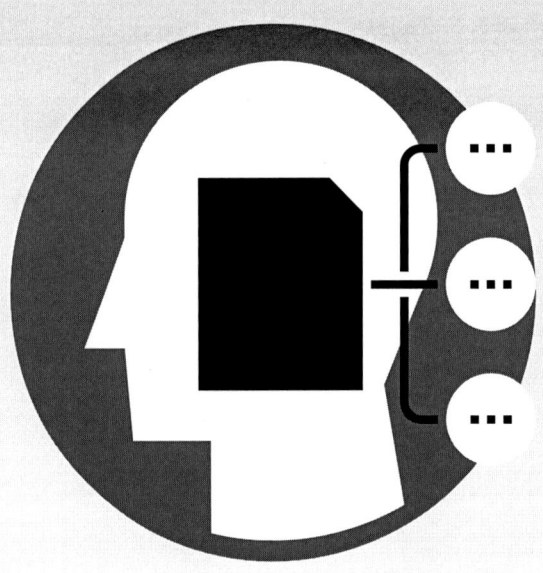

CHAPTER ONE

THE ESSENTIALS

PART ONE

||||||||||||||||||||||||||||||||||||||||||||||||||||||||||||||||||||||||||||||||||||||||||||||||||||||||||||||||||||||

CRITICAL THINKING AND LOGIC

 ## THINKING CRITICALLY: GOOD VS. BAD THINKING

All of us go through school, i.e., elementary school, junior high school, and most of us, high school, etc. All of us are graded on how well we are able to translate what we think in our heads to the written word in the form of papers and essays. Much of high school however is spent on the mechanics of writing and less on analyzing how well we think. To this point, logic as a specific course takes as its foundation, the study of how well we think or reason. It is often not built into the elementary, junior high, or high school curricula. One usually does not take a logic class until college, albeit, this is not to say that all college students end up taking a logic class either. In other words, those who do not find oneself in college taking a critical thinking class assume they have learned to think well, because they made it through high school and especially if they earned all As. Yet these folks have never had any formal or even informal training in the area. This is a problem, a personal and social one. We are allowed to have babies, get married, make decisions that impact our futures, vote on future presidents and political candidates, smoke, drive cars, and have jobs before we learn how to think well. For many of those who do not attend college and some that do can literally spend their entire lives without ever knowing how to think well and understand what is good thinking. Without knowing how to recognize our mistakes in thinking, we are unable to improve in the skill of thinking well and thus persist in our delusion that we are thinking well when in fact we may not be.

The task of this handbook is practical in nature, but its practicality does not diminish its significance. This handbook is designed for the beginner or intermediate thinker, a high school student, or first or second year college student to help students unpack the basic elements of thinking and understand what, for example, makes for good thinking. In other words, this handbook is to help students think about their own thinking to ensure good thinking and avoid bad thinking.

There are two different but often related ways to learn how to distinguish good from bad thinking: one is a) critical thinking, and the other is b) logic. In distinguishing them, we do not mean they are wholly distinct. Rather in distinguishing them, we mean to only highlight that critical thinking per se is broader than logic and includes the types of reasoning we perform every day in our lives and represents more than just argument structure. Logic on the other hand is quite narrow and involves the formal study of the normative structure of reasoning and argumentation – i.e., the science of reasoning. In short, critical thinking employs the particular tools of logic to carry out its agenda, but is not limited to logical analysis only. Logic as a tool however remains particular and does not carry out all the techniques of critical thinking.

A CAVEAT: GOOD THINKING IS NOT SYNONYMOUS WITH BEING A GOOD PERSON - OR IS IT?

When we use the term "good thinking," we are not claiming that the person using good thinking is a good person. "Good thinking" and "good persons" are two different types of judgments. Good thinkers can equally be good or bad persons. Yet many of us equate being a good person with the skill of thinking well, i.e., critically. Those who can think critically through all possibilities and offer an intelligent position often leads to decisions or positions that achieve their desired ends. Too often however critical thinking can be used for wicked ends as easily as it can be used to achieve good ends.

Many cases can be cited as excellent examples of how critical thinking can be used for wicked ends: Historically we just have to look at the Nazi regime during World War II, Stalin of the Soviet Union, etc. But we could easily just look to any great story either in print or film. Most movies have a protagonist and a villain, both of which exercise critical thinking to achieve their intended goals. Why do you think many films, at least in the United States, end with the protagonist winning – is it because of culture, tradition, wishful thinking, or is there something intrinsic about good critical thinking that leads to positive ends?

Quick Exercise

- Take a moment to make a list of books, films, or personal experiences where critical thinking was used effectively for both wicked and good ends.

Debate

- What do you think the relationship between thinking well and being a good person actually is and how it ought to be? Should they be distinct or should good critical thinking only be associated with good persons?

To help frame this debate, the Association of Certified Fraud Examiners (ACFE), a professional organization created in 1988 and centered on understanding fraudulent behavior, developed a list of ten critical thinking errors employed by those who commit fraud: • rationalization • instant gratification • disregard for authority • being overly

optimistic • sense of entitlement • lack of remorse •
peer or financial pressure •
inadequate fear of punishment • egoism/narcissism
• diffusion of harm.

Thus, the ACFE orga-
nization does argue that
psychological factors
ought to be included in
evaluating whether or not
critical thinking ought to
be considered good or
erroneous. Critical thinking under the influence of
these psychological factors

10 CRITICAL THINKING ERRORS

Rationalization
Instant gratification
Disregard for authority
Being overly optimistic
Sense of entitlement
Lack of remorse
Peer or financial pressure
Inadequate fear of punishment
Egoism/narcissism
Diffusion of harm
                    −ACFE 2013

PART ONE

do create thinking errors. What do you think? Do you think psychological states ought to be factored into the debate as to when we
should consider the employment of thinking well as good or bad?

WHAT IS CRITICAL THINKING

Critical thinking is the skill of thinking purposely in a clear, reasonable, and consistent manner. Broader in scope than logic, it not only
includes the structure, process, or evaluation of argument's, but it
considers all aspects of the thinking that goes into constructing and
evaluating arguments. Critical thinking and logic critical thinking
are often times informal and employ the power of logic to evaluate
the relationship between many of claims made in an argument. Logic

however is more formal and employs normative rules. Let's turn our attention to logic.

WHAT IS LOGIC

Some of you might be surprised to learn that there is a structure to thinking – there is an internal system of relationships and patterns that make up thinking. Logic in particular is the study of that type of thinking that leads directly to claims, or inferences, drawn from information we already know – in other words, logic is the study of how we reason, of how we infer one claim from another, of how we make a new claim that we did not know before from ones we already know to be true. Things we know to be true are often treated like facts and these facts then act as support or evidence for something we do not know. In other words, logic involves the relationship between what we call a premise, or the evidence or supporting claims, and the conclusion, the claim that is being supported. Often times, logic is explained as the science of reasoning because it seeks to identify, unpack, and make known this internal structure of making claims. In this way, logic is the study of the principles of reasoning and these principles help us determine whether one's way of reasoning is correct or incorrect – or good or bad respectively.

In practical terms, we can see logic as useful in making decisions, where in approaching a problem we at first do not know what to do, but drawing on information we do know or gather, we try to figure out the best course of action. That decided action is your claim, or inference, and the process of deriving it, is logic. Later on, we will use the term "conclusion" more often than the term "inference." That said, sometimes philosophers use inference as both a) the decided claim (aka the conclusion) and b) the process of inferring that claim, as in "her focus on ritual and order, and by inference organizational religion." This book will use the term inference in both ways and the term logic will often be used interchangeably with inference. With this in mind, we can see that logic is both a) a study of reasoning and b) the process of reasoning, i.e., of deriving a new claim from other claims, or the process of deriving a new claim from other claims.

Another way to think about logic is to view it as the science of argument making and evaluation. Logic helps us objectively evaluated whether a presented argument is either good or bad by form or by support. The latter we call formal logic and the latter informal logic. Before we can get at how to make or evaluate an argument which generates an inference, we have to understand what an argument is.

PART TWO

||||||||||||||||||||||||||||||||||||||||||||||||||||||||||||||||||||||||||||||||||||||||||||||||||||||||||||||||||||||||||||||||||||

ARGUMENTS

 WHAT IS AN ARGUMENT

We come across argument making everywhere in our daily lives, in the newspapers, on the news, among our friends and family, and of course in school. That said, however, what we mean by an argument is very specific and does not usually include the informal discussions we have with our peers or family members that often involve emotions and causal commentary.

> *An argument is a series of statements whereby at least one statement claims to support another statement.*

What we like about this definition is its simplicity, which makes it easy to remember and easy to unpack. There are three separate but interrelated parts to this definition:

- **First Part**: "a series of statements"
- **Second Part**: "at least one statement claims to support"
- **Third Part**: "another statement"

Let us break down each of these three different parts:

FIRST PART OF THE DEFINITION "A SERIES OF STATEMENTS"

The emphasis here is on two items: "series" and "statements."

1. By "**series**" we only mean that there must be "more than one." So by a series of statements," the definition means that for an argument to be an argument, there must be "more than one" statement present. This is the most basic rule of an argument.

If there is only one statement, then an argument is not present, even if the statement is an opinion, such as "Hilary Clinton should have won the 2016 Presidential Election." We will come back to this point shortly. For now, single statements, even if they are opinions, are not arguments. Arguments must have two or more statements in order to be present. This does not mean however that if you have any two statements present then you have an argument. An inference must be made in terms of support. More about this when we discuss the second part of the definition. Suffice it to say here that before you can even consider whether an argument is being made, you must have at least two statements. But how are we to understand what a statement is?

WHAT ARE STATEMENTS

2. By "**statement**," we mean something very specific, namely "a declarative sentence that can be relatively proven true or false." By **declarative** we refer to only sentences that explain or declare something, such as the world is round." While all logic books will agree that statements must be declarative, not all however will use the soft definition of statement that this book is using. For example, many logic books will use a strict definition of a statement, namely that "a

sentence that is true or false." Here, a declaration of any kind must be either true or false in order to be used in an argument. And really there is a huge debate in logic about what constitutes a statement or not. For example, the concept of a nonexistent object, like a white elephant, God, or Pegasus, has puzzled many logicians over the years. How do we handle objects that do or may not exist? That said, the approach taken here in this textbook is to introduce students to the basic elements of logic and critical thinking in order to help them think well. Thus, we want to introduce declarative statements as broadly as we can and show students the functionality of these as it pertains to argument making. That said, let's take a moment to further explain why we are not using the strict definition, but instead using the softer version of "relatively proven true or false."

By defining a declarative statement as strictly as "a sentence that is true or false" certain problems emerge – it does not allow for the reality that some sentences are statements that do not have a simple true or false value. Let's first look at some statements that have a simple true or false value: if I say "the grass is green," this statement is simply true, unless it's winter and the grass is brown, in which case the statement is false. But the point here is that the truth value of these types of statements are simply either true or false. One way we can prove truth value here is by looking outside and observing the grass. Other statements that have clear truth-value include the following:

Declarative statements that have *obvious* truth-value

- Ronald Reagan was president in 1985.
- Amazon.com is the largest online retailer.
- Batman is also Bruce Wayne.

- Bob Kane and Bill Finer created the DC comic fictional superhero, Batman, in 1939.
- The Santa Claus of the United States originally wore a green winter coat in Washington's Irving' *History of New York* (1809).
- Brad Pitt and Angelina Jolie split up in 2016.

Each of these statements is true. They are facts. How can you know the truth-value? A responsible google or library search will result in confirming or denying these facts. These are statements that are simple to verify. However, there are some statements that are a bit more complicated. Take opinionated, moral or religious statements such as the following:

> Declarative statements that have *less obvious* truth-value

- God is love.
- Polygamy is morally acceptable.
- The Harry Potter literary series by J.K. Rowling are the most creative adolescent fantasy novels of the early 21st century.
- Science fiction movies are the most progressive movies of our times.
- A president should not use the phrase "radical Islam" in a public speech.

These statements require more than a simple observation to determine truth or falsity. Yet, each of these statements can be relatively proven true or false based on the strength of the support or evidence provided. For example, let's take the statement "God is love" and provide support for this statement:

If God represents the best part of humanity, then God is love. God does represent the best part of humanity. Therefore, God is love.

I think we would all agree that based on this evidence, i.e., if we just assume for the moment that the statements #1 and #2 are true regardless as to whether we actually do believe them to be true, then the statement "God is love" must be true. That said, however, we could equally provide other support that does not support this claim.

IF GOD IS LOVE, THEN THERE WOULD BE NO SUFFERING IN THE WORLD. BUT THERE IS SUFFERING IN THE WORLD. THEREFORE, GOD IS NOT LOVE.

I think we would all agree that based on this evidence, i.e., if we just assume for the moment that the statements, #1 and #2 are true, then the statement "God is not love" must be true. But "God is not love" contradicts "God is love." So, here we have a case where the statement "God is love" can be equally true or false based on the support provided. And it is precisely because of this relativity that this textbook uses the soft definition for statements – "a sentence that can be relatively proven true or false."

The statement "God is love" is unlike the statement "The grass is green," and yet is it "relatively provable true or false." For the purpose of this textbook, both types of declarative statements are considered within the broad range of statements. We can conclude from this discussion that only statements are used in arguments.

Should you come across any non-statements in an argument, such as a question or exclamation, you must seek to do one of two things, either a) eliminate them from the argument by omitting them or b) restate the sentence in such a way that it becomes a statement.

3. DO NOT USE THESE IN ARGUMENTS: What are sentences that are not statements and thus not used in argument making?

These include three important types of sentences: a) imperative, b) exclamatory, and c) interrogative sentences.

Imperative sentences
These sentences issue commands or express wishes, suggestions, desires, warnings, or requests that end in a period or exclamation mark.

- Stop!
- Watch for falling rocks.
- Meet me at the movies.
- Respond immediately.
- Let us study together.

Exclamatory sentences
These are sentences that express strong emotion and always are punctuated with an exclamation mark. These sentences are often avoided from use in an argument because they act to persuade by emotion and often cloud the actual facts involved in the evidence.

- The inauguration is going to be great!
- Finally, someone who listens to me!
- I have to pass this class!
- You are the best!
- I do not know what to do!

Interrogative sentences
These are the easiest sentences to spot and should never be used in an argument, because they do not express a clear and specific claim. Interrogative sentences are nothing other than questions and sentences that end in a question mark.

- Who does this person think he is?
- Don't you like logic yet?

- Why are you doing that?
- Are you going to the movies?
- How are you?

One Caveat: Often times people will use what we call **rhetorical questions**, or questions that either already assume an obvious response or do not have a clear answer. These figures of speech in the form of a question are designed to create a particular effect, whether the effect be to persuade, to emphasize a significant point, or to create a literary mood. Whatever the reason, rhetorical questions are not encouraged and can often be misleading in an argument. Examples of rhetorical questions to avoid:

- What is the meaning of life?
- Are you really that naïve?
- Doesn't everyone strive for success?
- Don't you value your life?
- Is an Imam Muslim?

Whenever you encounter a rhetorical question such as these, the arguer often expects you to know the answer. Thus, when you recreate the arguer's argument, you will want to restate the question as an answer in the form of a declarative statement.

For example, let's take the following argument where one of the premises is acting as a rhetorical question:

DOESN'T EVERYONE STRIVE FOR SUCCESS? THEREFORE WHEN PEOPLE AT FIRST DON'T SUCCEED, THEY WILL TRY TO DO BETTER THE SECOND TIME AROUND.

We would rewrite the question in the form of a declarative statement, which gives us the following argument:

PEOPLE STRIVE FOR SUCCESS. THEREFORE WHEN PEOPLE AT FIRST DON'T SUCCEED, THEY WILL TRY TO DO BETTER THE SECOND TIME AROUND.

The second version is an argument, while the former is not as written. Just remember, you may have to rewrite some sentences in order to turn non-statements into statements in order to make the series of statements an argument.

SECOND PART OF THE DEFINITION
"AT LEAST ONE STATEMENT CLAIMS TO SUPPORT"

Now that we understand that an argument must have more than one statement and the most commonly used and accepted statements are declarative statements, this does not mean that any two or more statements make an argument. An argument must claim to establish a specific inferential relationship, or a relationship of support, between statements in order for an argument to occur. Let's take a look at the full definition again and recognize that we are unpacking the second part of this definition, which we now know involves some kind of inference:

> *An argument is a series of statements whereby* **at least one statement claims to support** *another statement.*

Now let's get back to unpacking.

MORE THAN ONE STATEMENT

First, we must explain that the statement that claims to support another statement is called a premise and the definition emphasizes the idea that "at least one statement" or "at least one premise" is providing, or claiming to provide, the support of another statement. In other words, for any given argument, there must be at least one premise.

Every argument must have one or more premise(s). Arguments then can be quite simple containing one premise and one statement that is being supported by that statement, such as the following:

ARNOLD SCHWARZENEGGER SHOULD NOT HAVE WON THE GUBERNA-
TORIAL RECALL ELECTION IN 2003, BECAUSE HE HAD NO EXPERIENCE
AS A POLITICIAN AT THE TIME.

or

SCHOOL VOUCHERS THAT PROVIDE PARENTS WITH FINANCIAL SUPPORT
TO SEND THEIR CHILDREN TO A PRIVATE SCHOOL SHOULD BE ACCEPT-
ABLE BECAUSE SCHOOL VOUCHERS GIVE PARENTS MORE CONTROL
OVER WHICH SCHOOL IS BEST FITTED FOR THEIR CHILD.

Here each argument contains only one premise, or supporting state-ment: in the first argument the premise is "he had no experience as a politician at the time" and, in the second argument, the premise is "school vouchers give parents more choice and control over which school is best fitted for their child."

Yet arguments can be more complicated containing more than one premise, such as the following:

ARNOLD SCHWARZENEGGER SHOULD NOT HAVE WON THE GUBERNA-
TORIAL RECALL ELECTION IN 2003, BECAUSE HE HAD NO EXPERIENCE
AS A POLITICIAN AT THE TIME, HE WAS MORE WELL-KNOWN FOR
HIS BODY-BUILDING THAN HIS CAPACITY TO LEAD POLITICALLY, AND
WAS A CELEBRITY.

In this example there are three premises that claim to support another statement. This just goes to show that arguments can come in a variety of shapes and sizes so to speak, where the more premises you add, the more dynamic the argument becomes.

WHAT DOES A PREMISE REALLY DO

2. So what does a premise really do? Premises essentially are bits of evidence that are used to support, or at least claim to support, another statement, which is called a **conclusion, or inferential claim**. A conclusion is a statement that is being supported by the premises. By "support," we mean that some inference, or new piece of information, can be drawn from the evidence or premises given. For example, consider the following two statements:

PAUL MCCARTNEY WAS ONE OF THE LEAD SINGERS FOR THE BEATLES.
ALL MEMBERS OF THE BEATLES WERE MILLIONAIRES.

From these statements, we can make the following inference, or conclusion:

PAUL MCCARTNEY MUST BE A MILLIONAIRE.

So, this gives us a whole argument, one that includes evidence or support, namely a premise, and a statement that is being supported, namely the conclusion:

PAUL MCCARTNEY WAS ONE OF THE LEAD SINGERS FOR THE BEATLES.
ALL MEMBERS OF THE BEATLES WERE MILLIONAIRES. THEREFORE, PAUL
MCCARTNEY MUST BE A MILLIONAIRE.

Now we can see what we mean by "support." The last statement is a statement containing a new piece of information, namely "Paul McCartney must be a millionaire," and it only makes sense when it is supported or inferred from the two pieces of evidence/premises that are acting as facts.

What is important here is that premises are only **claiming to** support a conclusion, but they do not in fact always do. **So an argument can occur even if the premises or evidence provided do not in fact support the conclusion**.

> IF IT RAINS, THEN THE GRASS IS WET. WELL, THE GRASS IS WET. THEREFORE, IT MUST HAVE RAINED.

> SOME MUSICIANS WENT TO SCHOOL WITH PARIS HILTON. KATY PERRY IS A MUSICIAN. THEREFORE, KATY PERRY WENT TO SCHOOL WITH PARIS HILTON.

Here we have two arguments, each of which that have two premises, but neither set of premises support the conclusion drawn. The first argument contains premises, "If it rains, then the grass is wet" and "Well, the grass is wet," and the second argument has two premises: "Some musicians went to school with Paris Hilton" and "Katy Perry is a musician." Even if we accepted each of these two supporting statements in each of the arguments as true, the conclusion for each do not follow. In the first argument, the conclusion "It must have rained" is not true because certainly the grass could have gotten wet by sprinklers, not the rain. In the second argument, the conclusion, "Katy Perry went to school with Paris Hilton, is not true as well, because the term, "some" means "at least one," and since the premise states that at least one mucisian went to school with Paris Hilton, there is no reason to believe that Katy Perry was one of them. Moreover, just for fun, we do know that Katy Perry briefly went to Dos Pueblos High School in Santa Barbara and Paris Hilton briefly went to Dwight School in New York. Thus, each of these arguments are bad. Despite this, each of the passages do meet our criteria of an argument, because the premises are nevertheless claiming to support the conclusion, even though they do in fact not.

Obviously, on the other hand, we can have passages where the premises do support the conclusion:

> IF IT RAINS, THEN THE GRASS IS WET. WELL, IT IS RAINING OUTSIDE. THEREFORE, THE GRASS IS WET.

> ALL MEN ARE MORTAL. SOCRATES IS A MAN. THEREFORE, SOCRATES IS MORTAL.

These two passages are also arguments, because the premises claim to support the conclusion and in fact since the premises do support the conclusion, the argument is a good argument. In the end, arguments can be good or bad, based on how well the premises do in fact support the conclusion. If an argument contains premises that do not support the conclusion, then the argument is a bad one. If the argument contains premises that do in fact support the conclusion, then it is a good argument. But again the take away here is that in order for a series of statements to be an argument, there must be at least two statements, whereby at least one, i.e., the premise, claims to support (yet even if it turns out it does not) another statement, the conclusion.

PATTERNS OF NON-ARGUMENTS

3. Patterns of Non-arguments: We have learned that arguments occur provided that some support is given, regardless of whether the support actually proves the inference or conclusion true. There are however some passages that look like arguments, but they are in fact not arguments. In logic, we call these passages **non-arguments** precisely because these passages meet the criteria of having more than one statement, but an argument is in fact not present. Non-arguments do not makes claims and do not provide evidence for those claims. Let's briefly introduce some of these common non-argument patterns to give you an idea of what we mean.

Expository Passages

Let's start with one non-argument pattern called **expository**. Expository passages are passages that provide information about a given topic, often in terms of describing something. But no inference is being made. For example:

> CAYUCOS IS A TOWN OF ABOUT 2,000, OVERLOOKING THE PACIFIC OCEAN. IT HAS ONLY ONE MAIN STREET AND HAS ONE STOPLIGHT.

Here we get four bits of information about Cayucos, namely it's "a town of about 2,000," "it overlooks the Pacific Ocean," "it has only one main street," and it "has one stoplight." But notice that there is no claim that is being suppored by those four other statements of facts. For this reason, this series of statements is not an argument and since it only provides factual pieces of data about Cayucos, this is an expository passage.

However, if I added the additional statement below, then the non-argument pattern becomes an argument:

> CAYUCOS IS A WONDERFUL PLACE TO GET AWAY FROM ALL THE PRESSURES OF EVERYDAY LIFE.

Now we have the following series of statements:

> CAYUCOS IS A TOWN OF ABOUT 2,000, OVERLOOKING THE PACIFIC OCEAN. IT HAS ONLY ONE MAIN STREET AND HAS ONE STOPLIGHT. THUS, CAYUCOS IS A WONDERFUL PLACE TO GET AWAY FROM ALL THE PRESSURES OF EVERYDAY LIFE.

With this additional statement, we have created an argument, because the other four statements do in fact claim to support the conclusion that "Cayucos is a wonderful place to get away from all the pressures of everyday life."

There are other types of passages that are common non-argument patterns. Two key ones here include **conditional statements** and **explanations**.

Conditional Statements

One important point that may not be intuitive is that a conditional statement, i.e., a statement that uses the operators, "if...then...", is understood in logic as one statement. Conditional statements however do not just come in the form of, for example, "If A, then B." Conditional statements can look like the following as well:

A IF B
B ONLY IF B
A IS A SUFFICIENT CONDITION FOR B
B IS A NECESSARY CONDITION FOR B

Each of these types of statements are conditional statements and can be rewritten in the form of "If A, then B." Knowing this will however be more important later in the book. For now, let's just focus on conditional statements that take the form of "If A, then B," where statement A is called the **antecedent**, and statement B is called the **consequent**. Conditional statements are made up of an antecedent and a consequent, much like any hypothetical situation. An antecendent is a statement that sets up, precedes, or anticipates another event, and the consequent is the event that is expected to occur or follow the antecendent. Statements A and B are thus not linked by inference, but only *relationship*, whereby should A or the antecendent occur, then B or the consequent is expected to occur.

PART TWO

No conditional statement that only states "If A (antecedent), then B (consequent)" provides evidence to support another statement. For this reason, all conditional statements are treated as one claim or statement. As one statement, no conditional statement by iteself can be considered an argument.

For example:

> IF THE RUSSIANS DID NOT INTERVENE IN THE 2016 PRESIDENTIAL ELECTIONS, **THEN** DONALD TRUMP WOULD NOT HAVE BEEN ELECTED AS THE PRESIDENT OF THE UNITED STATES.

An argument is not present here. Why? Because *all conditional statements are treated as single statements in logic* and as single statements, conditional statements cannot constitute an argument. All arguments need at least two statements and a conditional statement is treated as one statement. Moreover, what is being expressed in this conditional statement is a relationship between the Russians intervening and an elected president of Donald Trump. This example is not saying that the Russians intervention caused or proves that Donald Trump won. It just merely creates a relationship between them.

Let's take another conditional statement and stay with the political theme but from another perspective.

> IF SUSAN RICE UNMASKED THE NAMES OF TRUMP'S CAMPAIGN ASSOCIATES WHO WERE CAUGHT UP IN SURVEILLANCE EFFORTS AND SPREAD THOSE NAMES TO OTHER INTELLIGENCE AGENCIES FOR POLITICAL PURPOSES, **THEN** SHE COMMITTED A CRIME AND IS SUBJECT TO JAIL TIME.

While this looks like an argument because it appears to create some causal or correlational links between two ideas, namely "unmasking" and "spreading of names," in what appears to result in some kind of inference, namely "she committed a crime and is subject to jail time," this statement is still just one conditional statement. It acts simply as one "if…then…" statement. And, in logic, conditional statements by themselves are not treated as arguments. This is precisely because it is a conditional statement. Another example:

> IF PRICEWATERHOUSECOOPERS PROMOTES ALL GENDERS EQUALLY, THEN DELOITTE PROMOTES ALL GENDERS EQUALLY.

When we write a statement like this, we are not proving that Deloitte promotes all genders equally because PricewaterhouseCoopers does; but instead we are saying that as long as PricewaterhouseCoopers promotes all genders, then it's reasonable to expect Deloitte does too. *A relationship between antecedent and consequent is drawn, not a conclusion.*

Let's take one more example:

> IF TODAY IS WEDNESDAY, THEN TOMORROW WILL BE THURSDAY.

This example is not actually claiming that it is Wednesday. Nor is it being claimed that tomorrow will be Thursday. Rather, the conditional statement claims that there is a relationship between Wednesday and Thursday, such that if Wednesday occurs, Thursday will follow. So a conditional statement is a statement, for it does make a claim. It is not an argument, because no support for that claim is given. Remember this.

That said, however, like many non-argument patterns, you can transform a conditional statement into an argument. Taking the last conditional statement, we can make modifcations:

> TODAY IS WEDNESDAY. THEREFORE, TOMORROW WILL BE THURSDAY.

Now two definite claims are made, the first of which is that today is Wednesday and that tomorrow will be Thursday. We thus have a premise and a conclusion, and therefore an argument. We can also transform a conditional statement into an argument by adding additional statements to the conditional statement:

> IF TODAY IS WEDNESDAY, THEN TOMORROW WILL BE THURSDAY. TODAY IS IN FACT WEDNESDAY. THEREFORE, TOMORROW WILL BE THURSDAY.

Here we have a conditional statement, yes, but the passage also gives us another claim, namely "Today is in fact Wednesday." We now can see that the second claim or premise is a fact and acts to affirm the antecedent in the conditional statement.

> IF TODAY IS WEDNESDAY (**antecedent**), THEN *TOMORROW WILL BE THURSDAY* (**consequent**).
> TODAY IS IN FACT WEDNESDAY (**affirms the antecedent**)

So, from these two premises, a third statement can be inferred, namely the the consequent in the original conditional statement, "Tomorrow will be Thursday. We have an argument. In summary, remember, if you have only one conditional statement that includes both an antecedent and consequent, but no other premises, then an argument is not present.

Explanations

Now, with conditional statements it is quite easy to distinguish them from arguments, due to their "if/then" form. Unfortunately, explanations have no such distinguishing form that will enable us to separate them from arguments by using form only. Adding to our difficulty is the fact that explanations often use the same types of forms and the same types of words that we associate with arguments. Premise and conclusion indicators, a topic covered later in this chapter, occur frequently in explanations.

So how are we to distinguish explanations from arguments? Well, there is one crucial difference between an explanation and an argument. An argument expresses an inference. It attempts to prove a claim. An explanation, on the other hand, is designed to explain an accepted fact. It states the fact and tries to show how it occurred. So, an explanation is not proving anything. It is trying to explain something already accepted.

Two parts

Explanations, like arguments, can be broken into two parts: the **explanandum**, which is the fact to be explained, and the **explanans**, which are the statements that do the explaining. In terms of structure, the explanandum roughly corresponds to the conclusion of an argument and the explanans roughly corresponds to the premises. A few things are crucial in distinguishing explanations from arguments:

1. First for any passage, identify the main point, or what you would consider to be the conclusion or **explanadum**.
2. If you find that the main point is an accepted fact, then the passage is most likely an explanation. However, if the main point is debatable, then you are most likely reading an argument.
3. To help distinguish whether the main point is either an accepted fact or conclusion, ask yourself whether the other statements in the passage intend to shed light on the main point, or prove the main point. If they are intended to shed light on the main point, then you are dealing with an explanation. If they attempt to prove the main point, it is an argument. For example:

THE EPITAPH ON JIM MORRISON'S GRAVE BEARS THE GREEK INSCRIPTION "ΚΑΤΑ ΤΟΝ ΔΑΙΜΟΝΑ ΕΑΥΤΟΥ" BECAUSE HIS FATHER, GEORGE MORRISON, PLACED A FLAT STONE ON JIM MORRISON'S GRAVE IN THE EARLY 1990S.

and

GERMANY LOST WORLD WAR II DUE TO THE FACT THAT HITLER ORDERED THE GERMAN 6TH ARMY AT STALINGRAD NOT TO WITHDRAW IN ORDER TO SEEK MORE FRIENDLY GROUNDS.

These are explanations. Why? Because if we take what we think would be the supported statements, or conclusions, namely "the epitaph on Jim Morrison's grave bears the inscription of the Greek insciprtion 'kata ton Δaimona eaytoy', and "Germany lost World War II," we realize these are already facts. In other words, what appears to be conclusions are facts that we all already know to be true, or explananda. Explanandum/a are facts that are often easily known to be true through a simple google search.

In each of the two explanations, the supporting evidence, or the unkown reasons, are attempting to shed light upon how we know these facts to be true. They explain why the facts are facts. For example, in the Jim Morrison example, we learn that Jim Morrison's dad placed the engraved stone on his grave and that is why the gravestone contains the greek phrase. In the second example, we learn that the reason why Germany lost was because of a failed tactical decision on the part of Hitler. These are not proving but shedding light upon the explandanda.

Let's break this down:

Distinguising Explanations from Arguments

Explanations	Provides unknown reason(s) to explain a known fact
Arguments	Provides known fact(s) to prove unknown conclusion

Let's try to turn the Jim Morrison example into an argument:

JIM MORRISON'S FATHER, GEORGE MORRISON, PLACED A FLAT STONE
ON JIM MORRISON'S GRAVE IN THE EARLY 1990S CONTAINING THE
GREEK INSCRIPTION OF "KATA TON ΔAIMONA EAYTOY," WHICH MEANS
"TRUE TO YOUR OWN SPIRIT." THUS, MORRISON'S FATHER MUST HAVE
CONSIDERED HIS SON TO HAVE BEEN TRUE TO HIMSELF EVEN UP UNTIL
HIS UNTIMELY DEATH.

Notice in this example, the conclusion is actually something we did
not know before, and we proved this statement true by drawing on
the fact of an action that Jim Morrison's father did. In this way, the
evidence proves the conclusion true but the conclusion could also
end up being false all the while the premises still be true. This is the
nature of an argument. The truth-value of the conclusion is proven
true or false based on the premises provided.

Let's take a look at the other example about Germany losing WWII
and try to turn that into an argument:

GERMANY LOST WORLD WAR II. THEREFORE, HITLER, THE LEADER OF
THE GERMAN MILITARY AND STATE, MUST NOT HAVE BEEN AS INTEL-
LIGENT AS MANY MAKE HIM OUT TO BE.

In this passage, we actually use the known fact, "Germany lost WWII"
to make a debatable and unknown statement about the intelligence
of Hitler. In this way, we are proving that Hitler was not as smart as
we might have once thought.

At this point, let's quickly identify all the main non-argument patterns
and recognizing that each of them may at a certain point and given a
certain rearragment of statements turn out to be arguments:

PART TWO

Common Non-argument Patterns

Descriptions	Passages that describe things
Conditional statements	A single statement of the form, "if x then y"
Reports	Provide information about events
Expositions	Develop a theme or idea, but not prove anything
Illustrations	Demonstrate a point being made, not prove it
Explanations	Explain accepted fact
Suggestions	only implies or suggests an action or feeling

In the end, here, we learned that arguments CLAIM TO PROVE something we did not know was true. Non-arguments do not provide proof.

Let us turn now to the third and final part of the definition of an argument.

> *An argument is a series of statements whereby* **at least one statement claims to support** *another statement.*

⚡ THIRD PART OF THE DEFINITION "ANOTHER STATEMENT"

By now, you probably have guessed that the "another statement" that is being supported by the premise(s) is in fact what we call the

conclusion. The third part of the definition involves understanding the conclusion.

> FOR
> EVERY ARGUMENT, THERE IS ONLY ONE CONCLUISON

As we learned when distinguishing explanations from arguments, conclusions are statements that are technically not known yet, and based on the evidence provided, we infer that they are either true or false. Conclusions tell us something new.

Moreover, conclusions are the statements towards which all the premises points. It is the main point of any passage and all other points are tertiary to this one. This means that for every argument there is only one conclusion.

While we say that every argument has one conclusion, we will come to realize that by "one conclusion," we mean one main conclusion. For example:

IF A NATION OF IMMIGRANTS DOES NOT HAVE A COMMON LANGUAGE, THEN PEOPLE WITH DIVERSE BACKGROUNDSCH CANNOT UNITE. A MULTILINGUAL SOCIETY DOES NOT PROMOTE A COMMON LANGUAGE. THEREFORE, A MULTILINGUAL SOCIETY DOES NOT PROMOTE UNITY OR A COMMON BOND.

In this example, one conclusion is presented and is a bit obvious. The conclusion is "multilingual society does not promote unity or a common bond." But let's say that we wanted proof for one of the premises, namely "A multilingual society does not promote a common language." Now, we would have to provide a evidence, or a premise, that supports or claims to prove true, one of other premises. We could add a premise that shows multicultural societies speak in various languages, none of which are the same. This would definitely complicate our simple rule that every argument has one conclusion, as the premise used to support the obvious conclusion would in fact be a subconclusion to this new premise. This notion that arguments are a bit more complex will be the main topic of discussion in the next chapter when we learn to diagram arguments. We will suffice it to say for now that every argument has only one conclusion and all the other statements are acting to in one way or another claim to support the conclusion. And in logic, we like to write arguments using what is called **standard form**, where each premise is labeled on top of a solid line that represents an inference. The single conclusion should be placed below the solid line.

A Note About Writing Arguments

USING STANDARD FORM

In logic, we like to use what is called **standard form** when we try to identify and isolate each of the premises from each other and from the conclusion, where each premise is labeled on top of a solid line. the single conclusion should be placed below the solid line.

Argument With Four Premsises in Standard Form

Premise 1 (P1)
Premise 2 (P2)
Premise 3 (P3)
Premise 4 (P4)
conclusion

Some arguments do have multiple conclusions, but on a technical level, when an argument uses a premise to support two different conclusions, then two different arguments are being made. For example:

> A STUDY CITES THAT HIGH SCHOOL GRADUATES ARE UNDERPREPARED FOR COLLEGE, WHICH LEADS TO LOW COLLEGE GRADUATION RATES. THEREFORE, TO INCREASE COLLEGE GRADUATION RATES, WE NEED TO DEVELOP MORE EFFECTIVE WAYS OF TEACHING BASIC SKILLS TO HIGH SCHOOL STUDENTS, AND, ALSO, WE SHOULD RETHINK THE HIGH SCHOOL CURRICULUM TO ENSURE COLLEGE SUCCESS.

This argument shows that there is one piece of evidence, namely "A study cites that high school graduates are underprepared for college, which leads to low college graduation rates." From this one fact, two totally different conclusions are drawn. On a technical level, what you have here in this passage is two different arguments, each one with one premise and one conclusion.

For the purpose of this textbook, we will always treat arguments with mulitiple conclusions as two separate and individual arguments.

PART TWO

⚡ SUMMARY

As we have learned, in order for an argument to be present several things have to be present: all arguments have four features:

An argument must:

1. contain more than one statement
2. make an infential claim, something we did not know before (a conclusion)

3. claim to support that inferential claim (a premise)
4. not be a non-argument passage

Be sure to write these four features of an argument down.

PART THREE

||||||||||||||||||||||||||||||||||||||||||||||||||||||||||||||||||||||||||||||||||||||||||||||||||||||||||||||||||||||||||||||||||||||

INDICATOR WORDS

 IDENTIFYING PREMISES AND CONCLUSIONS

Now that you understand what an argument is, let us move to how to identify the difference between premise and conclusion. Previously, we learned that a premise is a statement that claims to support, or prove, another statement, the conclusion. In the arguments already discussed it is quite apparent what are the premises and what is the conclusion. In most arguments it is generally not that easy to distinguish the premises from the conclusion. This is a problem, because in order to analyze an argument, you have to be able to distinguish between premises and conclusion. This illustrates a basic rule: before you can analyze (or criticize) an argument, you must first understand it.

The first step in understanding an argument is breaking it down into its parts. Therefore, to correctly evaluate an argument, you have to know what the argument is claiming, i.e., "what its conclusion is," and what evidence is being offered in support of the claim, i.e., "what the premises are."

The best way to make this determination is by looking for **the main point** of the argument. Look at the argument carefully, and determine **its focal point**. This will be the argument's conclusion.

How do you then distinguish between premises and conclusions? By looking closely at the argument. You have to ask yourself what is the arguer's intent. You have to determine what is his or her main point.

What is the arguer claiming? That is going to be the conclusion. Identifying the conclusion will give you a good idea of what the premises should look like. Moreover, by identifying the conclusion, you know the other statements in the argument have to be premises, whereas if you first identified a premise, any remaining statement might be a premise or a conclusion.

Consider this example:

> SMITH SHOULD WIN THE ELECTION. WE NEED MORE QUALIFIED WOMEN IN OFFICE AND SHE IS QUALIFIED. ADDITIONALLY, HER OPPONENT, JAMES BOZO, IS INCOMPETENT.

The main point here is "Smith should win the election." The other statements all support that claim. For example, the claim that Smith's opponent is incompetent supports the claim she should win the election. The reverse is not true: the statement "Smith should win the election" tells us nothing about the competency of her opponent. One way of determining whether a statement in an argument is a premise or the conclusion is by determining whether the other statements support it, or whether it supports another statement. The premises should provide the support: the conclusion is what should be supported.

Do not be discouraged if it is difficult for you to identify the conclusion of an argument at first. It takes practice. Make sure you carefully read the arguments you are analyzing. Don't try to make snap judgments.

INDICATOR WORDS

One tool that can help you identify the different parts of arguments are **premise and conclusion indicators.** These indicators are words and phrases that serve as signposts within an argument, pointing out premises or conclusions. You do not want to be overly reliant upon indicators, because many arguments will lack indicators entirely. If you cannot analyze an argument without relying on indicators, you will have trouble with such arguments. Indicators are best used as a means of confirming your analysis: you should try to analyze the argument and then use the indicators as confirmation. If indicators are present, you should use them. One of the most common mistakes students make is to overlook the presence of indicators.

Conclusion indicators are words and phrases that occur right before a conclusion in an argument. They provide a clue that the statement following the indicator is the conclusion. For example:

> BRUCE SPRINGSTEEN IS A MAN. (PREMISE). ALL MEN ARE MORTAL. (PREMISE). **THEREFORE**, BRUCE SPRINGSTEEN IS MORTAL. (CONCLUSION).

Obviously, when we read this argument, we all recognize that the statement, "Bruce Springsteen is mortal" is the conclusion and that the other two statements are premises, or pieces of evidence that are claiming to support the conclusion. But how do we know this so easily. One way is to recognize the word, "therefore," as a conclusion indicator word. A conclusion indicator word forces us to consider the other statements as evidence or proof of accepting the truth value of the claim being made. As such there are other examples of conclusion indicator words:

Some typical conclusion indicators

therefore	thus	consequently
we may conclude	so	it follows that
as a result	entails that	we may infer
accordingly	hence	it must be that

Whenever a statement follows one of the indicators, it can generally be identified as the conclusion. Some examples (the conclusion indicator is in bold, the conclusion is in italics):

> BRUCE SPRINGSTEEN MAKES GOOD MUSIC. SINCE ALL PEOPLE WHO MAKE GOOD MUSIC HAVE WON GRAMMY AWARDS, **IT FOLLOWS THAT** *SPRINGSTEEN HAS WON A GRAMMY AWARD.*

or

> NO MAN WHO WOULD DEFRAUD HIS MOTHER IS FIT TO HOLD PUBLIC OFFICE. CONGRESSMAN SLEAZE DID THAT; **CONSEQUENTLY,** *HE IS NOT FIT FOR OFFICE.*

or

> **WE MAY INFER** *BATMAN IS NOT AFRAID OF THE DARK* BECAUSE HE OPERATES EXCLUSIVELY AT NIGHT.

Sometimes, though, there will be no conclusion indicators. In such cases, one should search for premise indicators. Premise indicators are as important in telling you the intended structure of the supporting evidence and the main point as the conclusion indicators are. Thus, just as you should memorize all the of conclusion indicators, you should memorize the following list of premise indicator words:

Some Typical Premise Indicators

because	since	for
in that	seeing that	for the reason that
given that	provided that	owing to
inasmuch as	as	as indicated by

A statement following these indicators can generally be taken as a premise. Some examples (the premise indicator is bold, the conclusion is italics):

Bolivia lost its struggle for access to the sea **because** *its army was smaller than those of Chile and Peru.*

or

There is no life on Venus **since** *the temperatures are too high and the circulating winds are too powerful.*

or

As indicated by *the story in the Daily Planet and the articles written by Lois Lane,* Clark Kent is really Superman.

If we were to take the second argument about no life on Venus, we would see that there are two premises being identified by the premise indicator word "since," both of which support the conclusion – this is also true of the last argument as well. Let's take a look at what the argument about Venus would look like in standard form:

Premise 1: The temperatures are too high (on Venus)
Premise 2: The circulating winds are too powerful (on Venus)
Conclusion: There is no life on Venus.

HIDDEN PREMISES

Often, the conclusion of an argument will rely on an assumption that is not explicitly stated as a premise in an argument. Such assumptions are called **hidden premises**. Even though such statements are not explicit in the argument, they are considered part of the argument because without these assumptions, the conclusion makes no sense.

When a person looks at an argument with a hidden premise, she generally supplies the missing information on a subconscious level without realizing that the information is missing. This is fine when the hidden premise is a trivial assumption:

FIDO IS A CAT. (PREMISE) THEREFORE, FIDO IS AN ANIMAL. (CONCLUSION)

Here the hidden premise is "All cats are animals." This is a trivial assumption, since most people already know that cats are animals.

Sometimes hidden premises conceal more controversial assumptions. In such cases, hidden premises are problematic. Unless they are identified, people may buy into these questionable premises without realizing it. For example:

LIKE SO MANY IRISH ROCK BANDS, U2 HAS A GREAT SINGER. BONO WORKS HARD AT DEVELOPING HIS VOICE AND SINGS VERY PASSIONATELY.

The conclusion is "Bono is a great singer." There are three explicit premises: "Many Irish rock bands have a great singer," "Bono works hard to develop his voice," and "Bono sings passionately." The argument also has four hidden premises, two are which are trivial, and two of which are problematic. The two trivial hidden premises are "Bono is the lead singer of U2," and "U2 is an Irish rock band." The two problematic assumptions are "If you work hard to develop your voice, then you are a great singer," and "If you sing passionately, then you are a great singer." Each of these is questionable. Bob Dylan is noted for singing passionately, but is he a great singer? I sing passionately when I'm in the shower. Does that assure you I am a great singer? And if someone who is tone deaf and who has a two-note range works hard at developing his voice, will he then be a great singer? No, he will be Michael Bolton.

When analyzing an argument, it is always best to identify any hidden premises in an argument to determine whether they are trivial. This way you can be sure you are dealing with all of the argument.

CHAPTER TWO

VISUALIZING ARGUMENTS

PART ONE

||||||||||||||||||||||||||||||||||||||||||||||||||||||||||||||||||||||||||||||||||||||||||||||||||||||||||||||||

PRESENTING ARGUMENTS LINEARLY

 ## FEATURES OF STANDARD FORM

The **standard form of presenting an argument** helps us take an argument and break down its parts into premises and a conclusion. It helps us strip away the pieces from the original prose used in order to simplify the structure of the argument. Many times an argument looks quite convincing and elegant when they are written out in prose form, but in the final anaysis the argument may not be a good one when it is unpacked. In this way, presenting arguments in standard form is very useful in logic and understanding the actual main point of an argument.

Let's take an example.

> GOD IS ALL THAT IS PERFECT. NOTHING IS PERFECT UNLESS IT EXISTS. THEREFORE, GOD MUST EXIST.

When you put an argument written in prose into standard form, you must first isolate the premises and the conclusion. Here we clearly see the first two statements are the premises and the last the conclusion. Conclusion indicator word, "therefore," makes this quite easy. First thing is to number each of the statements and place them vertically in line with one another like this:

> 1. GOD IS ALL THAT IS PERFECT.
> 2. NOTHING IS PERFECT UNLESS IT EXISTS.
> 3. THEREFORE, GOD MUST EXIST.

When presenting the argument you must identify how the premises fit together in a logical manner. Here, we realize that premise 1 clearly sets up the idea that leads to statement 2, which based on 1 and 2, gives us statement 3. We have satisfactorily set up the argument in a logical way. Also, indicator words are usually not included as part of any statement, but you can keep the conclusion indicator, as we did here, or add one if you think it helps you.

Finally, we complete the form by drawing a line above the conclusion like this:

1. GOD IS ALL THAT IS PERFECT.
2. NOTHING IS PERFECT UNLESS IT EXISTS.
3. THEREFORE, GOD MUST EXIST.

The conclusion is always at the bottom and below the line that indicates that an inference is being made from the evidence stated above. Not all arguments are simple like this one and will require a little more work. The benefit of standard form is that you can always clearly and quickly identify the conclusion, because it is always at the bottom.

ESSENTIAL FEATURES OF STANDARD FORM

- Number every statement
- Eliminate any nonstatement from the argument
- Make sure the statements are clear and concise, which requires sometimes having to rewrite them
- Remove any indicator words, unless you want to keep the conclusion indicator for clarity
- Add hidden premises if there are any

PART ONE

- Draw line above the last statement which is the conclusion indicating an inference is being made

STANDARD FORM VS. MAPPING ARGUMENTS

As we mentioned above, not all arguments are simple in that all the premises logically lead to the one conclusion. As often is the case, many arguments that we make in everyday life are more complicated, meaning we sometimes use premises that only make sense when stated with another premise, use premises that do not relate to one another and so act independently to support a conclusion, or use premises in such a way that some premises act as both a sub-conclusion to other premises or a premise to the main conclusion.

One of the greatest weaknesses of standard form is that it cannot clearly highlight for you how each of the premises act toward each other, and it is for this reason that mapping or diagramming arguments is often a more enlightening way of visualizing the structure of an argument.

PART TWO

||||||||||||||||||||||||||||||||||||||||||||||||||||||||||||||||||||||||||||||||||||||||||||||||||||||||

PRESENTING ARGUMENTS DYNAMICALLY

 ## MAPPING ARGUMENTS

Argument mapping is another way to visually show the logical structure of arguments, but it is much more instructive than standard form. Just like standard form, you will want to number each of the premises. Let's take the previous argument in standard form:

Original Argument
1. GOD IS ALL THAT IS PERFECT.
2. Nothing is perfect unless it exists.
3. THEREFORE, GOD MUST EXIST.

While this is easy to spot the conclusion, standard form fails to show us how premise 1 and premises 2 are acting toward each other in supporting the argument. Let us explain.

Notice that if we were to imagine this argument as having only one premise, either statement 1 or statement 2, the conclusion would not be obvious.

Example One
1. GOD IS ALL THAT IS PERFECT.
2. THEREFORE, GOD MUST EXIST.

OR

Example Two
1. Nothing is perfect unless it exists.
2. THEREFORE, GOD MUST EXIST.

What we realize quickly is that in order for our original argument to make sense, we NEED both premises 1 and 2. Without both of them neither argument, example one or example two, is clear. We can not logically see or infer the conclusion. In fact, in order to infer the conclusion, namely "God must exist," we need both Premise 1, "God is all that is perfect," and Premise 2, "Nothing is perfect unless it exists." Thus, this is where mapping helps us considerably.

1. When we map an argument, we want to do several things:
2. We want to visualize the relationship of each premise to each other

We want to visualize how, independently or dependently, each premise supports the conclusion.

When we diagram, we want to first identify the conclusion and from there ask yourself whether each of the premises independently or dependently support the conclusion. When we do this with our original argument, we learn that the first premise, statement 1, is acting dependently with the second premise, statement 2, to support the conclusion. So, we would diagram this argument as follows:

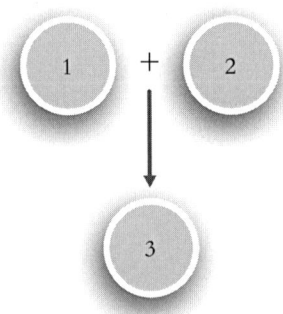

By mapping the argument, we can now quickly visualize more information about the nature and structure of this particular argument.

We can, for example, see that if we were to challenge premise 1 and show that it is in fact false, then we would show that the entire argument fails, because where two premises depend on one another: if you remove one, you remove the other. It's like an axle of a car. If one of your vehicle's operational axles is broken, your car won't go very far. On the other hand, if we had an argument where each of the premises acted independently of one another in supporting the conclusion, then we could eliminate one premise and the argument would still be intact - you would not have effectively undermined the argument as a whole. It's like a twin-engine jetliner that loses one of its propellers midflight - it can still land safely. For example:

BEFORE A TORNADO IN OKLAHOMA, (1) ALL DOMESTIC DOGS WITHIN A 30 MILE RADIUS BEGAN BARKING VOCIFEROUSLY AND (2) THE HORSES STARTED BUCKING UNCONTROLLABLY. THEREFORE, (3) ANIMALS ARE GOOD PREDICATORS OF TORNADOS.

Here we have three statements, and a conclusion indicator before statement 3 provides us with an easy way to identify the conclusion. In mapping this argument, we want to ask ourselves, does premise 1 independently or dependently, support the conclusion and we do the same for premise 2. As it turns out, we can see by way of this inquiry that premise 1, which discusses the behaviour of domestic dogs before an tornado, and premise 2, which discusses the behaviour of horses before an tornado, are not at all dependent on each other in order to support the conclusion. The conclusion talks about the broad range of "animals" and each premise provides a different example of an animal that acts strangely before a tornado. In this way, we can see that the behaviour of dogs is not depenedent on the behaviour of horses, and so we know each of the premises act independently of one another to support the conclusion. Thus, the map of this argument looks like this:

PART TWO

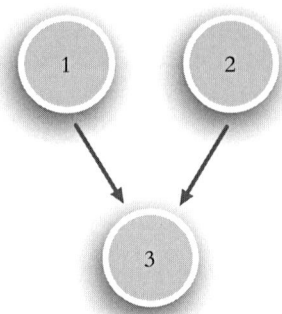

There are many other ways in which an argument can be diagrammed depending on how the premises support the conclusion, and in many arguments there are several conclusions, even though there is only one main conclusion. Here is an example:

THE NEW DESIGN OF THE APPLE IPHONE 7 IS BETTER THAN THE OLD DESIGN OF THE 6, BECAUSE THE IPHONE 7 IS WATER RESISTANT AND THE SCREEN IS MORE DIFFICULT TO CRACK. SALES OF THE IPHONE SHOULD INCREASE THIS YEAR.

First, thing you want to do is number each statement like this:

(1) THE NEW DESIGN OF THE APPLE IPHONE 7 IS BETTER THAN THE OLD DESIGN OF THE 6, BECAUSE (2) THE IPHONE 7 IS WATER RESISTANT AND (3) THE SCREEN IS MORE DIFFICULT TO CRACK. (4) SALES OF THE IPHONE SHOULD INCREASE THIS YEAR.

When you try to identify the conclusion you will notice that there really are two conclusions. There is the first statement which is a conclusion to statement 2 and 3, and we know this because of the indicator "because." Remember, "because" is a premise indicator, and here we have the following:

STATEMENT (1), BECAUSE STATEMENT (2) AND (3). (4).

Statement (1) is "the new design of the Apple iPhone 7 is better than the old design of the 6," and statement (2) is "the iPhone 7 is water resistant." Statement (3) claims that "the iphone 7 screen is more difficult to crack." So, we know because of the indicator "because" that statements 2 and 3 are supporting statement 1. But that makes statement 1 the conclusion. As it turns out, however, statement 1 also serves as a premise to statement 4, which claims "sales of the iphone should increase this year." In this way, statement 1 acts as both a sub-conclusion to premises 2 and 3, but in turn acts also as a main premise to the main conclusion 4. We map this type of arrangement as follows:

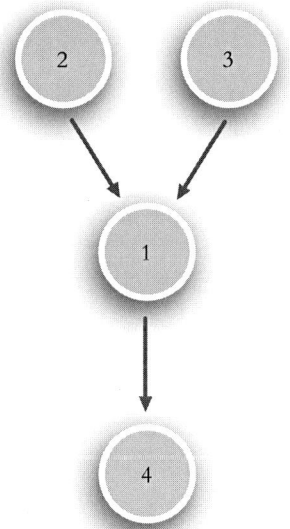

We see that premises 2 and 3 are not the main premises, but only act to support the main premise, which is statement 1. An argument like this is more likely to be similar to the ones you will encounter with your friends, colleagues, parents, and politicians.

There are many other variations of these types of maps or diagrams, but essentially we can say in mapping arguments, there are two types of arguments, simple arguments containing one-level of support and complex arguments containing multi-levels of support.

SIMPLE ARGUMENT MAPS

Simple arguments are like the first two arguments we mapped earlier in this chapter. There is one-level of support and only a few ways that the diagram can look.

Example one: *horizontal pattern with independent premises*

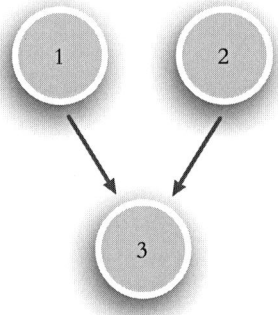

Example two: *horizontal pattern with dependent premises*

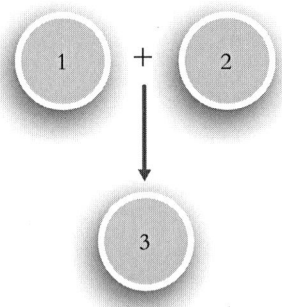

Example three: *horizontal pattern with combination*

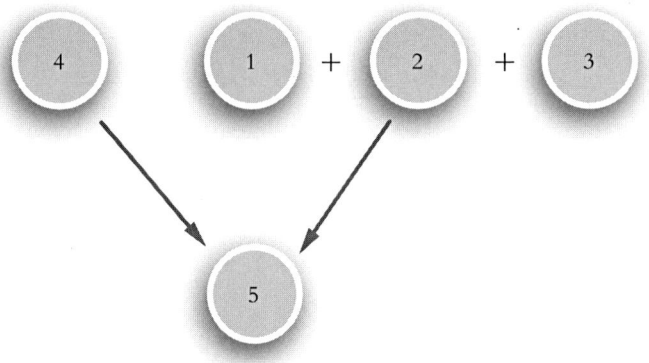

⚡ COMPLEX ARGUMENT MAPS

Complex arguments are arguments such that there are more than one level of support and because of this, there will always be at least one sub-conclusion and always one main conclusion. Let us look at some of these maps:

Continued on next page...

Example one: *Vertical pattern with indepedent premises*

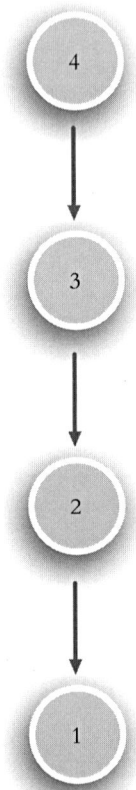

What kind of complex argument would take this pattern? Let us look at an example:

(1) EVERYONE SHOULD BE ALLOWED TO CHOOSE WHEN AND HOW THEY DIE, BECAUSE (2) PEOPLE WANT TO LIVE A LIFE AS LONG AS THAT LIFE IS WORTH LIVING. THIS IS BECAUSE (3) PEOPLE HAVE DIGNITY. THIS IS BECAUSE (4) GOD GAVE EVERYONE A SENSE OF SELF-WORTH.

This argument shows that each premise is providing evidence for a sub-conclusion, which in turn acts as a premise for the next sub-conclusion, until it reaches the main conclusion, which is statement 1, "Everyone should be allowed to choose when and how they die."

***Example two*:** *Vertical pattern with dependent premises*

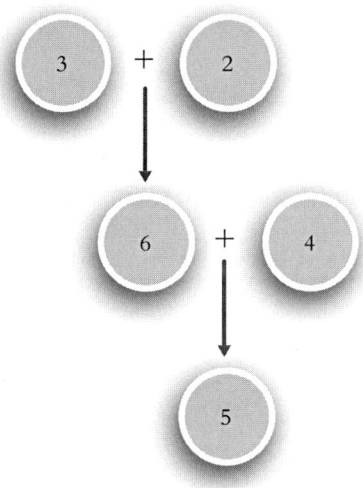

***Example three*:** *Vertical pattern with combination*

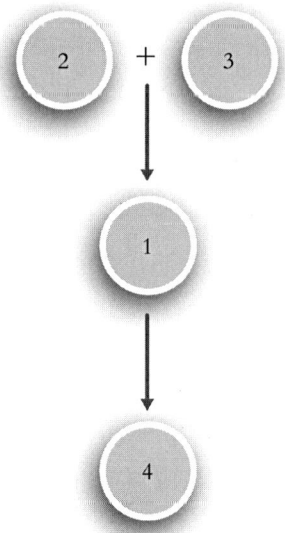

Let us look at an argument that follows this last argument map:

(1) PEOPLE WANT TO LIVE A LIFE AS LONG AS THAT LIFE IS WORTH LIVING. THIS IS BECAUSE (2) PEOPLE HAVE DIGNITY AND (3) THIS MEANS PEOPLE HAVE SELF-RESPECT. THEREFORE, (4) EVERYONE SHOULD BE ALLOWED TO CHOOSE WHEN AND HOW THEY DIE.

Now with complex arguments, the number of premises, the ways in which the premises support the sub-conclusions and main conclusion, and the number of sub-conclusions will all factor into the shape or map of the argument diagram. Thus, there are many more maps than the ones we have provided. In order to get an idea of just how various these maps can be, go pick up a local paper and turn to the opinion or editorial section - and start mapping!

CHAPTER THREE

UNDERSTANDING REASONING

PART ONE

‖‖

TYPES OF REASONING

DEDUCTIVE & INDUCTIVE REASONING

There are two basic argument types based on what type of reasoning is employed: deductive and inductive. **Deductive arguments** are arguments in which the conclusion *claims to* follow *necessarily* from the premises. By *necessarily*, we mean that the conclusion follows from the premises one-hundred percent of the time - there should be no exceptions. **Inductive arguments** however are arguments in which the conclusion *claims to* follow *with probability* from the given premises. By *with probability*, we mean that the conclusion is supported by the given premises greater than fifty-percent of the time, meaning there may be times when the premises do not always support the conclusion but the argument's reasoning may still be strong. There will always be exceptions when using this type of reasoning and yet these exceptions do not always undermine the strength of the argument.

Importantly, notice when we provide the definitions of a deductive and inductive argument we used the clause "claims to." For **deductive arguments** we say the conclusion *claims to* follow *necessarily* from the premises, and for **inductive arguments** we say the conclusion *claims to* follow *with probability* from the given premises. What this means essentially is that we can identify the types of reasoning without evaluating the actual strength of the argument - we identify only the intent of strength. Since we know that *necessity* means the conclusion follows the premises one hundred percent of the time, when we add the clause "claims to," we are saying that for an argument to be deductive, the premises are expected to support the conclusion one hundred percent of the time, even if, in the evaluation stage, we discover that the conclusion does not follow necessarily. Same for induction. An argument is inductive provided that the premises are expected to support the conclusion *with probability*, or greater than fifty percent of the time. This does not however mean that the argument provides such support.

Let's see how this idea of intent of strength plays out in the following deductive argument. A good deductive argument, one with with good logic and true premises, the conclusion will *necessarily* be true. The conclusion of a good deductive argument, then, is *certain*. For example:

ALL CATS ARE FELINES.

ALL FELINES ARE MAMMALS.

THEREFORE, ALL CATS ARE MAMMALS.

The premises in the above argument are true and *necessarily* support the conclusion. The conclusion is therefore certain. In a good deductive argument, there is no way for the premises to be true and the conclusion false. In such an argument, if you accept the premises, you must also accept the conclusion one-hundred percent of the time.

Not all deductive arguments are good, however, as we mentioned. Some have false premises and/or bad logic. This means many deductive arguments will fail to have a necessarily true conclusion. For example, this is a bad deductive argument:

ALL DOGS ARE MAMMALS.

ALL CATS ARE MAMMALS.

THEREFORE, ALL CATS ARE DOGS.

What distinguishes such arguments as deductive is the type of reasoning employed. If the arguer intends to prove the conclusion is certain,

PART ONE

then that argument is deductive even if the argument fails. The key is to separate the intent behind a deductive argument (trying to prove a conclusion is certain) from the actual result. When we judge an argument deductive, we are judging the intent, not the result.

Fortunately, we have identified several argument patterns that indicate the intent of an argument. There are two types of argument patterns, both of which will be covered in this section. There are **common deductive argument patterns** and **common inductive argument** patterns. The nice thing about knowing these patterns is that when you spot them, you will easily be able to know the intent behind the argument made and correctly identify the type of reasoning that the arguer is using. This will prove extremely invaluable when evaluating arguments later in the book.

Some textbooks refer to certain words and phrases that indicate whether an argument is deductive or inductive. For example, when you come across a words like "necessarily" or "probably" then you can anticipate the argument being deductive or inductive respectively. Other inductive words include "plausible," "likely," "unlikely," or "improbable," etc. Other deductive words include "certainly," absolutely," "must," etc. That said, however, these indicator words are not particularly reliable. This is true especially of deductive indicators. Inductive arguments often have deductive indicators like "necessarily true" in them, because when people construct arguments they want to make their conclusion appear as strong as possible. This leads them to use deductive indicators in inductive arguments. Therefore, do not rely on such indicators.

The manner in which the premises support the conclusion or the argument form employed are more reliable guides in determining whether an argument is deductive or inductive.

PART TWO

||||||||||||||||||||||||||||||||||||||||||||||||||||||||||||||||||||||||||||||||||||||||||||||||||||||||||||||||||||||||||||

INDUCTIVE REASONING

COMMON INDUCTIVE ARGUMENT FORMS

There are several types of inductive arguments. All of these arguments possess one feature in common: they all have conclusions based upon probability, rather than necessity. Remember, these types of arguments have premises that intend only to support the conclusion *with probability*, meaning the premises are not expected to support the conclusion all the time - only some of the time. Good or bad inductive reasoning depends on the strength of the probabilty, a point covered more in detail next chapter. The point here is to be able to identify the intent of an argument by examining the pattern of reasoning in it.

Let us now turn to examine some common inductive argument types.

PREDICTION

A **prediction** reasons by using the past to make claims about the future. The prediction holds that since past events have behaved in a certain fashion, they will behave in that fashion in the future as well. For example:

> ALL PREVIOUS LOGICIANS HAVE BEEN DEVASTATINGLY HANDSOME. THEREFORE, ALL FUTURE LOGICIANS WILL BE DEVASTATINGLY HAND-SOME.

or

EACH OF THE 5000 TIMES I DROPPED THIS PEN, IT HAS FALLEN. THEREFORE, WHEN I DROP THIS PEN AGAIN, IT WILL FALL.

(This is a primitive version of the theory of gravity.)

The key thing to look for in a prediction is whether the past events cited are relevant to the future being predicted. Reasoning that since objects have fallen when dropped in the past, they will also fall when dropped in the future is fine. But predicting that since Harvard's football team beat Notre Dame in 1923 and in 1925, they will beat them next year is problematic, since the two teams may have changed a great deal in terms of ability. The number of past events sampled is also important. If you refer to only one or two past events, your prediction is likely to be very poor. For instance, consider this example:

EACH OF THE THREE TIMES I DROPPED THIS PEN, IT FELL TO THE GROUND. THEREFORE, WHEN I DROP IT AGAIN, IT WILL FALL.

This is poor reasoning. The number of past events upon which the prediction is based is too small.

ANALOGIES

The **argument by analogy** reasons by comparing two (or more) objects. Such an argument notes a feature that the two objects hold in common. It then notes a second feature that one of the objects has and claims that this means that the other object must have that same property. For example:

MARTY AND TED BOTH HAVE PORSCHE 911S.
MARTY'S 911 WILL GO FASTER THAN 140 MPH.
THEREFORE, TED'S 911 WILL GO FASTER THAN 140 MPH.

or

BORDER COLLIES AND DOLPHINS ARE BOTH MAMMALS.
DOLPHINS CAN SWIM UNDERWATER FOR 15 MINUTES AT A TIME.
THEREFORE, BORDER COLLIES CAN SWIM UNDERWATER FOR 15
MINUTES AT A TIME.

It should be clear that an argument by analogy is not going to be a good argument unless the similarity between the two objects being compared is relevant to the conclusion. In our first example, the similarity was relevant. The make and model of a car is relevant to how well it performs. The similarity cited in the second example is not relevant to the conclusion. The fact an animal is a mammal tells you little about its ability to survive underwater, because mammals can be aquatic and land dwelling. In analyzing an argument of this type, therefore, one of the first things you should do is determine whether the analogy drawn is relevant.

GENERALIZATIONS

The third type of inductive argument to consider is the inductive **generalization**. This is where one bases a conclusion about a whole group based on what is true for a sample of that group. For example:

THE FIRST TWO MICHAEL BOLTON SONGS I HEARD WERE MINDLESS
DRIVEL. THEREFORE, ALL MICHAEL BOLTON SONGS ARE MINDLESS DRIVEL.

or

EVERY DIAMOND FOUND IS HARDER THAN GLASS. THEREFORE, ALL
DIAMONDS ARE HARDER THAN GLASS.

Here, the strength of the argument depends upon the size of the sample with which you are dealing. The first argument is rather weak but true, because it is dealing with a small sample size. The second argument is dealing with a much larger sample size and is much stronger. Imagine if we look at several different cars, all of them 1993 Honda Accords, and then draw a conclusion about the quality of that type of car. If we only look at 2 Accords, and are unhappy with the quality of the car, we would not be justified in concluding that Accords are not good cars. The two cars we looked at might not be typical. If we sampled 300 Accords, though, and found that all of them were roughly the same quality, our conclusion would be much stronger.

Bias is also an issue. If a sample is not randomly selected from the group of objects you are testing, then your argument is suspect. Imagine we received our sample Accords from GM. Would we be able to trust that the samples are typical Accords? No, for it may be that GM has tampered with the cars. So using them in our sample would bias the generalization.

You will note that a generalization is much like the prediction. The difference is that in the prediction, you are using what has occurred in the past to judge the future. In the inductive generalization, you are making a judgement about an entire group of objects based on what is true about individual members of the group.

AUTHORITY

An **argument from authority** is when one draws a conclusion based on what an expert has claimed. The idea is that since the expert has made the claim, the claim must therefore be true. For example:

THE BATMAN SAYS THE STREETS OF GOTHAM ARE NOW SAFE AT NIGHT. THEREFORE, THE STREETS OF GOTHAM ARE SAFE AT NIGHT.

Or

MIKE TYSON SAYS WE SHOULD SEND 100 BILLION DOLLARS IN ECONOMIC AID TO AFGHANISTAN. THEREFORE, WE SHOULD SEND 100 BILLION DOLLARS IN ECONOMIC AID TO AFGHANISTAN.

The issue here is whether the authority is a relevant one. In the first example, the degree of relevance is quite high. Batman is an expert on crime. (Ignore the fact that he is a fictional character). Now, consider the second example. Do you think Afghanistan should get that much aid because Tyson says so? When analyzing these sorts of arguments, you have to judge how reliable the authority being cited actually is.

SIGNS, SIGNS, EVERYWHERE A SIGN

The next argument form is the **argument based on signs**. These are not astrological in nature: we are not talking about arguments like "He's a Scorpio, so he must be philosophical." Rather, an argument based upon signs is closely related to the argument from authority. This where you state a conclusion based upon some information conveyed by a sign. (For our purposes, we will define "sign" very broadly. Food labels, messages on blimps, vanity plates on cars etc. will all count as signs.) For instance:

THE SIGN ON THE BUILDING SAYS "GOTHAM POLICE HEADQUARTERS."
THEREFORE, THIS MUST BE THE HEADQUARTERS OF THE GOTHAM POLICE.

Or

THE SIGN SAYS CAYUCOS IS 14 MILES FROM SAN LUIS OBISPO.
THEREFORE, CAYUCOS IS 14 MILES FROM SAN LUIS OBISPO.

The question here is whether the sign in question is reliable. If there is no reason to doubt the reliability of the sign, then the argument is fine. A billboard informing you about the location of a restaurant is usually reliable, because a restaurant is not likely to deceive you about its location. However, if that same sign claimed that this restaurant has the best food in town, that is questionable, since the restaurant might well lie about that.

PART TWO

CAUSE AND EFFECT

The final type of inductive argument to be looked at is the cause and effect relationship, or what some call **causal inference**. (This is a causal inference, not a casual inference. This is not the type of argument you make while wearing shorts and sitting on a beach). A causal inference occurs when one reasons based on causal relationships of cause and effect.

Of course this type of reasoning pattern recalls the infamous Merovingian in the film, Matrix Reloaded.

Morpheus: WE ARE LOOKING FOR THE KEYMAKER.

Merovingian: OH YES, IT IS TRUE. THE KEYMAKER, OF COURSE. BUT THIS IS NOT A REASON, THIS IS NOT A 'WHY.' THE KEYMAKER HIMSELF, HIS VERY NATURE, IS MEANS, IT IS NOT AN END, AND SO, TO LOOK FOR HIM IS TO BE LOOKING FOR A MEANS TO DO... WHAT?

Neo: YOU KNOW THE ANSWER TO THAT QUESTION.

Merovingian: BUT DO YOU? YOU THINK YOU DO BUT YOU DO NOT. YOU ARE HERE BECAUSE YOU WERE SENT HERE, YOU WERE TOLD TO COME HERE AND YOU OBEYED. [LAUGHS] IT IS, OF COURSE, THE WAY OF ALL THINGS. **You see, there is only one constant, one universal, it is the only real truth: causality. Action. Reaction. Cause and effect**.

So, a causal relationship is a cause and effect situation - action, reaction. For example, consider a ball hitting a window and breaking it. The ball hitting the window would be the cause. The effect would be the window breaking.

A causal inference can work two ways: from cause to effect or from effect to cause. Reasoning from cause to effect works this way: we see the ball headed for the window and conclude that the window is about to break. Here we have moved from the cause (the ball) to what the effect will be (the broken window). What we need to consider here is whether the cause cited is likely to produce the effect. Is the ball likely to break the window? If yes, then this is a good causal inference.

Reasoning from effect to cause works this way: we see a broken window, and admist all the broken glass, we see a baseball. We therefore conclude the ball broke the window. We have therefore moved from the effect (the broken window) back to the cause (the baseball). The crucial question here is whether the effect sited is likely to have been produced by some other cause. If we see a broken window and a baseball surrounded by glass, is it likely something else caused the window to break? If the answer is no, then this is a good causal inference.

PART THREE

||||||||||||||||||||||||||||||||||||||||||||||||||||||||||||||||||||||||||||||||||||||||||||||||||||||||||||||

DEDUCTIVE REASONING

 COMMON DEDUCTIVE ARGUMENT FORMS

There are several types of deductive arguments. All of these arguments possess one feature in common: they all have conclusions based upon necessity, rather than probability. Remember, these types of arguments have premises that intend only to support the conclusion necessarily, meaning the premises are expected to support the conclusion one hundred percent of the time. Good or bad deductive reasoning depends on whether the conconclusion does in fact follow one hundred percent of the time, a point covered more in detail next chapter. Again, the point here is to be able to identify the intent of an argument by examining the pattern of reasoning in it.

Let us now turn to examine some common deductive argument types, beginning with what we call the three most common syllogisms: disjunctive, categorical and hypothetical syllogisms.

SYLLOGISMS

Many, but not all, deductive arguments have the form of a syllogism. A syllogism is a deductive argument that consists of two premises and a conclusion. All syllogisms must meet this requirement. There are three different types of syllogisms, each of which has additional characteristics.

Disjunctive Syllogism

The **disjunctive syllogism** is a syllogism that has a disjunction as one or both of its premises. A disjunction is a statement of the form

"Either A or B." A disjunctive syllogism commonly offers two choices as possibilities. The non-disjunctive premise then eliminates one of the choices, leaving the remaining choice as the only possibility:

EITHER THE COWBOYS OR THE PATRIOTS WILL WIN THE SUPERBOWL. THE PATRIOTS WILL NOT WIN THE SUPERBOWL. THEREFORE, THE COWBOYS WILL WIN THE SUPERBOWL.

Either the Cowboys or the Patriots will win the Superbowl. (This is the disjunctive premise.) The Patriots will not win the Superbowl. (Second premise: One of the two alternatives is eliminated.) Therefore, the Cowboys will win the Superbowl. (We conclude that the remaining alternative is true.)

Categorical Syllogism

The **categorical syllogism** is a syllogism that meets two added requirements (besides being a deductive argument with two premises and a conclusion):

1) All the statements in the argument begin with one of the words "all," "no," or "some." These three words are known as quantifiers. All statements in a categorical syllogism must begin with a quantifier.

Premise and conclusion indicators do not count when you are determining whether a statement begins with a quantifier. For example, if the conclusion of an argument reads." Thus, all dogs are mammals," that statement is considered to start with a quantifier. The word "thus" is not considered the beginning of the statement.

2) The argument uses three terms, each of which occurs twice in the argument. A term is a word or phrase that names a group or class of objects. For example, "cats," "people who listen to Michael Bolton without gagging," "aquatic mammals," and "full-time students" are all terms. Here is an example of a categorical syllogism:

ALL MICHAEL BOLTON FANS ARE LOVERS OF INSIPID MUZAK. SOME
LOVERS OF INSIPID MUZAK ARE PEOPLE WHO ENJOY THE MUSICAL
STYLINGS OF KENNY   G. THEREFORE, NO MICHAEL BOLTON FANS
ARE PEOPLE WHO ENJOY THE MUSICAL STYLINGS OF KENNY G.

Note that the argument has two premises and a conclusion. Each
statement begins with one of the words "all," "no," or "some." There
are three terms used in the argument: "Michael Bolton fans," "lovers
of insipid muzak," and "people who enjoy the musical stylings of
Kenny G." Each of these terms occurs twice in the argument. Thus,
the argument is a categorical syllogism.

Hypothetical Syllogism

The final type of syllogism we will examine is the **hypothetical syllogism**. This syllogism has a conditional statement as one or both of
its premises. The argument may be composed entirely of conditional
statements. Here are some examples of hypothetical syllogisms:

IF CHRISTINA AGUILERA SINGS LIKE A WARTHOG IN HEAT, THEN
PEOPLE CANNOT STAND HER. CHRISTINA AGUILERA SINGS LIKE A
WARTHOG IN HEAT. THEREFORE, PEOPLE CANNOT STAND HER.

or

IF ELVIS IS ALIVE, THEN HE WAS CAPTURED BY ALIENS FROM PLANET ZOG.
IF ELVIS WAS CAPTURED BY ALIENS FROM PLANET ZOG, THEN HE
NOW LIVES ON ZOG. THEREFORE, IF ELVIS IS ALIVE, THEN HE NOW
LIVES ON ZOG.

Affirming the Antecedent & Denying the Consequent

In logic, there are particular types of hypothetical syllogisms that are
so common, we have designated them by giving them their own
individual names: **Affirming the Antecendent** (or **Modus Ponens**)

and **Denying the Consequent** (or **Modus Tollens**). Each of these are deductive argument patterns that include a conditional statement of "If A, then B," but include two different ways of drawing a conclusion from it. For example:

> IF YOU RESPECT YOURSELF, THEN YOU KNOW WHAT IT MEANS TO RESPECT ANOTHER. YOU DO IN FACT RESPECT YOURSELF. THEREFORE, YOU KNOW WHAT IT MEANS TO RESPECT ANOTHER.

This is **Affirming the Antecedent** for two reasong, the first of which is because the second premise, namely "You do in fact respect yourself," affirms the antecedent of the first premise, "You respect yourself." Secondly, from these two premises, one of which is a conditional statement, a conclusion is drawn that is in fact the consequent of the original conditional statement. This particular form has an inverse called **Affirming the Consequent** and operates in much the same way but instead of affirming the antecdent of the given conditional statement, it affirms the consquent and then draws a conclusion as the antecedent.

Another way of drawing a conclusion from a premise that is a conditional statement is when one of the premises denies or rejects the consequent of a conditional statement and then draws a conclusion as the denial or rejection of the antecendent. This type of deductive argument syllogism is called **Denying the Consequent**. For example,

> IF YOU RESPECT YOURSELF, THEN YOU KNOW WHAT IT MEANS TO RESPECT ANOTHER. YOU DO NOT KNOW WHAT IT MEANS TO RESPECT OTHERS. THEREFORE, YOU DO NOT RESPECT YOURSELF.

Like Affirming the Antecedent, Denying the Consequent also has an inverse pattern called **Denying the Antecedent**, where the antecedent is rejected and from that the argument rejects the consequent as the conclusion.

OTHER TYPES OF DEDUCTIVE ARGUMENT PATTERNS

Math or Algebra

Another type of deductive argument is the **argument based on mathematics**. This is any argument that relies on purely mathematical computation to support its conclusion. Arguing that since Peter has 5 oranges and Ted has 3 oranges, that together they have 8 oranges is an example of this type of argument. Note that even illegitimate mathematical reasoning will fall into this category. For example, arguing that since A + B = 7, and A = 3, that therefore B = 5 is an argument by mathematics. It is a bad argument, since B must actually equal 4, not 5, but that does not change the type of reasoning being employed. It just indicates that the reasoning was poorly done.

Someone might object to the above and say that the last argument is not deductive because the conclusion is not necessarily true. But remember, not every deductive argument has a necessarily true conclusion. The goal when constructing a deductive argument is a necessarily true conclusion, but poorly constructed deductive arguments will fall short of this goal. They still are deductive arguments, however.

Objective Standards - Measurements, Age, Spatiality & Timelines

Any argument that uses support drawn from objective standards such as measurements, age, space or timelines will be using deductive reasoning. For example:

> EMMA IS EXACTLY 5 YEARS OLDER THAN ELEANOR, AND NIKO IS EXACTLY 5 YEARS YOUNGER THAN EMMA. THUS, NIKO AND ELEANOR ARE THE SAME AGE.

or

Lara is taller than Olivia, but Olivia is shorter than Josh. Therefore Josh is shorter than Lara.

or

Boston is east of California and California is west of Nevada. Therefore Boston is east of Nevada.

Using Definitions

The **argument from definition** is a deductive argument that relies upon the definition of a word used in the argument to justify its conclusion. For example, I note that Bruce Wayne is a bachelor. I then conclude he is unmarried. This is an argument by definition because the conclusion, "Bruce Wayne is unmarried," depends upon the definition of the word "bachelor."

It is worth noting that while the argument from definition has a very distinct form, all deductive arguments rely upon definitions in some sense. For example, mathematical arguments rely upon the definitions of the rules of math and the definitions of terms such as "square" or "circle." Categorical syllogisms also rely upon definition. Consider the first premise of the categorical syllogism used as an example earlier:

All Michael Bolton fans are lovers of insipid muzak.

This premise defines Michael Bolton fans as lovers of insipid muzak. If you look at the remaining propositions in the argument, you will see similar definitional moves being made.

Disjunctive syllogisms also use definition. A typical disjunctive syllogism offers you two alternatives, then excludes one of those two choices. The disjunctive premise is a definition, for it defines what two choices are available to you. Hypothetical syllogisms also rely upon definition, for hypothetical syllogisms employ conditional statements, and every conditional statement defines both a necessary and a sufficient condition. To sum up, while the argument from definition is a type of deductive argument, all deductive arguments will rely on definition in some way.

CHAPTER FOUR

ARGUMENT EVALUATION

PART ONE

||||||||||||||||||||||||||||||||||||||||||||||||||||||||||||||||||||||||||||||||||||||||||||||||||||||||||

EVALUATING INDUCTIVE ARGUMENTS

 TWO-STEP EVALUATION PROCESS

Remember from last chapter there are two basic argument types based on what type of reasoning is employed: deductive and inductive. An argument is deductive provided that the premises are expected to support the conclusion by necessity, or one hundred percent of the time. An argument is inductive provided that the premises are expected to support the conclusion with probability, or greater than fifty percent of the time. This does not however mean that the argument provides such expected support. This section provides ways in which we can determine whether the argument does what it intended to do - does the conclusion in fact follow the given premises by necessity (deductive) or with probability (inductive). To this end, let's start with inductive arguments.

For inductive arguments, we stated that a conclusion which is supported by given premises with probability is intended to follow those given premises greater than fifty-percent of the time, meaning there is more likely a chance of the conclusion occurring than not occurring. As such, the first step of evaluating an inductive argument is that we must evaluate the actual strength of the inductive reasoning in order to determine if that conclusion follows from the premises in the way that it is intended to do.

FIRST STEP - TEST REASONING - STRENGTH

Our first criterion for inductive arguments is strength. Inductive arguments can be said to be strong or weak. Strong inductive reasoning would include a conclusion that is supported by the evidence in such a way that if you were to put a percentage on the likelihood of the con-clusion occuring provided the premises were true that percent would be greater than fifty percent. Any conclusion in an inductive argument that does not meet the **greater than fifty percent rule** would indi-cate that the reasoning is weak. In other words, in a strong inductive argument, the premises are more likely than less likely to support the conclusion and, a weak inductive argument is one where there is a more likely chance that the premises do not support the conclusion. In a weak argument, the premises do not support the conclusion.

You should recognize that strength, like validity for deductive argu-ments, is a judgement about the logic of an argument, rather than the content of an argument. A strong argument may have false premises and a false conclusion. The only issue is whether those premises support that conclusion. For example:

SCIENTISTS AT NASA SAY THAT THE MOON IS MADE OF GREEN CHEESE.
THEREFORE, THE MOON IS MADE OF GREEN CHEESE.

This is a strong argument. It is an argument from authority. Are scien-tists at NASA relevant experts on the composition of the moon? Yes. So, the premise of this argument supports the conclusion. However, both the premise and the conclusion are false.

Like deductive arguments, an inductive argument can take 4 possible forms. By definition, a strong argument is one where if the premises are true, the conclusion is probably true. An argument with true prem-ises and a probably false conclusion contradicts that definition and has to be weak. However, the other three possibilities, true premises and a probably true conclusion, false premises and a probably true conclusion, false premises and a probably false conclusion, are open to both strong and weak arguments. As with the distinction between

PART ONE

valid/invalid, there is one sure way to distinguish between weak and strong inductive arguments: a strong argument will never have true premises and a probably false conclusion.

Hint: the best way to judge strength is by imagining that the premises as true and then asking if the conclusion follows. If the answer is "yes," then the argument is strong. If the answer is "no," then it is weak. (Please note that this does not mean you actually believe the premises to be true. You are just asking, "what if they are true?".)

⚡ STRONG ARGUMENTS ARE NOT ALWAYS GOOD

ARGUMENTS

Because strong arguments may have false premises, strong arguments are not necessarily good. When an inductive argument is called strong, it is being described as having good logic. Its content may still be bad.

Degrees of strength are possible

Now, the concept of strength in inductive arguments is parallel to the concept of validity in deductive arguments. There are some important differences to be noted, though. First, as previously noted, valid and invalid are absolute judgements. An argument is either valid or it is not; there is no such thing as a slightly valid argument. However, strong and weak are judgements of degrees. Among strong inductive arguments, some can and will be considered stronger than others. Why? Remember that the conclusion of an inductive argument is based on probability rather than necessity. When we say an inductive argument is strong, we are saying that its conclusion is very probable, given the truth of its premises. Two arguments may both have probable conclusions, but one may be more probable than the other. For example:

There has been a dawn every day in the past.
Therefore, there will be a dawn tomorrow.

U2's last six albums have sold over million copies each.
Therefore, U2's next album will sell over a million copies.

Now, both of these examples are strong inductive arguments. However, although the chances of U2's next CD going platinum are quite high, it is even more likely that the sun will not go nova or otherwise be destroyed in the next 10 or 12 hours. Therefore, the first argument is stronger than the second because it has a conclusion that is more likely.

What we should realize from these examples is that the concept of strength allows for degrees. Some strong arguments are stronger than others are; some weak arguments are weaker than others.

SECOND STEP - TEST TRUTH-VALUE

After testing the argument for reasoning, and only if the argument passes, can you move to the second step of argument evaluation, i.e., evaluating truth-value of the premises. Should the premises be found to all be true, then and only then can you say you have a good inductive argument. All good inductive arguments are called cogent arguments.

A **cogent argument** is an inductive argument that meets two conditions:

1) It is strong - passes the reasoning test

2) It has true premises - passes the truth-value test

Failure to meet both of these conditions means the argument is uncogent. Because true premises support the conclusion of a cogent argument, it follows that the conclusion stands a high probability of being true, that is, there is more of a likelihood than less likelihood

PART ONE

that the conclusion will occur. Therefore, a cogent argument is the ideal type of an inductive argument. It is an inductive argument with good logic (it is strong) and which has true premises. An example of a cogent argument:

PEOPLE WHO DRESS LIKE GIANT BATS FREQUENTLY ARE USUALLY VERY STRANGE.
BATMAN DRESSES LIKE A GIANT BAT VERY FREQUENTLY.
THEREFORE, BATMAN IS VERY STRANGE.

To say that an argument is cogent is say that both of our questions of argument analysis are answered "yes." Yes, the premises are true, and yes, the premises support the conclusion in the way the way the argument intended. If you accept an argument as cogent, you should accept its conclusion as probably true. A cogent argument is a good inductive argument.

PART TWO

||||||||||||||||||||||||||||||||||||||||||||||||||||||||||||||||||||||||||||||||||||||||||||||||||||||||||||||||||||||||||||||||||

EVALUATING DEDUCTIVE ARGUMENTS

 TWO-STEP EVALUATION PROCESS

For decutive arguments, we stated that a conclusion which is supported by given premises by necessity is intended to follow those given premises one hundred percent of the time, meaning there is no chance that the conclusion can be false if the premises are accepted. As such, the first step of evaluating a deductive argument, like that of an inductive argument, is that we must evaluate the actual strength of the reasoning in order to determine if that conclusion follows from the premises in the way that it is intended to do. And the intention of all deductive arguments is to produce a conclusion that follows the evidence one hundred percent of the time.

FIRST STEP - TEST REASONING - VALIDITY

The criteria for evaluating deductive arguments has us begin with the notion of **validity**. Deductive arguments can be said to be valid or invalid. A valid deductive argument is one where assuming the premises are true, then the conclusion is necessarily true. In other words, in a valid deductive argument, the premises support the conclusion one hundred percent of the time. An invalid deductive argument however is one where even if we assume the premises are true, the conclusion is not necessarily true. In an invalid argument, the premises do not support the conclusion one hundred percent the time. Much of our work this semester will be aimed at determining the validity or invalidity of arguments. Validity and invalidity are not matters of degree like it is for inductive arguments. An argument is either valid or invalid. There is no such thing as a slightly valid argument.

There are no degrees of validity

You need to notice something about our definition of validity: a valid argument need not have true premises. We just assume the premises are true when we test for reasoning. Because of this, it follows that the premises of a valid argument can be false, and so can the conclusion. For example:

> MADONNA IS FROM ENGLAND.
> ALL PEOPLE FROM ENGLAND HAVE RED HAIR.
> THEREFORE, MADONNA HAS RED HAIR.

This is a valid argument. The premises support the conclusion one hundred percent of the time: if we assume that those premises are true, the conclusion would necessarily be true. The premises, though, are quite obviously false and yet the argument is still valid, because validity only tests for reasoning.

Validity, then, is not a judgement about the content of an argument. Rather, it is a judgement about the logical form or reasoning of an argument. If one says an argument is valid, one says nothing about whether the argument's content is true or false.

Validity is a concept that deals only with whether the premises actually support the conclusion in a very particular way – out of necessity. To say an argument is valid is to say only that the premises support the conclusion one hundred percent of the time assuming of course that the premises are true.

Importantly, a valid argument will never have true premises and a false conclusion. An argument with actually true premises and a false conclusion must be an invalid argument. Why? Think of it this way: arguments can be bad in one of two ways. Either an argument uses bad information -- they contain false premises-- or use bad logic or reasoning. Now, consider our argument with true premises and a false conclusion. It must be bad: the false conclusion tells us that. But it doesn't have bad content: the premises are true. So, that means the logic must be bad. A deductive argument with bad logic is termed invalid.

Valid arguments, though they cannot have actual true premises and a false conclusion, can have a) true premises and a true conclusion, b) false premises and a true conclusion, or c) false premises and a false conclusion.

VALIDITY IS NOT TRUTH VALUE

Hint: the best way to judge validity is by accepting the given premises as true and asking yourself assuming the premises are true does the given conclusion follow one hundred percent of the time from those premises. If the answer is "yes, the conclusion always follows" then the argument is valid. If the answer is "no, the conclusion does not always follow" then the argument is invalid. (Please note that this does not mean you actually believe the premises to be true.)

SECOND STEP - TEST TRUTH-VALUE

To say that an argument with false premises and a false conclusion is valid may bother you, because it seems you are saying the argument is good. Yet clearly there is a problem with the argument: the content is false. Keep in mind that validity passes no judgement on the content of an argument. When you judge an argument to be valid, you are not saying it is good. The argument could still have a false premise.

PART TWO

Because of this, we need another criterion by which to evaluate both the content and the logic of a deductive argument. This is the criterion of soundness. A **sound argument** is an argument that meets two conditions:

1) It is valid – passes the reasoning test
2) It has true premises– passes the truth-value test

Any argument which does not meet both of these conditions is unsound. Unlike validity, then, soundness is not a judgement that applies simply to logical form: it is also concerned with the argument's content. It takes into account both of our questions in argument analysis, for it asks whether the premises are true and whether those premises necessarily support the conclusion. A sound argument is the ideal type of deductive argument: it has a valid logical form and true content. Such an argument will have a necessarily true conclusion. Sound arguments are what one should strive for in a deductive argument. An example:

> BRUCE SPRINGSTEEN LIVES IN NEW JERSEY.
> NEW JERSEY IS NEAR NEW YORK.
> THEREFORE, BRUCE SPRINGSTEEN LIVES NEAR NEW YORK.

To say that an argument is sound is to say that both of our questions of argument analysis are answered "yes." Yes, the premises are true, and yes, the premises support the conclusion. If you accept an argument as sound, you should accept its conclusion. A sound argument is a good argument.

PART THREE

||||||||||||||||||||||||||||||||||||||||||||||||||||||||||||||||||||||||||||||||||||||||||||||||||||||||||||||||||||||

SUMMARY OF ARGUMENT EVALUATION

 SUMMATION

To briefly recap all of this: there are three things to consider when accessing an argument. First, is the conclusion supposed to be necessary? Or only probable? That will tell you whether you have a deductive or inductive argument. In answering this question, do not worry about whether the conclusion actually is necessary or actually is probable. Instead, focus on what the intent of arguer is.

Second, ask whether the premises offer firm support for the conclusion. That tells you if the argument is valid/invalid or strong/weak.

Finally, ask if the premises are true. That will determine whether the argument is good or bad. After you have done this, you will be in a position to analyze the argument.

THREE STEPS FOR EVALUATING ARGUMENTS

1. Test for deductive/inductive: Does arguer intend for the conclusion to follow *necessarily* or *with probability* from the premises?
2. Test for validity/invalidity or strong/weak: Do the premises actually support the conclusion in the way it was intended?
3. Test for goodness: Are the premises true?

CHAPTER FIVE

DEFECTIVE REASONING – FALLACIES

PART ONE

‖‖

UNDERSTANDING FALLACIES

FORMAL VS INFORMAL FALLACIES

All arguments that have premises that do not support their intended conclusion uses faulty or misleading reasoning. We call arguments that have faulty or misleading reasoning, fallacies. A **fallacy** is a failure in reasoning or a defective argument containing faulty, misleading, or deceptive reasoning.

There are two types of fallacies: formal and informal. **Formal fallacies** are arguments that are defective because of their logical structure, or form. An argument that is formally fallacious, then, is one that has a defective structure. The argument forms of Affirming the Consequent and Denying the Antecedent are examples of formal fallacies. Here is an example:

> If Michael Bolton sings like a warthog in heat, then he is a terrible singer. He is a terrible singer. Therefore, Michael Bolton sings like a warthog in heat.

This is an example of Affirming the Consequent, which takes the form of a particularly incorrect type of a hypothetical syllogism, where, since the consequent is affirmed in the given conditional statement, then the antecent is (incorrectly) argued to also be true. This is also called an inverse Modus Ponens as we learned a couple of chapters ago. Affirming the Consequent is a formal fallacy because any argument with this structure will be defective. The specific content, that is, the information about Michael Bolton, has no bearing on this. The argument's form is itself defective and so is considered a formal fallacy.

The other type of fallacy is the informal fallacy. This is when the content of the argument causes it to be fallacious. The structure of the argument is not the problem; it is the *content* that is the problem. For example:

ALL LAWS ARE CREATED BY A LEGISLATIVE BODY. THE LAW OF GRAVITY IS A LAW. THEREFOR, THE LAW OF GRAVITY WAS CREATED BY A LEG-ISLATIVE BODY.

This argument is defective because the word "law" is being used in two different senses. In the first premise, "law" refers to political laws; in the second premise, "law" refers to natural or scientific laws. This is a content problem. An argument with different content, but with the same structure as the above example, may commit no fallacy. For example:

ALL LAWS ARE CREATED BY A LEGISLATIVE BODY. THE LAWS REGULAT-ING TARIFFS ARE LAWS. THEREFORE, THE LAWS REGULATING TARIFFS WERE CREATED BY A LEGISLATIVE BODY.

Informal fallacies are quite common in everyday language. Politicians, lawyers, used car salesmen, your friends and family use them all the time. Virtually every commercial commits an informal fallacy. The danger is that this type of bad reasoning is often very persuasive. In order to avoid being conned, one must recognize the dubious reasoning being employed. Also, since commercials are repeated so often, after a time the reasoning displayed by commercials begins to look legitimate because one is so often exposed to them. Knowing the different fallacies can prevent one from falling into bad reasoning

PART ONE

habits. To this end, this chapter discusses the most **common defective argument patterns**.

Fallacies can be categorized by the general way in which an argument proves to be defective. This chapter will break down fallacies in three categories: Exploitation, You're Fired, and Off Topic.

PART TWO

||||||||||||||||||||||||||||||||||||||||||||||||||||||||||||||||||||||||||||||||||||||||||||||||||||||||||||||||||||||||||||

INFORMAL FALLACIES - EXPLOITATION

⚡ COMMON FALLACIES OF WEAK REASONING

One group of inductive fallacies that all of us may find ourselves making on a daily basis, either inadvertently or advertently, are what we are calling Exploitation Fallacies. **Exploitation fallacies** are common arguments that use a kind of defective reasoning that takes a common argument form but abuses it to generate a corrupted conclusion. In other words, these are arguments with premises that are ineffective or misapplied in order to generate a certain conclusion. The premises exploit the general argument pattern. While the premises may be relevant to the conclusion and bear a relationship to the conclusion, they just are not up to the task of adequately supporting a probable conclusion.

Important note: Informal fallacies frequently occur, or most often occur, in inductive arguments, and less so in deductive. With this in mind, we are mostly evaluating the reasoning to see if the conclusion is supported *with probability*. Remember, *with probability* means the conclusion has a greater than fifty percent chance of occuring than not occuring given the premises are assumed to be true. You will use the Greater Than Fifty Percent Rule a lot in this chapter. Exploitation fallacies covered here include, hasty generalization, false cause, weak analogy, unfit authority, accident, composition, and division.

HASTY GENERALIZATION

Hasty generalizations are based on the argument form of inductive generalization, a common inductive argument patterns studied earlier.

This is where one takes a sample of a group, and reasons that what is true for the sample will be true for the group as a whole. Such arguments are justified so long as the sample that one is basing one's conclusion on is a large and randomly selected set. The fallacy of hasty generalization occurs when the sample set the generalization is based upon does not accurately represent the group, either because the sample set is too small or is not randomly selected. For example:

I'VE KNOWN TWO PEOPLE FROM ALABAMA IN THE PAST AND THEY WERE BOTH BIGOTS. CLEARLY, EVERYONE FROM ALABAMA IS A BIGOT.

TWO WEEKS AGO THEY ARRESTED THE JOHNSON BOY FOR PIMPING AND HE LOVES METALLICA. THEN YESTERDAY, THE FREDRICKSON KID WAS PICKED UP FOR SELLING DOPE AND HE LISTENS TO METALLICA, TOO. METALLICA FANS MUST BE NOTHING BUT A PACK OF CRIMINALS.

In both cases, a sample group of two is used to generalize about a group that has million of members. That is insufficient. Such large groups require much larger samples. In general, the larger the small, the more accurate the generalization (assuming all other factors remain the consistent). However, there is a point at which increasing the size of the sample yields diminishing returns. A sample of 4,000 is accurate to within +/– 2% for groups of 100,000 or 100 million. Your book details this on p. 527.

Small sample sizes are not the only factor that can lead to the fallacy of hasty generalization. Non-random samples are also a problem. By a random sample, statisticians mean that every member of the group being sampled has an equal chance of being included in the sample. If one took a sample of voters in the Bakersfield area by randomly selecting people from the phone book, it would fail to be random, since voters not in the phone book would not be included in the sample. A lack of randomness can bias the sample, leading to an incorrect generalization. An example:

A SURVEY OF 4,000 AMERICANS SHOWED THAT 97% ARE OPPOSED TO AFFIRMATIVE ACTION. IT MUST BE THE CASE THAT THE VAST MAJORITY OF AMERICANS ARE OPPOSED TO SUCH POLICIES.

This might seem creditable. A sample size of 4,000 is large enough to generalize about the entire country. Imagine, however, that the survey was taken at a Ku Klux Klan convention. Would you then trust the results? Clearly not, since such a sample would be biased-- and in more ways than one.

FALSE CAUSE

This fallacy is based on the inductive argument type known as the **causal inference**. This is where one reasons that a particular event has a certain cause. This becomes the fallacy of false cause when the cited cause is not likely to have produced the effect in question. The fallacy seeks to establish a causal connection that does not actually exist. For instance:

I GOT MY CAR WASHED THE OTHER DAY AND THE ALTERNATOR GAVE OUT. THEREFORE, TO KEEP YOUR ALTERNATOR FROM GIVING OUT, DON'T GET YOUR CAR WASHED.

THOMAS IS A DRUNKEN BUM AND HAS A DEGREE IN PHILOSOPHY. THEREFORE, DON'T MAJOR IN PHILOSOPHY UNLESS YOU WANT TO BE AN ALCOHOLIC.

In these cases, we have a cause being offered which seems to have no relation to the effect cited. Having your car washed is not likely to cause your alternator to fail; majoring in philosophy is unlikely to cause one to have a substance abuse problem.

This fallacy can also be committed when one takes a complicated situation, which has a number of causes, and claims instead that the situation has only one cause. For example:

PART TWO

REAGAN'S MILITARY BUILDUP DURING THE 1980S CAUSED THE DOWN-FALL OF THE SOVIET UNION.

The collapse of the Soviet Union was caused by many factors, including economic factors dating back twenty years or more. The military buildup in question may have helped caused the collapse, but it was not the sole cause. This argument is therefore reducing a complicated situation to a simplistic one.

Another way this fallacy can occur is where one takes a legitimate cause and effect relationship and inverts it, mistaking the effect for the cause. For example:

SUCCESSFUL PERFORMERS ARE GENERALLY ON LATE NIGHT TALK SHOWS LIKE LETTERMAN AND LENO. SO IF YOU WANT TO BE A SUCCESSFUL PERFORMER, YOUR BEST BET IS TO GET BOOKED ON A TALK SHOW.

Here, the causal order has been reversed. Success gets one booked on a talk show, but the argument supposes that being on a talk show brings success. It has reversed the connection.

WEAK ANALOGY

The **weak analogy** is based upon an argument from analogy. This is where you compare two items and, on the basis of that comparison, conclude that since something is true of one item, it must be true of the other. This is a legitimate argument if the similarity cited between the two items is strong enough to support the conclusion, meaning there is not something substantial that undermines the analogy made; and if there is a substantive problem with the analogy, then you have an ineffective analogy. For example:

JAY'S BICYCLE AND TODD'S NINJA MOTORCYCLE BOTH HAVE TWO WHEELS. SINCE TODD'S NINJA DOES 0-60 IN 5 SECONDS, JOE'S BIKE DOES TOO.

Here, the similarity cited-- that the two vehicles both have two wheels-- is not strong enough to support the conclusion, and we know that the number of wheels is substantially ineffective at establishing a correlation to speed. Another example:

> BART SIMPSON IS A COOL DUDE AND IS ON TV. BART HAS A GREAT HAIRCUT. MICHAEL BOLTON HAS A GREAT HAIRCUT, AND IS ON TV, TOO. SO MICHAEL IS COOL.

Having a great haircut and being on TV does not create an effective relationship to being cool. Again, the similarities cited are not strong enough to support a probable conclusion.

UNFIT AUTHORITY

The **unfit authority fallacy** is based on the argument from authority, which is an argument where you base your conclusion on what a given authority has said. This is legitimate so long as the authority cited is relevant to the conclusion, but if the authority is not relevant it becomes the fallacy of the unfit authority. Here is an example:

> ROBERT URICH SAYS PURINA ONE IS THE BEST DOG FOOD AVAILABLE. THEREFORE, PURINA ONE MUST BE THE BEST.

Is Robert Urich an expert on dogfood? No, he is an actor. He is not a vet. How can he know which dog food is best? Did he eat it himself? Here, we have an appeal to an illegitimate authority, but the pattern here is such that should Robert Urich be an legitimate authority, the argument would have succeeded; but since he is no such authority, we can say this authority is "fired."

This fallacy can also be committed if the authority being cited in the argument is biased. A biased authority might be someone who is indeed an expert in the field, but whose integrity we have reason to question. An example:

> MICHAEL JORDAN SAYS AIR JORDAN BASKETBALL SHOES ARE THE BEST
> ON THE PLANET. THEREFORE, THEY ARE THE BEST ON THE PLANET.

Jordan may be an expert on basketball shoes (that is debatable); however, since Nike pays him close to $80 million a year to endorse Air Jordans, his credibility is questionable. This is not an argument against the person, ad hominem circumstantial, because Jordan is not making an argument. He is endorsing a product, and with an endorsement we have to trust the person making the endorsement. Whether we trust someone is a question of character, so character is relevant here.

COMPOSITION

Composition is where one reasons illegitimately from the properties of a part to the properties of the whole. In other words, you reason that since the parts of an object possess certain characteristics, the object itself will, too. While this is not alway wrong to argue this way, there are instances in which this type of reasoning can be obviously wrong. For example, imagine if you reasoned that since the individual parts of a machine were light in weight, the machine itself was light:

> EVERY PART OF THIS REFRIGERATOR WEIGHS LESS THAN 10 POUNDS.
> THEREFORE, THIS REFRIGERATOR WEIGHS LESS THAN 10 POUNDS.

Another example:

> HYDROGEN AND OXYGEN ARE BOTH MOST COMMONLY FOUND AS
> GASES. THEREFORE, SINCE WATER IS MADE OF HYDROGEN AND OXYGEN,
> ITS MOST COMMON FORM IS AS A GAS, TOO.

These examples are obviously fallacious. Sometimes the fallacy can be more subtle. For example:

EVERY SHIP IS READY FOR BATTLE. THUS, THE FLEET IS READY FOR BATTLE.

This is an illegitimate argument because the fleet itself may not be ready for battle-- the overall battle plans, for example, may have yet to be drawn.

The move from part to whole can be legitimate however. For example:

EACH COMPONENT OF THE TABLE IS VISIBLE. THEREFORE, THE TABLE IS VISIBLE.

EVERY CELL IN THE HUMAN BODY IS 90% WATER. THEREFORE, THE HUMAN BODY IS 90% WATER.

These examples demonstrate why composition is an Off Topic fallacy, as while the pattern of using composition may sometimes be relevant to drawing a conclusion about the whole, there are times when we just mistakenly misapply this pattern and in doing so the premises become Off Topic from the conclusion. However, like every Off Topic fallacy, composition can be reworked to be legitimate, as we saw with the last two arguments which are similar in structure to the earlier fallacious examples, yet commit no fallacies. The only way to distinguish the good arguments from the bad arguments is by a careful examination of each.

Collective distribution

There is another version of the composition fallacy that turns on a confusion over the way a term is used. Terms refer to groups: the term "cat," for example, refers to the group of cats. Terms can be used either collectively or distributively. When a term is used collectively, it refers to a group as a whole. When a term is used distributively, it refers to the individual members of the group. If this difference is overlooked, it can lead to confusion. Consider these two statements:

HARVARD STUDENTS GENERALLY TAKE NO MORE THAN 5 CLASSES A SEMESTER.

HARVARD STUDENTS ENROLL IN HUNDREDS OF COURSES PER SEMESTER.

These statements might at first appear to be contradictory. However, they are not. The term "Harvard students" can refer to the student body as a whole (collectively) or can be used to each individual student (distributively). The first statement refers to individual students and illustrates the distributive use of the term. The second statement refers to all students as a group. Here, the term "Harvard students" is used collectively. While it is true that individual students rarely take more than 5 classes at a time, it is also true that students as a group take hundreds of classes. The fact the two statements use the same term in a different way explains why they are not contradictory.

When this distinction between the collective use of a term and the distributive use of a term is overlooked, it can lead to a fallacy of composition. Such fallacies of composition reason that since something is true of a term distributively, it must be true collectively, as well. For example, consider this argument:

YACHTS COST MORE THAN CARS. THEREFORE, MORE MONEY IS SPENT EACH YEAR ON YACHTS THAN ON CARS.

This is fallacious. While yachts do cost more than cars, far fewer yachts than cars are sold. That means more money is spent, in total, on cars each year. So, while it is true, distributively, that more money is spent on yachts, it is not true collectively.

Note: often times people confuse composition with hasty generalization. With a generalization, one moves from a sample to the entire group. With composition, one moves from the parts of an object to the object itself. For example, a generalization about the parts of a refrigerator will move from some parts to all parts but will never refer to the refrigerator as a whole. The composition fallacy, on the other hand, will go from part to whole.

DIVISION

Division is the exact opposite of composition. Here, you reason that since something is true of the whole, it must be true of the part. As with composition, there can be arguments that seem to be of this type which are not fallacious. For example:

ALL DOGS ARE MAMMALS. THEREFORE, THIS DOG IS A MAMMAL.

This is a perfectly fine move from whole to part. But consider this argument:

IBM IS AN IMPORTANT AMERICAN CORPORATION. MR. SMITH IS A JANITOR THERE, SO HE IS IMPORTANT.

Here, we have falsely reasoned that since it is true that IBM is important that its janitor is important. Another example:

THIS REFRIGERATOR WEIGHS MORE THAN 300 POUNDS. THEREFORE, EACH PART MUST WEIGH 300 POUNDS.

This is illegitimate. The fact that the whole object weighs 300 pounds does not imply that each part weighs that much.

Just as with composition, there is a second variety of the fallacy of division. This version also turns around the distributive/collective difference. If one argues that since something is true collectively of a group, it is also true distributively for members of that group, one

PART TWO

is committing the fallacy of division. Again, here we are no longer speaking of part/whole but of a word being applied in two different ways, collectively and distributively. An example:

> CALIFORNIAN CONDORS ARE DISAPPEARING. THAT BIRD IS A CONDOR, SO IT IS DISAPPEARING.

Here, we are using the term condor collectively first. We then reason that since something is true collectively for the term, it is also true distributively. This is fallacious.

ACCIDENT

The **Accident fallacy** occurs when you misapply a rule, generally accepted as true, to a specific case where the rule does not apply. This is a fallacy of exploitation because the general rule, while may be valid, is misapplied to a different situation. An example:

> (GERMANY, 1942) YOU SHOULD ALWAYS TELL THE TRUTH. THEREFORE, YOU SHOULD TELL THE GESTAPO OFFICER ABOUT THE TWO JEWS YOU ARE HIDING IN YOUR BASEMENT.

It is generally accepted as true that one should tell the truth, but the above situation is one where the rule does not seem to fit. Another example:

> YOU SHOULD NEVER TAKE SOMEON'S PROPERTY. THEREFORE, YOU SHOULDN'T TAKE YOUR FRIEND'S CAR KEYS EVEN THOUGH HE IS DRUNK AND WANTS TO DRIVE HOME.

Again, taking someone's property is usually considered stealing. However, in this case, taking your friend's car keys seems justified.

FALSE DICHOTOMY

False dichotomy fallacy occurs when an argument has a disjunction as a premise. This disjunction presumes that there are only two possible choices when, in fact, there are actually more options. This argument is generally valid, since it often has the form of a disjunctive syllogism:

P OR Q. IT IS NOT THE CASE THAT P. THEREFORE, Q.

Since the disjunctive premise in a false dichotomy is false, though, the argument is unsound. What makes this a fallacy is the attempt to deceive the listener into believing only two choices exist. You probably used this fallacy as a teen:

EITHER YOU LET ME GO TO THE PARTY OR MY SOCIAL LIFE WILL BE RUINED. YOU DON'T WANT TO RUIN MY SOCIAL LIFE, SO YOU GOTTA LET ME GO TO THE PARTY.

Here, the choices are limited to either going to the party or having a ruined social life. But surely, that is not the full story. There are other choices.

This is a common fallacy. Commercials use it. For example, the commercial for Sure deodorant has a tag line that states:

"RAISE YOUR HAND IF YOU'RE SURE!"

Breaking this apart, we find the following disjunctive syllogism:

EITHER YOU USE SURE OR YOU WILL NOT BE ABLE TO RAISE YOUR HAND. YOU WANT TO BE ABLE TO RAISE YOUR HAND. THEREFORE, YOU MUST USE SURE.

PART TWO

However, is the first premise true? Are the only options available either using Sure or not raising our hands? There are obviously other options: wearing a T-shirt, taking a shower, or using another brand of deodorant. So, we are falsely being limited to two choices.

It needs to be stressed that false dichotomies can occur only when the disjunctive premise falsely limits the listener to two choices. If the flaw with the argument is not with the disjunctive premise, then false dichotomy does not occur. For example:

> SAN ANTONIO IS IN TEXAS OR NEW YORK.
> IT IS NOT IN TEXAS.
> THEREFORE, SAN ANTONIO IS IN NEW YORK.

This is not a false dichotomy. The problem with the above argument is not with the disjunctive premise. San Antonio is in Texas: the disjunction is therefore not excluding a legitimate alternative. The problem is that the second premise is false. This is therefore an unsound argument, but it does not commit a fallacy. Now, consider this example:

> SAN ANTONIO IS IN MICHIGAN OR NEW YORK.
> IT IS NOT IN MICHIGAN.
> THEREFORE, SAN ANTONIO IS IN NEW YORK.

This does commit false dichotomy: the disjunctive premise is limiting us to two options, both of which are false. It is therefore failing to account for a legitimate alternative. The key to recall here is that a false dichotomy must use a false disjunction. False dichotomy = false disjunction.

SLIPPERY SLOPE

Slippery slope fallacy is a variant on the false cause fallacy. This occurs when someone claims that a certain event will trigger a chain of consequences that are undesirable. A slippery slope argument is fine if the chain of events being mentioned actually is likely to occur. But if the chain of events is unlikely to occur, the argument turns fallacious. Here's an example of a legitimate and a fallacious slippery slope:

> WE MUST NOT CUT EDUCATION FUNDING DRASTICALLY. IF WE DO, THE QUALITY OF OUR SCHOOLS WILL SUFFER. THIS IN TURN WILL HURT OUR STUDENTS, MAKING THEM LESS COMPETITIVE WITH OTHER STUDENTS AROUND THE WORLD. SINCE THESE CHILDREN WILL BE THE BASIS FOR OUR COUNTRYÂ€™S FUTURE, CUTTING EDUCATION FUNDING DRASTICALLY WILL HARM OUR FUTURE. (THE CHAIN OF EVENTS CITED HERE SEEMS REASONABLE)

We should censor rock music. The continued exposure of our formerly God-fearing children to rock and roll will undoubtedly lead to more immorality and Satan worship among them, causing them commit crimes. Since these children will grow up to lead this country, this means our future leaders will be immoral Satan worshippers unless we act now. (Here, the causal chain is not likely).

The question as to whether a slippery slope is a fallacy depends entirely on whether the chain of events being cited is likely to occur. If not, it is fallacious: if it is likely, it is not a fallacy.

PART THREE

||||||||||||||||||||||||||||||||||||||||||||||||||||||||||||||||||||||||||||||||||||||||||||||||||||||||||||||||

FALLACIES – YOU'RE FIRED

 COMMON FALLACIES OF QUESTIONABLE PREMISES

Whereas Exploitation fallacies offers relevant but inadequate premises, inadequate in that they often either misapplied or ineffective, **You're Fired fallacies** results from arguments whose premises are fundamentally questionable or flawed in their assumptions or wording. In this way, when you encounter such evidence presented in an argument, you can say "You're fired" on the grounds that you are not an acceptable premise.

BEGGING THE QUESTION

Begging the question is one of the most common fallacious patterns that use questionable premises. Begging the question occurs when an arguer uses some type of linguistic trick to conceal the questionable nature of a premise. There are essentially two versions of this fallacy. The first version is when a premise restates the conclusion. This version uses **circular reasoning**. The second form uses a **hidden premise** that is problematic in nature. Without this premise, the conclusion does not follow. Yet, the premise is not one that should be hidden. To begin, let us look at the use of circular reasoning.

Circular reasoning occurs when the conclusion of an argument is also used as a premise: the conclusion is used to justify itself. While such arguments are always questionable, they do not commit begging the question unless there is an attempt to conceal the circularity. For example, this is a circular argument:

WATER IS WET. THEREFORE, WATER IS WET.

Although this is circular, no fallacy is committed here, because the circularity of the argument is not concealed. However, the following example does commit the fallacy:

TV EVANGELISTS ARE SLIMY INDIVIDUALS BECAUSE THEY WOULD NOT BE ON TV PREACHING UNLESS THEY ARE INDIVIDUALS COATED IN SLIME.

Again, this is circular. The premise is saying the same thing as the conclusion. However, there is an attempt to conceal the circularity by restating the information in a different form.

The problem with all arguments using circular reasoning is that no real justification is supplied for the conclusion, because the premises assume the very thing the conclusion claims. In the above example, no evidence to support the claim that TV evangelists are slimy is ever produced.

Don't break the chain

Another common form of begging the question that uses circular reasoning occurs in **chain arguments**, where the conclusion of one argument is used as the premise of a second argument, which then justifies a premise in the original argument. Such arguments have the following form:

A
THEREFORE, B.

B
THEREFORE, A.

PART THREE

The conclusion B is supported by A; but A in turn is supported by B. Again, we have circular reasoning. We know B because of A; we know A because of B. No outside evidence is provided. Here is an example of this type of begging the question:

> APPLE COMPUTER MAKES THE BEST PERSONAL COMPUTERS IN THE WORLD. THIS IS DUE TO THEIR HAVING THE BEST COMPUTER DESIGNERS. THEY HAVE THE BEST COMPUTER DESIGNERS BECAUSE APPLE'S REPUTATION FOR QUALITY ATTRACTS THEM. APPLE HAS THAT REPUTATION BECAUSE THEY MAKE THE BEST PERSONAL COMPUTERS IN THE WORLD.

Here, the overall conclusion is Apple makes the best personal computers in the world. This is justified by a series of arguments, the last one of which uses the overall conclusion as a premise. Thus, the conclusion is assumed true, creating a circular argument. The overall conclusion is supported by reference to itself. What makes these arguments difficult to recognize is that each step in the chain of reasoning seems reasonable. It is only when you view the argument as a whole that it seems questionable. Someone looking at each individual move made in the argument would miss the fallacy.

What is hidden must be revealed

The other form of begging the question occurs when a questionable premise, needed to make the argument true, is hidden. Often times, people will not state all the information that a conclusion is based on. If the information omitted is trivial, then no fallacy occurs. Here is an example:

> FIDO IS A CAT.
> THEREFORE, FIDO IS AN ANIMAL.

The hidden premise is that "all cats are animals." This is common knowledge. Omission of this information therefore creates no fallacy.

Sometimes, though, an argument will depend upon a questionable assumption that is not explicitly stated. The person making the argument may fail to realize that she is making the assumption; or, may deliberately conceal the premise to forestall any possible objections. For example:

DISCRIMINATION IS IMMORAL. GIVEN THIS, IT IS CLEAR THAT AFFIRMATIVE ACTION IS IMMORAL.

Here, a premise is left out: "affirmative action is discrimination." This argument, by being stated as it is, is designed to hide the fact that an additional premise is needed to complete the argument. Since the stated premise is obviously true, if one concentrates only on that premise, one might accept this argument. The premise that is hidden, though, it is not a trivial one. The claim that affirmative action is a type of discrimination is highly debatable and must therefore be explicitly made.

COMPLEX QUESTION

Complex question fallacy occurs when one asks a question that presumes the existence of a set of circumstances. Any presumptions in a premise must be fired. For example:

HAVE YOU STOPPED CHEATING ON YOUR SPOUSE?

This question does not just pose a simple factual inquiry. It presumes that a certain situation is in existence: it assumes you have been cheating on your spouse. Therefore, it makes certain presuppositions about your character. There is no easy way to answer the question without implicating yourself in some fashion. If you answer "yes," that indicates you have cheated on your spouse in the past: a "no" answer indicates you still are cheating on him/her. Either answer implicates you. To avoid the implication, you must not answer the question either yes or no. Since the question is designed to evoke a yes or no response, though, this is not an easy thing to do.

The complex question is not explicitly an argument. However, an implied argument is being made: in the above example, it is being argued that you are a spouse-beater. The question presupposes the conclusion is true, and then tries to trick you into providing the evidence needed to support the assumption. The arguments posed by complex questions are generally designed to trap the person the question is directed at into admitting something he might not otherwise admit to. Here's another example:

ARE YOU STILL ABUSING CRYSTAL METH?

Here the argument assumes you are using crystal meth and is attempting to use your answer to this question as confirmation for that assumption.

Note: Complex question always involves the posing of a question.

SUPPRESSED EVIDENCE

Suppressed evidence fallacy occurs when an arguer deliberately ignores evidence that undermines the conclusion of his argument. Whenever obvious information is omitted, the premises of the argument must be fired. When suppressed evidence occurs, one presumes the argument is true despite evidence to the contrary. This fallacy is common whenever someone has a strong desire for a certain conclusion to be true. For example:

OF COURSE, HILLARY CLINTON IS A MORAL PERSON. SHE IS A WONDERFUL MOTHER, A DECORATED POLITICIAN AND HAS BEEN PRAISED BY FORMER PRESIDENT OBAMA.

This argument ignores the fact that Hillary broke the law when she deliberately destroyed 30,000 emails requested in a subpoena. Whether you agree with the conclusion or not, this is still fallacious because it is ignoring relevant evidence that casts doubt on the conclusion. The issue here is not political. If one is going to argue in favor of Hillary Clinton, the email scandal must be dealt with. Another example:

> THE YUGO IS A WONDERFUL CAR. IT GETS GREAT GAS MILEAGE AND USES VERY LITTLE FUEL AND HAS A GREAT DEAL OF CARGO SPACE FOR A LITTLE CAR.

What is this example ignoring? It ignores that the Yugo is poorly made and needs constant repair. To detect these fallacies, you must determine if all the relevant evidence is presented. This can be quite difficult to do if you do not know anything about the subject of the argument. In the last example, if you did not know anything about the Yugo, you would be unable to detect the fallacy.

PART THREE

EQUIVOCATION

Equivocation fallacy occurs when the definition of an ambiguous word or phrase is changed during the course of an argument. Premises whose meaning can change must be fired. This redefinition is necessary in order to justify the conclusion. For example:

> HITLER'S TALK OF A MASTER RACE WAS HARMLESS. HE WAS JUST REFERRING TO A SPORTING EVENT.

> A SHEEP IS A MAMMAL. THEREFORE, A SMART SHEEP IS A SMART MAMMAL.

In the first example, the term race is being used in two ways, to refer to ethnicity and to refer to a sporting event. Clearly, that redefinition is unjustified. In the second example, a relative term is being used inappropriately. Sheep are rather dumb as far as mammals go. Therefore, even a smart sheep is still dumb. The term smart, being a relative term, changes its meaning in relation to its context. For example, what we mean when we refer to "smart" when talking about dogs is clearly very different than what we mean when we speak of someone's wife as being smart, even though in both cases we are referring to intelligence. Similarly, when the term smart is applied to mammals it has a different meaning than when it is applied to sheep, since mammals, as group, include things like humans, apes, whales and dolphins.

Generally, speaking, equivocation is used in a far more subtle fashion than in the examples just given. What will happen is that during the course of a speech, a speaker might gradually redefine a term so that it means something very different from what it did at the beginning of the speech. For example, a politician might gradually redefine the meaning of the term "taxes" during the course of a speech, or over the course of a campaign. A politician might pledge to not raise taxes-- and then raise registration rates for your car. What exactly a tax is has been redefined.

AMPHIBOLY

Amphiboly fallacy occurs when a statement that has a structural defect is misinterpreted by someone. This person then draws a conclusion based on the faulty interpretation. (Note: it is a statement that is being misinterpreted, not an argument. This is the difference between amphiboly and straw man.) The structural defect in the statement being misinterpreted is usually due to poor sentence construction, which makes the statement unclear. And all unclear premises should be fired. For example:

MOLLY TOLD PEGGY THAT SHE IS 9 MONTHS PREGNANT. PEGGY MUST BE DUE ANY DAY NOW.

Here the difficulty lies with the use of the pronoun "she." Generally, a pronoun should refer back to the person last named, which in this case is Peggy. Replacing "she" with "Peggy" changes the first statement to this:

MOLLY TOLD PEGGY THAT PEGGY IS 9 MONTHS PREGNANT.

Assuming Molly is not Peggy's doctor, is this a likely interpretation? Would Peggy need to be told by someone else that she is 9 months pregnant? This is unlikely. In fact, the pronoun "she" actually refers to Molly. That changes the first statement to this:

MOLLY TOLD PEGGY THAT MOLLY IS 9 MONTHS PREGNANT.

This makes much more sense. So, the original conclusion that Peggy must be due any day now is incorrect. It is based on a misinterpretation of the original statement.

Another example:

THE DESERT COOKBOOK SAYS TO SERVE CHERRIES JUBILEE DRENCHED IN BRANDY. THEREFORE, WE MUST POUR BRANDY OVER OURSELVES BEFORE SERVING THE DESERT.

The first premise does not specify what is to be drenched in brandy. Common sense would suggest that it is the cherries that are to be drenched, but the person making this argument has misinterpreted the initial premise.

Amphiboly differs from equivocation in that equivocation involves reinterpretation of a word during the course of an argument while amphiboly involves an entire statement being ambiguous.

PART FOUR

||||||||||||||||||||||||||||||||||||||||||||||||||||||||||||||||||||||||||||||||||||||||||||||||||||||||||

FALLACIES - OFF TOPIC

COMMON OFF-TOPIC FALLACIES

Whereas You're Fired fallacies draws conclusions using inappropriate or questionable premises, **Off-Topic fallacies** employ premises that totally do not relate to the conclusion at all. While many of these are persuasive because they use emotion, threats, violence, sexuality, character, circumstance, or hypocrisy, all these nevertheless try to deceive the listener into accepting a certain desired conclusion based on an irrelevant premise, or a premise that is off-the-topic.

INVOKING PITY

Invoking pity fallacy tries to instill sympathy and uses this sympathy as the premise to persuade the listener to accept the conclusion. For example:

> PLEASE DON'T FIRE ME. I HAVE 4 CHILDREN AND NO OTHER WAY TO SUPPORT THEM.

The conclusion is that the speaker should not lose his job. But is the fact that the speaker has no other way to support his children relevant? No. What is relevant to the issue of whether one should be fired is the quality of the work the employee produces and the company's ability to afford the worker. Here the speaker is trying to make the listener feel sorry for the speaker, so that the listener will accept the speaker's conclusion. The appeal to pity is a fallacy professors hear all the time:

OH, PLEASE, MR. GEORGE, I KNOW I DESERVE A D BUT I'VE GOT TO GET A B. OTHERWISE, I CAN'T GET INTO LAW SCHOOL AND MY FUTURE WILL BE RUINED AND MY MOM AND DAD WILL HATE ME.

Sometimes, an appeal to pity needs no words. Students just come into the office, wave their test and cry. Again, the idea is to try to persuade the professor to change their grade, not on the basis of any relevant evidence, but out of pity.

INVOKING FORCE

Invoking force fallacy is where the person posing an argument warns the listener that some harm will come to them if they do not accept the argument. This fallacy always involves a threat to the listener. It is not necessarily a physical threat. It could be a psychological threat as well. But some threat must be made for the fallacy to be an appeal to force. We are sure you can remember various examples of this from childhood:

PART FOUR

MY DAD IS BETTER THAN YOUR DAD, AND IF YOU DON'T AGREE, I'LL BEAT YOU UP.

The conclusion here is the statement "My dad is better than your dad." The problem here is that the sole evidence for the conclusion is that the speaker will beat up the listener. Is that logically connected to the conclusion? No. However, there is an emotional appeal being made here: fear is being used as motivation. The listener is being told "agree or else," and the arguer expects that fear will motivate the listener to accept the conclusion.

Another example:

WELL, BOB, YOUR PROPOSAL SEEMS INTERESTING BUT YOU REALLY SHOULDN'T BRING IT BEFORE THE BOARD. I'M SUGGESTING WE GO A

DIFFERENT ROUTE AND IF YOU PRESENT YOUR PROPOSAL, I'LL HAVE
TO ARGUE AGAINST IT AND MAKE YOU LOOK BAD.

The conclusion here is that Bob should not bring his proposal before
the board. No evidence supports this. Instead, Bob is being warned
against making his proposal because he will end up looking bad. Again,
the speaker is trying to make the listener fearful of what will happen
to him if he doesn't accept the conclusion. (It is for this reason that
the appeal to force is sometimes called the appeal to fear.)

INVOKING SEXUALITY & TRADITION

Invoking sexuality or tradition is a lot like invoking pity and
force patterns of fallaciously reasoned arguments. All you have to do
here is make an appeal to sex or one's own context of family history
or tradition, and make a conclusion that because of the persuasive
emotional appeal of sexuality or the nostalgia of past tradition, you
should accept the conclusion as true.

INVOKING IGNORANCE

Invoking ignorance fallacy occurs when someone argues that since
something cannot be shown to be true, it must be false-- or, since
something cannot be shown to be false, it must be true. Essentially,
this boils down to the following claim: since we do not know anything, we know something. Ignorance is therefore used as a basis for
knowledge. That is a very strange way to reason, to claim that since
you are ignorant, you are in fact knowledgeable. An example:

NO ONE HAS EVER BEEN ABLE TO SHOW THAT GOD DOES NOT EXIST.
WE SHOULD THEREFORE CONCLUDE GOD DOES EXIST.

NO ONE HAS EVER BEEN ABLE TO SHOW THAT GOD EXISTS. WE
SHOULD THEREFORE CONCLUDE GOD DOES NOT EXIST.

That this is problematic is shown by the fact that the above examples both start with essentially the same premise-- God's existence has never been proven-- and reach contradictory conclusions. These types of arguments depend on an appeal to some vaguely defined "authority," whose inability to reach a conclusion is supposed to prove something definite. For example, the above examples appeal to "no one" as an authority. Appeals to ignorance will refer to "exhaustive testing" without telling you who did the testing, or refer to "countless experts" without identifying any of the individuals, or might refer to "no one." In any case, it is the reference to these vaguely defined authorities that is the main problem. If a legitimate group of experts has failed to find evidence of a given event, that is evidence that the event did not occur. An example:

> SCIENTISTS AT NASA HAVE FOUND NO EVIDENCE OF LIFE ON MARS. THEREFORE, THERE IS LIKELY NO LIFE ON MARS.

Here, there is no fallacy. Scientists at NASA are a very specific group, and are legitimate authorities on Mars. The fact that they have found no evidence of life on Mars supports the claim that there is no life on Mars. Who is going to qualify as a legitimate authority will differ from argument to argument. Certainly scientists would not be acceptable authorities in proving/disproving the existence of God.

APPEAL TO PEOPLE

Appeal to the People fallacy tries to justify a conclusion by noting that "everyone else" does it. This fallacy is using the fact that all humans have a desire to belong to social groups. Even nonconformists find other nonconformists to associate with. As Aristotle noted, "man is a social animal." The fact that this fallacy manipulates people by using this basic need makes it quite dangerous.

There are two basic types of this fallacy: the **direct version** and the **indirect version**.

Appeal to the People – Direct

The **direct version** makes no argument: a person who commits a direct appeal to the people fallacy is not trying to support a conclusion. Instead, the speaker tries to whip up the listener or listeners into a mob mentality. The idea is to fire up the listeners so that they will stop thinking and blindly follow the speaker. An example:

> TRUE AMERICANS BELIEVE IN THEIR NATION AND CHERISH THE FREEDOMS FOUGHT FOR AND NURTURED BY OUR ILLUSTRIOUS ANCESTORS. TRUE AMERICANS ARE PROUD OF THEIR HERITAGE AND BELIEVE IN THEIR WAY OF LIFE. BY BEING TRUE AMERICANS, WE SHALL RESTORE OUR COUNTRY'S PRIDE.

The direct version of appeal to the people is a powerful persuasive force. One only needs to look at the examples provided by Hitler, Manson and the Rev. Jim Jones to see this. This is what we meant when we called this fallacy dangerous.

Appeal to the People – Indirect

The other type of appeal to the people is the indirect version. Indirect appeals to the people are arguments: the speaker or writer is trying to establish a conclusion. There are three variants: the **bandwagon** argument, the **invoking vanity** and the **invoking snobbery**.

Bandwagon argument

The bandwagon argument is the classic form of the indirect appeal to the people. It plays upon our desire to belong, to fit in and be part of the crowd: to be part of the majority, or part of a large group of people. This is often a fallacy children use on their parents:

Tina: "Oh, mom, you got to let me go. Everyone else's parents are letting them go."

Is the fact that everyone else's parents are letting their children go evidence that Tina's parents should let her go? If the activity in question is driving through Crips turf and throwing paint bombs at them, Tina's parents are showing reasonable caution in saying no. The fact that other parents are being incautious does not imply Tina's parents are incorrect in saying no. This fallacy is one we are cautioned against when we are young. When you tried this type of reasoning on your mother, how did she respond? "If everyone else jumped off a cliff, would you do it too?"

Another example of a bandwagon fallacy:

Dumb and Dumber is the #1 movie in the country. It must be a great movie.

Is the fact that a movie is popular an indication that it is good? Before you answer, please recall that all of the Porky's movies were popular in the 1980s, and that Duran Duran was once the biggest selling band in the world. Case closed.

Invoking Vanity

Invoking vanity fallacy is a variant on the appeal to the people. It plays on the same desire to be a part of a group, except instead of appealing to our desire to be part of the majority, it appeals to our desire to be thought of as having excessive pride in oneself, one's appearnace, abilities, and achievements.

Cher works out at Bally's gym. You should work out there, too.

The assumption here is that by working out at Bally's, one can look as good as Cher. But does Cher look as she does because she works out at a particular gym? Surely working out at another gym would work as well.

Invoking Snobbery

The appeal to snobbery works much the same way, except it appeals to our desire to be seen as rich and successful. It is an appeal to elitism:

> A MERCEDES ISN'T FOR EVERYONE, JUST THE LUCKY FEW. IF YOU ARE ONE OF THOSE FEW, SEE YOUR MERCEDES DEALER.

The idea is that only the very special can have a Mercedes. Of course, this is not true. All it takes is sufficient credit.

ARGUMENT AGAINST THE PERSON (AD HOMINEM)

The next fallacy we will look at is the **argument against the person (ad hominem)**. This is a fallacy that always involves two people. A person makes an argument. A second person responds to the first person's argument. It is in this response that the fallacy is committed. Rather than responding to the actual argument, the second person instead attacks the person who made the argument. Thus, the second person tries to discredit the argument not by showing it to be weak, but by discrediting the person who made it. The person responding makes the character of the other person the issue, rather than the argument itself. But the character of a person making an argument is irrelevant, making the premises totally off-topic in an attempt to decieve. For example, consider the following argument:

P > Q
P
THEREFORE, Q

This is a modus ponens argument. This is a valid argument, even if it turns out that it was made by Charles Manson. The character of the person making an argument is not relevant when examining the quality of that argument.

This does not mean that character is never relevant. A daycare center may refuse to hire a child molester precisely because of character. But the daycare center is not responding to an argument. Character can be relevant in hiring decisions. It is never relevant in analyzing arguments.

Three versions of ad hominem

The argument against the person fallacy comes in three flavors: ad hominem abusive, ad hominem circumstantial, and two wrongs make a right.

Ad hominen abusive

In the **ad hominem abusive**, the person responding to the original argument verbally abuses the person who made the argument.

> MY ESTEEMED COLLEAGUE FROM THE STATE OF NORTH CAROLINA HAS PRESENTED HIS ARGUMENT. BUT BEING A GODLESS COMMUNIST, WHAT HE THINKS IS IRRELEVANT.

Here, we have no idea what the original argument is. Instead, the person responding simply insults the person who made the argument. Another example:

> PRESIDENT BUSH THINKS CAPITAL PUNISHMENT IS OK BUT WHAT DOES HE KNOW? HE'S A DWEEB.

Again, no discussion of Bush's position is given. Instead, an insult is made. Certain radio talk-show hosts are fond of this style of repartee.

Ad hominem circumstantial

The next version of the argument against the person is the **ad hominem circumstantial**. Rather than insulting the person who made an argument, the second person instead points to their motives for making the argument. The thing to realize is that everyone has a motive for making an argument. Otherwise, they would not make one. Thus, motives are irrelevant in evaluating arguments. The only relevant issues are whether the premises are true and whether the logic is good. An example:

> SURE HUFFINGTON WANTS TO REDUCE THE CAPITAL GAINS TAX. HE'S RICH AND THAT'S WHOM THE REDUCTION WOULD BENEFIT: THE RICH.

The fact that Huffington might personally benefit from a capital gains tax reduction does not show that his argument in favor of such an argument is bad. His reasoning in support of a reduction might still be quite good. Another example:

> JESSE HELMS ARGUES THAT SMOKING ISN'T DANGEROUS. OF COURSE, HE REPRESENTS A STATE THAT DEPENDS ON THE TOBACCO INDUSTRY SO HE WOULD SAY THAT.

The fact that Jesse Helms has a strong motive for arguing smoking is not dangerous does not show his argument to be wrong. Questioning his motives will not prove him wrong: medical evidence is needed for that.

Ad hominem Two Wrongs Make it Right

The final version of the argument against the person is **two wrongs make a right fallacy**. With this fallacy, someone responds to an argument by noting that the person making the argument is guilty of the very thing she is criticizing. The idea is that since the person making an argument is a hypocrite, that this undermines her criticism.

DON'T TELL ME I SHOULDN'T HAVE AN AFFAIR; YOU CHEATED ON
ME THREE YEARS AGO.

This fallacy essentially reasons that two wrongs make a right; that the
affair three years ago justifies the current one. However, this is not
the case. The fact that the person making an argument is a hypocrite
does not show that the criticism is unjustified: it only shows that the
person is a hypocrite. That is not relevant to the issue of whether it
is right to have an affair, though. Another example:

(SON TO FATHER): "HEY, YOU TRIED HEROIN WHEN YOU WERE MY
AGE, SO YOU CANNOT TELL ME IT IS WRONG."

The fact that a parent tried heroin when he was younger does not
undermine his warning against heroin. Indeed, such a warning might
be all the stronger because it is based on personal experience. In
any case, the father is being accused of being a hypocrite and that is
irrelevant. His criticism has not been addressed by the son's argument.

SUMMATION OF ARGUMENT AGAINST THE PERSON

1. **Ad hominem abusive**: Employs insulting character.
2. **Ad hominem circumstantial**: Attacks motives for making
   an argument.
3. **Ad hominem two wrongs make a right**: Accuses the
   other of hypocrisy.

Two other points need to be raised with regard to this fallacy: first,
as noted earlier, there are situations where character is relevant. For
example, if a lawyer brings up the fact that a witness was previously
convicted of perjury, that is not a fallacy. A witness is not making an
argument. She is offering testimony. It is the jury's duty to determine
the credibility of a witness's testimony. Character is directly relevant
in such a situation.

PART FOUR

131

Second, the argument against the person fallacy must be committed in response to an argument. If another person simply insults you, then that is rude, but is not a fallacy.

STRAW MAN

Straw Man fallacy, like the argument against the person, always involves two people. The fallacy occurs when a person is responding to an argument made by the first person. The second person distorts the argument by reinterpreting it. This reinterpretation exaggerates the argument and makes it weaker. The second person does this because the weaker version is easier to refute than the actual argument. This is a fallacy of relevance because the weaker version of the argument has no relevance to the argument actually made. Here is an example:

> SCIENTISTS WOULD HAVE US BELIEVE IN EVOLUTION. BUT EVOLUTION TELLS US THAT WE ARE ANIMALS, JUST LIKE BABOONS OR APES. BUT CAN BABOONS OR APES REASON? COULD THEY THINK UP SCIENTIFIC THEORIES, EVEN A FALSE ONE, LIKE EVOLUTION? CERTAINLY NOT. OBVIOUSLY, THE SCIENTISTS ARE WRONG.

The original argument was the theory of evolution. But does evolution claim that humans are "just like" baboons or apes? No, it does not. This is a distortion. It is quite clear that humans are not just like baboons and apes, so such a claim is easy to refute. However, that shows nothing about the theory of evolution.

Another example:

> THE TEACHERS IN OUR SCHOOL DISTRICT HAVE ASKED FOR A PAY RAISE. WHAT ARE THEY EXPECTING, TO BE PAID AS MUCH AS BILL GATES? NO SCHOOLTEACHER IS WORTH THAT MUCH.

The original argument is that teachers have asked for a pay raise. This is distorted: it is claimed that teachers want to be paid like Bill Gates. Again, such a claim is easy to refute, but since the teachers did not make such a request, the refutation shows nothing about whether teachers should be given a pay raise.

MISSING THE POINT

All of the fallacies we have looked at up to this point have had premises which were not relevant to the conclusion - they were off topic. Missing the point reverses this: it features a conclusion that is not relevant to the premises. What happens in this fallacy is that evidence is introduced in the premises that supports an obvious conclusion, but a completely different and unsupported conclusion is drawn. The fact that the premises suggest an obvious conclusion is why we say that the conclusion is not relevant, rather than the premises. In any instance of missing the point you should be able to identify what the correct conclusion should be. If you do not have at least a rough idea of what the conclusion actually should have been, then the fallacy is not missing the point. An example:

PART FOUR

TEEN GANGS ARE COMMITTING CRIMES AT AN ALARMING RATE. MOST TEEN GANGS ARE MADE UP OF LOWER CLASS YOUTHS, WHO ARE ECONOMICALLY DISADVANTAGED. WE SHOULD THEREFORE KILL ALL TEENAGERS WHOSE PARENTS MAKE LESS THAN $15,000 A YEAR.

The conclusion here does not follow from the premises. The correct conclusion is something like this: We should target social (or crime prevention) programs at low-income families to reduce gang related crimes. Killing all teenagers whose parents make less than $15,000 a year is not a reasonable response, though.

Another example:

ELECTED OFFICIALS OFTEN TAKE BRIBES AND ABUSE THEIR OFFICE JUST TO ENSURE THAT THEY ARE REELECTED. WE SHOULD THEREFORE STOP HOLDING ELECTIONS.

The conclusion is that we should stop having elections. But this leaves the corrupt officials in office. The conclusion that should be drawn is that political reform is needed.

RED HERRING

Red Herring fallacy is similar to the straw man fallacy. It also involves two people. Like straw man, red herring occurs in response to an argument made by someone else. The person responding to the argument does not actually deal with that topic:instead, the arguer diverts the attention of his audience to a completely different point. The subject is switched from one topic over to another, which is not relevant to the original subject. An example:

STUDENTS TALK ABOUT BEING OVERWORKED. BUT THEY DON'T REALIZE THAT THEIR INSTRUCTORS ARE OVERWORKED AS WELL. BETWEEN TEACHING 5 CLASSES, GRADING PAPERS AND TRYING TO DO RESEARCH WELL, IT'S A WONDER THAT PROFESSORS DON'T HAVE A NERVOUS BREAKDOWN.

The original topic is that students are overworked. However, this topic is changed to instructors being overworked. While both topics are about individuals being overworked, they are different subjects.

Another example:

PEOPLE TALK OF ANDY ROONEY BEING A RACIST. BUT ROONEY IS FUNNY AND ENTERTAINING. HE EASES THE BURDEN OF MANY BY MAKING THEM LAUGH. HIS CRITICS SEEM TO HAVE FORGOTTEN THIS.

The original topic is whether Andy Rooney is racist. Whether he is funny has no relevance to that topic.

Note: It can often be very difficult to recognize the difference between the straw man and the red herring fallacies. Keep in mind this distinction: the straw man fallacy distorts the original argument. The subject is not changed but the argument being responded to is reinterpreted so as to be weakened. In the red herring fallacy, the original argument is not considered in any form. Instead, a new topic is considered.

PART FIVE

|||||||||||||||||||||||||||||||||||||||||||||||||||||||||||||||||||||||||||||||||||||||||||||||||||||

SUMMARY - STUDY GUIDE

 **SUMMARY**

We have seen that arguments can be faulty in a number of ways. A fallacy is a way of specifying the nature of faulty reasoning in an argument by identifying common fallacious argument patterns. Here is a list of all the fallacies learned in this chapter:

Ad hominem abusive	False Cause
Ad hominem circumstantial	Suppressed Evidence
Ad hominem two wrongs make a right	Complex Question
Appeal to the People – Direct	Slippery Slope
Appeal to the People – Indirect	Accident
Invoking Pity	False Dichotomy
Invoking Force	Composition
Invoking Sexuality	Hasty Generalization
Invoking Tradition	Division
Invoking Ignorance	Missing the Point
Unfit authority	Weak Analogy
Begging the question	Straw Man
Composition	Red Herring

CHAPTER SIX

|||||||||||||||||||||||||||||||||||||||||||||||||||||||||||||||||||||||||||||||||||||||||||||||||||||||||||||||||||||||||||||||||||||

SENTENTIAL LOGIC

 **LEARNING OUTCOMES**

1. Learn the difference between simple & compound statements
2. Learn the five logical operators & their common English equivalent
3. Learn to translate statements from English into symbolic logic
4. Learn how to use parentheses
5. Learn how to use negations in statements with other operators
6. Understand the various meanings of conditional statements

Be patient: symbolic logic takes time to learn. You are essentially learning a new language.

PART ONE

|||||||||||||||||||||||||||||||||||||||||||||||||||||||||||||||||||||||||||||||||||||||||||||||||||||||||||||||||||||||||||||||||||||||||||||

PROPOSITIONAL LOGIC AND
UNDERSTANDING STATEMENTS

 UNDERSTANDING STATEMENTS

Symbolic logic is probably the most powerful way to identify the logical form of deductive arguments. (Symbolic logic deals only with deductive arguments.) The power of symbolic logic is derived from the fact that it deals with the statements in arguments on two levels: the simple and the compound. A simple statement is a statement that makes a single claim. A compound statement is a statement that makes multiple claims.

BATMAN EATS QUICHE.

MICHAEL BOLTON SINGS LIKE A WARTHOG IN HEAT.

SACRAMENTO WILL WIN THE NBA CHAMPIONSHIP.

These are all examples of **simple statements**. These statements all make a single claim. A simple statement has one subject and one verb. Any variation on that theme makes the statement not a simple statement. Contrast these statements with the following examples:

SACRAMENTO WILL WIN THE NBA CHAMPIONSHIP BUT THE CELTICS WILL BE IN THE NBA FINALS.

IF BATMAN EATS QUICHE, THEN ROBIN WEARS SHORTS.

These are **compound statements**. A compound statement is any statement that is not a simple statement. It must include a simple

PART ONE

statement, but a compound statement either a) modifies the simple statement using an operator, or b) adds another statement to a simple statement using an operator. In both cases, a compound statement uses operators. We will learn that there are only five operators: negation, conjunction, disjunction, conditional, biconditional.

In the examples given above about Sacramento and Batman, we clearly see that each of these examples makes two claims and each involves an operator. The first example claims that Chicago will win the NBA Championship and claims that the Spurs will be in the NBA Finals. These two separate statements are joined together by a conjunction, the operator "but." The second example makes a claim about Batman's eating habits and a claim regarding Robin's fashion sense. In this case, each statement is linked together using the conditional operator, "if... then..." You will note that these compound statements are formed from simple statements. "Batman eats quiche" is a simple statement. And in each case, each simple statement is either modified or another statement is added to the first simple statement, making the overall statement, a compound statement.

Remember in chapter one, we learned that conditional statements are treated as one statement. Let's clarify what we meant. A conditional statement is made up of an antecedent, which is in itself a statement, and a consequent, which is in itself another statement. So, the statement, "if it rains, then the grass gets wet," is considered one statement or claim in an argument, yet it is also made up of two separate statements that are being joined by an operator, yielding a compound statement. In this way, any compound statement is treated as one single claim in an argument and can represent any given premises or a conclusion. And when we translate for example a conditional statement using symbolic logic, we understand the conditional to be a compound statement, where at least two separate statements are joined together by an operator called implication symbolizing the "if...then..." relationship.

PART ONE

PART TWO

||||||||||||||||||||||||||||||||||||||||||||||||||||||||||||||||||||||||||||||||||||||||||||||||||||||||||||||||||||||||||||||||||

TRANSLATING STATEMENTS INTO SYMBOLS

 ## AN INTRODUCTION TO SYMBOLIC LOGIC

In **symbolic logic**, *simple statements* are represented by variables. These variables are capital letters. The letter selected to represent a simple statement is generally the letter that the statement begins with. The following is a list of our earlier examples. Next to each is the symbolic translation of that statement.

Statement	Translation
BATMAN EATS QUICHE.	B
MICHAEL BOLTON SINGS LIKE A WARTHOG IN HEAT.	M
SACRAMENTO WILL WIN THE NBA CHAMPIONSHIP.	S

Make the connection. All simple statements get translated with one letter.

As noted earlier, **compound statements** are formed out of simple statements. In symbolic logic, the way this is done is by taking simple statements and linking them to each other using operators, or modifying a simple statement with a negation. As mentioned, there are five operators:

COMMON ENGLISH TRANSLATION

Operators/ Connectives	Symbol	Meaning
Conjunction	• (dot)	and, but, yet, moreover, furthermore
Disjunction	v (wedge)	or, unless
Conditional or Implication	> (horseshoe)	if...then; if; only if; implies that; provided that; is sufficient condition for; is necessary condition for
Biconditional or Equivalence	≡ (triplebar)	if and only if; is a sufficient and necessary condition for
Negation ~ (tilde)	not; is	not the case that, it is false that

Some logic textbooks use slightly different symbols for the conjunction, conditional, and the biconditional than we use here. We have opted for student convenience over strict philosophical symbols. However, these symbols are similar to the ones used in traditional symbolic logic. Thus, the conditional symbol is still called the "horseshoe" even though we are using the greater than sign symbol (">") to represent it.

We have listed the common English translation of each of these operators in the chart above. However, each of these operators has multiple translations. For example, the conjunction is also used for "yet," "however," and "moreover," as well as "and" and "but." We advise you to memorize this table.

Compound statements are formed by using the above operators to link simple statements together. Which operator is used depends on the original compound statement. Consider an earlier example of a compound statement:

> Sacramento will win the NBA Championship but the Celtics will be in the NBA Finals.

In this example, the two simple statements, "Sacramento will win the NBA Championship" and "the Celtics will be in the NBA Finals," are linked together by the word "but." "But" is a conjunction, so the dot symbol should be used here. We will symbolize "Sacramento will win the NBA Championship" with the variable "S" and "the Celtics will be in the NBA Finals" is symbolized as "C." Our resulting symbolic statement is:

$$S \cdot C$$

Another example:

> If Batman eats quiche, then Robin wears shorts.

Here the simple statements are "Batman eats quiche" and "Robin wears shorts." These will be symbolized as "B" and "R" respectively. The operator connecting these statements together is "if/then." This is a conditional statement, which is also called an implication. This is symbolized with the horseshoe. The resulting symbolic statement is this:

$$B > R$$

Here are some other compound statements. The correct symbolic translation is listed beneath the English statement:

VICKI VALE DATES BATMAN OR CATWOMAN DATES BATMAN.

$$V \lor C$$

ATLANTA WILL WIN THE WORLD SERIES IF AND ONLY IF GREG MADDUX PITCHES A SHUTOUT.

$$A \equiv G$$

Note: When translating from English into symbolic form, you must recognize that you are symbolizing claims, not names. In the first of the examples above, three persons were named Vicki Vale, Batman, and Catwoman; yet the symbolic statement only had two variables. This is because only two claims were made by the statement.

Let's now unpack each of the operators or connectives, starting with negations.

OPERATORS OR CONNECTIVES

NEGATIONS

The first four operators, the conjunction, the disjunction, the implication and the biconditional, all link statements to other statements. For this reason, these operators are often termed connectives, because they enable us to connect simple statements together to form a compound statement. The last operator, the negation, does not connect statements together. Rather, it contradicts or negates whatever statement it is in front of. As an illustration, consider this statement:

BATMAN DOES NOT EAT QUICHE.

This statement should be symbolized as "~B," rather than "B." Why? Because the original statement is a compound statement. It expresses two claims: the claim Batman eats quiche and the denial of that claim. Thus, two assertions are made. This is why when we symbolize a negated statement, we must always make the negation explicit. B can never represent Batman does not eat quiche. To symbolize the statement in that way would hide one of the two claims being made. This is called burying the negation. It is to be avoided. Variables (letters) should always represent positive terms and phrases. Negations should always be expressed by a tilde and always precede that which it negates, meaning it is always placed in front of that which it negates. Negations in English include the word "not" and the phrase "it is false." Unless an English statement is explicitly negated, however, you generally do not negate it. The statement "Prices will soon decrease" is not a negation, because no explicit denial or contradiction is made.

We can also use a negation in statements involving two variables. To illustrate, let us look at an example used earlier:

SACRAMENTO WILL WIN THE NBA CHAMPIONSHIP BUT THE CELTICS WILL BE IN THE NBA FINALS.

We will change the example by adding a negation to the second part of the statement. The resulting compound statement will be:

SACRAMENTO WILL WIN THE NBA CHAMPIONSHIP BUT THE CELTICS WILL NOT BE IN THE NBA FINALS.

This is symbolized as follows:

$$S \bullet \sim C$$

On the other hand, negations can also negate a compound statement, as in this case:

NOT BOTH SACRAMENTO WILL WIN THE NBA CHAMPIONSHIP AND THE CELTICS WILL BE IN THE NBA FINALS.

This is symbolized as follows:

$$\sim(S \bullet C)$$

In this case, notice the negation precedes that which it modifies and what it is modifying is the conjunction (S • C). How do we know this? Because the negation, the "not," comes before the word "both" in the compound statement and as such we know the negation is modifying the entire conjunction and not one single simple statement.

Some things to remember about negations

The Tilde…
- Is always placed in front of proposition it negates

- *Cannot* be used to connect two propositions
  FOR EXAMPLE: G ~ H

- Is the only operator that can follow another operator
  FOR EXAMPLE: G • ~ H

Can be used to negate an entire compound statement

Examples of negating compounds

$$\sim (P \bullet \sim Q)$$
$$\sim (H > P)$$
$$\sim [(B \equiv Q) \bullet (C \equiv G)]$$

Negating Compound Statements – Conjunctions & Disjunctions

One aspect that can be especially difficult in translating statements into symbolic form is trying to figure out the role negations play in conjunctions and disjunctions. However, this can be easily resolved. You will find the following charts useful:

Statement	Translation
Not A and B	~A • B
A is false and B	~A • B
Not both A and B	~(A • B)
Both A and B are not	~A • ~B

The key to translating the above statements is to understand how negations work, and the use of the word "both." A negation only affects whatever it is in front of. In the first two examples in the chart above, the only variable that is being negated is "A." Neither statement indicates that the negation should be carried over to B.

In the second two examples, the word "both" indicates that "B" is affected by the negation. Why are the two statements translated differently? The third example has "not" in front of "both." This indicates it is not possible for both statements to be true at the same time: "they are not both true." Therefore, we need to first claim that they are both true: A • B. We then need to deny that claim. Since we are denying the entire claim, we put it in parentheses and then place the negation outside: ~(A • B).

In the fourth example, the word "not" occurs after the word "both." "Both are not." This indicates that both variables are not true. In other words, they are both false. How do we indicate a simple statement is false? By placing a negation directly in front of the statement. This gives us ~A • ~B.

We can sum this up with two rules:

1. If "not" occurs before "both," negate the entire statement.
2. If "not" occurs after "both," negate the individual variable.

Much the same is true for negations in disjunctions, as the following chart illustrates:

PART TWO

Statement	Translation
Not A or B	~A v B
A is False or B	~A v B
Not either A or B	~(A v B)
Neither A nor B	~(A v B)
Either A or B are not	~A v ~B

The main differences here are the use of the word "either" instead of "both," and the use of disjunctions rather than conjunctions. Note that "neither/nor" is the same as "not either." "Neither" is a contraction of "not either" and has the same meaning.

Again, we can sum this up with two rules:

1. If "not" occurs before "either," negate the entire statement.
2. If "not" occurs after "either," negate the individual variable.

CONJUNCTIONS

Conjunctions are indicated by connective words such as *and, but, yet, moreover, furthermore, nevertheless, also,* etc. These indicate that at least two statements are being joined together, but these two statements can be two simple statements, two compound statements, or a combination.

Joining two simple statements

W • K

Joining two compound statements

(W • G) • ~H

Joining a combination of statements

~(H • ~B) • M

DISJUNCTIONS

Disjunctions, like conjunctions, are indicated by connective words such as *either, or, unless.* These indicate that at least two statements are being joined together with a binary connective, a wedge, "v", where the truth-value output is true provided at least one of the disjuncts is true, and false if none of the disjuncts are true. Each disjunct can either be simple statements, compound statements, or a combination of simple and compound statements.

Joining two simple disjuncts

W v K

Joining two compound disjuncts

(W • G) v ~H

Joining a combination of disjuncts

$$\sim(H \bullet \sim B) \text{ v } M$$

CONDITIONALS OR IMPLICATION

Conditional statements provide their own order. A conditional statement can be broken into two parts, antecedent and consequent. The antecedent is the portion that occurs between "if" and "then." The consequent comes after "then." This needs to be kept in mind when translating conditional statements. If you have multiple statements in the antecedent, they should be grouped together. Similarly, if you have multiple statements in the consequent, they should be grouped together. For example:

IF F OR C, THEN D

"F" and "C" are both in the antecedent. They must be grouped together, as the following translation illustrates:

$$(F \text{ v } C) > D$$

Another example:

IF M, THEN W OR NOT X

This is translated as:

$$M > (W \text{ v } \sim X)$$

It can often at first be difficult to decide where parentheses are needed. The thing to keep in mind is that parentheses replace the grammar present in English statements that tell us how to group claims. If you keep this in mind, it will often make translating statements easier.

Sharing means togetherness

Another way that you can determine that statements need to be grouped together is when they share a predicate in English. Such a structure indicates that the two terms are to be kept together. For example:

> ATLANTA WILL WIN THE WORLD SERIES BUT THE DODGERS AND THE RED SOX WILL NOT.

Here the wording of the statement indicates clearly that the two claims about the Dodgers and the Red Sox should be grouped. This is because each of these claims shares the same predicate. If you divorce the claim about the Dodgers from the claim about the Red Sox, then there is no predicate associated with the subject, "Dodgers." Note that there is a negation affecting both of these claims as well. This makes the correct translation:

$$A \bullet (\sim D \bullet \sim R)$$

Flipping over conditional statements

Another puzzle when first trying to translate into symbolic form are conditional statements. Students are confused over the differences between "if," "only if," and "if and only if." Let's clarify how to deal with conditional statements.

The basic idea is that when we translate something as a conditional statement, we want the antecedent to come first and the consequent to come second. This is the order that is found in "if/then" statements, such as "If today is Monday, then tomorrow is Tuesday." Such a statement is translated in the order in which it is found:

$$M > T$$

However, not all conditional statements have an "if/then" form. Sometimes, "if" will occur in the middle of a conditional statement. For example:

YOU HAVE BAD TASTE IF YOU LIKE MICHAEL BOLTON

In translating this statement into symbolic form, we must make sure that the antecedent is listed first. The antecedent is the sufficient condition, the guarantee. Consider: does having bad taste guarantee you like Michael Bolton? No. You might hate Michael Bolton, yet love the Britney Spears. On the other hand, does liking Michael Bolton guarantee you have bad taste? Oh, yes! So "liking Michael Bolton" is the sufficient condition and must be the antecedent, although the English statement lists this part second. The correct translation is:

$$M > B$$

Where M stands for "you like Michael Bolton" and "B" stands for "you have bad taste." (Notice that I did not use "Y" to symbolize either part of the statement. "You" is such a common pronoun that it is avoided when symbolizing. Much the same is true for words such as "the" or "a.") So, when "if" is in the middle of a conditional statement, you flip the order of the variables.

On the other hand, when a conditional statement has "only if" in the middle, you do not flip the order of the variables. Why? Because "only if" designates a necessary condition, and necessary conditions always are found in the consequent. For example:

YOU GRADUATED ONLY IF YOU ENROLLED.

Enrolling is a necessary condition for graduating. Necessary conditions are found in the consequent. As noted above, the consequent should come second. In this example, it is listed second. Therefore, when we translate this, we have no need to flip the order of the variables:

$$G > E$$

Given all of this, it follows that sometimes with conditional statements you will need to flip the order of the variables, and sometimes you will not. The charts below will help serve as a guide to this.

Flip these conditionals	translation
A if B	B > A
A is necessary for B	B > A
A provided that B	B > A
A given that B	B > A
Do not flip these Conditionals	Translation
A is sufficient for B	A > B
A only if B	A > B
If a, then B	A > B
A implies B	A > B

BICONDITIONAL

Biconditionals are indicated only by connective words of *if and only if*, and *is a sufficient and necessary condition for*. These indicate that at least two statements are being joined together in such a way that should both parts have the same truth value then the enitre compound biconditional statement is true. Essentially this takes the form of the joining of a conditional statement and its inverse: (R > G) and (G >

PART TWO

R). When fully translated this would look like (R > G) • (G > R). Logicians, however, have simplified writing this form as a triple bar, =.

Some examples

R ≡ G

A ≡ (V • G)

(B v S) ≡ (A • P)

[K v (K > I)] ≡ [~L • (G v H)]

Creating Order from Chaos - When to Use Parenthesis

This should give you an idea of the various ways we can combine simple statements to form compound statements. As the last example also shows, however, we are not just limited to using simple statements when forming compound statements. We can also use other compound statements-- such as ~B-- as components of other compound statements. This presents a problem. Since compound statements consist of simple statements linked by an operator, if we have several compound statements as part of a larger compound statement, how do we determine which operator receives priority? This is not an issue with the tilde. A negation always affects whatever it is front of. But for other operators, this is a difficulty. Consider this statement:

F > R • H

How should we read this statement? Is it "F implies both R and H"? Or is it "both F implies R and H are true"? The two interpretations do not mean the same thing. Yet we cannot determine which interpretation is correct, given the symbolic statement above. In order to avoid this sort of confusion, we need to use parentheses and brackets to give order to compound statements of this type. For example, if our original statement was "F implies both R and H," we would write our symbolization as:

$$F > (R \cdot H)$$

On the other hand, if our original statement was "Both F implies R and H are true," then the symbolic statement would be as follows:

$$(F > R) \cdot H$$

By using parentheses, we make the meaning of the statement quite apparent. What will determine how parentheses are applied is the structure of the original statement itself. The idea is to accurately map out the logic embodied in the original statement. You must pay close attention to the wording and grammar of the original English statement. Words like "both" or "either" often indicate how to use parentheses. Commas and semicolons can also help. Below are some examples. We have already turned the simple statements into variables in the examples:

BOTH F AND R, OR C

The keys here are the word "both" and the comma. "Both" is almost always linked to an "and." Whatever is between "both" and "and" is one part of the conjunction. What comes after the "and" is the second part of the conjunction. The comma indicates that the "C" is separated from the conjunction, and should be grouped apart from it. The correct translation would then be:

$$(F \cdot R) \vee C$$

Notice that just as the comma blocks off "F" and "R" from "C", the parenthesis do the same. Another example:

F AND EITHER R OR C

Here the major clue is word "either." "Either" functions like the word "both," except that it is usually linked to disjunctions. "Either" tells us to group "R" and "C" together, since they make up the disjunction. The correct translation is then:

$$F \bullet (R \lor C)$$

Another example:

<small>EITHER R, OR C IMPLIES D</small>

Here the main clue is the placement of the comma. It separates R from the other two variables. The translation is:

$$R \lor (C > D)$$

This deals with conditional statements. But students often confuse "if" or "only if" with "if and only if." Where "if" and "only" are implications, the phrase "if and only if" requires the use of a biconditional. A biconditional is really two conditional statements combined. Think of the phrase, "If and only if." That combines "if" with "only if." So for a statement of this type, the triple bar symbol is used:

Batman finds the Riddler if and only if the Riddler leaves clues.

$$B \equiv R$$

CHAPTER SEVEN

||||||||||||||||||||||||||||||||||||||||||||||||||||||||||||||||||||||||||||||||||||||||||||||||||||||||||||||||||||||||||||

UNDERSTANDING TRUTH-TABLES

⚡ LEARNING OUTCOMES

- Learn the way the different operators affect truth value.

We strongly advise that you memorize this information. Each operator has 4 different possibilities, except for the negation, which has only 2 possibilities. Should you heed our advice and memorize these tables and how to set them up, most of the chapter should be much easier.

PART ONE

||||||||||||||||||||||||||||||||||||||||||||||||||||||||||||||||||||||||||||||||||||||||||||||||||||||||||||||||||||

TRUTH VALUE AND LOGICAL OPERATORS

TRUTH VALUE

You will recall in chapter 1 that we defined statements as having a truth value. That is, every statement has the potential to be either true or false. This is true in symbolic logic as well. Simple statements are either true or false. If we take the simple statement, C, to represent "Christina Aquilera sings like a warthog in heat," we have a statement that is either true or false. It has two possible values.

Now, when we link simple statements together to form a compound statement, the resulting compound statement also has a truth value. Two things determine this truth value: one, the truth value of the individual simple statements; and two, the nature of the logical operators linking the individual statements. The logical operators that link the simple statements together determine the nature of the compound proposition. Thus, these operators determine when the compound proposition will be true or false, because they specify the logical relationship existing between the simple statements.

Think of it this way. Imagine you have the statement A and the statement B. Now, if you say *A and B*, that is quite different from saying *A or B*. Yet both of these compound statements are made of the same simple statements. They have the same truth value in both cases. The only difference is the operator used. This means the operators must be the reason these statements differ. Since the simple statements are the same in both statements, and have the same truth value, the operator will determine the truth value of the compound statement.

PART ONE

For example, let us symbolize the statement given above. Let us also assume that A is true and B is false. This will give us the following situation:

> Assume A is T
> Assume B is F

$$A \star B$$

Replace A with T and B with F

$$T \cdot F$$

A conjunction ("and") claims that two things are true. Therefore, in this example, the conjunction is false. Both parts are not true.

Let's try another, but this time let's try a disjunction.

$$A \vee B$$

Replace each with their given corresponding truth-value from before.

$$T \vee F$$

A disjunction (the "v"), on the other hand, says that at least one of two choices will be true. The disjunction above will therefore be true. We can update the above example to illustrate this:

A • B	A v B
T • F	T v F
F	T

PART ONE

Both compound statements fed the same truth values into the operators. However, the operators gave different results, because of their different meanings. So, we can see that the operator will have the final say in deciding the truth value of the overall compound proposition, because it determines the logical relationships that exist between the simple statements. Each operator has its own logic in terms of assigning truth value, so what we want to do is look at each of the operators and see under what conditions they will be true or false.

LOGICAL OPERATORS & TRUTH-TABLES

CONJUNCTIONS

Let's start with the conjunction. The conjunction claims that each of the two statements it links is true. For example, the statement B • R is a claim that B and R are both true. Under what conditions will this claim be true? Only when both B and R are each true. We can illustrate this using a truth table. A truth table is a chart that shows all the different possibilities that exist for a given statement. In this case we have two variables. This gives us four possible cases: B and R can both be true, B can be true with R false, R can be true with b false or B and R can each be false. The truth table below shows all four cases and the result for the conjunction.

B	R	B • R
T	T	T
T	F	F
F	T	F
F	F	F

This chart represents each of the four possible situations and illustrates what we have just stated, namely that the conjunction of B and R will be true only in those cases where B and R are both true. If one fails to be true, the conjunction will be false. The conjunction is a strong statement, because it requires both statements to be true in order to be true itself. You will notice that it is true only 25% of the time.

Rule for Conjunctions: Both parts must be true.

DISJUNCTION

The disjunction is a weaker claim than the conjunction. The statement B v R does not claim that both B and R are true. Rather, it claims that at least one of the two options is true. "Either B or R," means "at least one of the two choices will be true." So when will the disjunction be false? Only when B and R are both false. We can map this out just as we did with the conjunction, again considering each of the 4 possible cases.

PART ONE

B	R	B v R
T	T	T
T	F	T
F	T	T
F	F	F

This truth table shows that a disjunction is false only when both statements linked by the disjunction are false. In every other case, it is true. Thus, a disjunction is a weaker statement than a conjunction, because it has fewer conditions to meet in order to be true. A disjunction has a 75% chance of being true.

Rule for disjunctions: At least one part must be true.

CONDITIONAL

The conditional statement is more difficult to understand than the conjunction or the disjunction. The easiest way to grasp how a conditional statement works is to recall that a conditional statement expresses a sufficient condition. B > R tells you that B is sufficient for R. A sufficient condition is a guarantee. With this in mind, consider the following analogy: imagine you buy a dishwasher at Circuit City. With the dishwasher, there is a warranty. Warranties are guarantees. The guarantee here is that if the dishwasher breaks, then Circuit City will repair it. This is represented by the following conditional statement: B > R. Again, there are four possible arrangements of truth value. This gives us this truth table:

B	R	B > R
T	T	T
T	F	F
F	T	T
F	F	T

To better understand these results, let us take them one by one. On line one, it is true that the dishwasher broke and true that it is repaired. (Both B and R are true.) In such a case, is it true we have a warranty? Yes. On line two, the dishwasher broke, but it was not repaired. (B is true but R is False.) Is it true we have a warranty in this case? No. The dishwasher broke, but they did not fix it. This indicates it was not under warranty. On line three, the dishwasher is not broken (B is false) but it is repaired anyway (R is true). Is it true we have a warranty? Yes, if they work on a dishwasher that is not broken, it is reasonable to assume they will also work on a broken dishwasher. On line four, the dishwasher is not broken (B is false) and it is not being repaired (R is false.) If you have a new dishwasher and it is working fine, do you not normally assume you have a warranty? Yes. So, the conditional statement is true.

Another way to think of conditional statements is to relate it to scientific hypothesis, which interestingly are always assumed to be true until proven false. Let's take the following conditional statement:

IF (W) THERE IS WATER ON MARS, THEN (L) THERE IS LIFE MARS.

We apply this conditional statement to our Mars expedition. If it turns out, as in the first case, line one, we discover water on Mars and we discover a life form (both W and L are true), then the conditional statement holds true. However, if we do discover water on Mars but we do not find any life-forms then it turns out the statement is false. In fact, this is the only scenario in which we can prove the condition false. Moving on. Let's say we do not find water on Mars but we do find life on Mars (W is false but L is true). In this case, the statement has not been proven false. Some scientists today argue life is possible without the presence of water. Thus, the statement remains true because the consequent, here statement L, may in fact be true based on a different factor than having water present. This makes water only a sufficient condition for life on Mars, not a necessary one. Finally, should we not find water on Mars and not locate any life-forms (both W and L are false), then the statement is still held to be true...until proven false. In other words, both the antecedent and the consequent may be false and the conditional statement true, precisely because we have no way in which to prove the statement false. So, as a theory, this statement can only be falsified should we find water and yet there be no life form on Mars.

In the chart above we can see that the only time a conditional statement is false is when the antecedent is true and the consequent is false. This means a conditional statement is true 75% of the time.

Rule for conditional statements: Only way to falsify a conditional statement is to have antecendent present (true) and the consequent not (false). Otherwise it's true.

BICONDITIONAL

The biconditional is an operator that links two simple statements together in both a necessary and sufficient relationship. Basically, B ≡ R is the equivalent of (B > R) • (R > B). B ≡ R claims R to be sufficient for B and R to be necessary for B. What does this mean? If B is sufficient for R, then if you have B, you must get R. And if B is necessary for R, then R cannot occur without B. In short, if we do not get B, we cannot get R, and if we do get B, we have to get R. They must either occur together or not at all. The chart for the biconditional looks as follows:

B	R	B ≡ R
T	T	T
T	F	F
F	T	F
F	F	T

Line one gives us a true result because the biconditional claims that both B and R must occur together, or not at all. Both B and R are true. They occurred together. On line two, B is true but R is false. But B is supposed to be sufficient for R: if B is true, we should get R. That failed to happen. The biconditional is false. On line 3, B is false and R is true. B is also supposed to be necessary for R. To get R, we must first get B. That did not occur here. Thus, the biconditional is false. The final case gives a true result. We said that either B and R would both occur or neither would occur. On line 4, they both fail to occur and this makes the biconditional true.

Now that we have explained the logic behind the truth value of the biconditional, let us point out something that will make this easier to remember. The triple bar looks much like an "equals" sign. Notice that in our chart, when B and R have the same truth value, the biconditional is true. When they have different truth values, they are both false. So, you should think of the triplebar as an "equals" sign. When the two parts of the biconditional match, i.e., when they are equal, the biconditional will be true. When they do not match, when they are not equal, the biconditional will be false. Biconditionals are true 50% of the time.

Rule for biconditionals: Both parts are equal.

NEGATION

The final operator to examine is the simplest: the tilde or negation. It just reverses the truth value of the statement it is in front of. For example, consider the statement "Bill Clinton is a former President of the United States." This is a true statement. If I added a negation to this statement, "Bill Clinton is not a former President of the United States," the result is a false statement. So adding a negation reverses the truth value of the original statement. The following truth table illustrates this:

B	~B
T	F
F	T

PART ONE

Here, again, we have 50% chance of getting a true statement as a result.

Rule for negations: The negation reverses the truth value of the original statement.

RECOGNIZING THE MAIN LOGICAL OPERATORS

In the above examples, the statements we have looked at only used one operator. But in complicated compound statements, there may be several operators at work. In order to be able to determine the overall truth value of such statements, you have to first recognize the main operator. The main operator is the operator that determines the truth value of the overall statement. For example, in the statement ~B v C, the main operator is "v." The tilde only affects B. The wedge, however, links the entire statement together and therefore determines the statement's overall truth value.

In order to determine the main operator of a statement, you should keep two things in mind: 1) the main operator is the operator that all other parts of the statement link into; 2) the main operator appears outside any parentheses or brackets.

For example:

$$X \cdot (Y \lor B)$$

In this statement the main operator is the conjunction. (In all of the following examples, I have made the main operator black in color.) It links X to the statement in parentheses. The disjunction links Y and B, but does not tie in with X: it therefore does not affect the entire statement. It is also the only operator outside. Another example:

$$(X \vee A) > (B \cdot C)$$

Here the main operator is the horseshoe. It links together both of the statements in parentheses. In order to figure out the truth value of the disjunction, we need to only know the truth values of X and A; in order to determine the truth value of the conjunction, we need to know the truth values of B and C. But to determine the truth value of the conditional statement, we first have to determine the truth values of the two statements in parentheses. Again, the conditional is the only operator outside the parentheses.

Another example:

$$\sim[B \cdot (Y > A)]$$

Here, the main operator is the negation. The rest of the statement is within the brackets and the negation is outside the brackets. So, the negation affects the entire statement.

One more example:

$$\sim A \vee [B > (Y \vee X)]$$

Here the main operator is the first disjunction. While the tilde is outside the brackets, it only affects "A." If there is more than a single operator outside the parenthesis or brackets, the main operator will be whichever operator is not a tilde. (There can only be one such operator.) A tilde can be the main operator only if it is the only outside operator (as it was in the prior example).

PART TWO

||||||||||||||||||||||||||||||||||||||||||||||||||||||||||||||||||||||||||||||||||||||||||||||||||||||||||||||||||||||||||||

CALCULATING TRUTH-VALUES OF COMPLEX STATEMENTS - *WITH A GIVEN DESIGNATED TRUTH-VALUE*

 ## DETERMINING TRUTH VALUE OF COMPLEX STATEMENTS

Now that we have seen how to recognize the main operators in compound statements, we can discuss how to determine the truth value of such statements. Take the statement (A v B) > X. Imagine we wish to determine whether this statement is true or false. For purposes of demonstration, assume that A and B are true, and that X and Y are false. We apply these values to the individual simple statements, replacing the simple statements with their truth values. For example:

$$(A \ v \ B) > X$$
$$(T \ v \ T > F$$

To determine the truth value of this statement, we must first determine the main operator. The conditional statement links the entire statement together, so it is our main operator. To determine the truth value of the conditional statement, we must obtain a truth value for the antecedent. The antecedent is the statement A v B. Therefore, we must first determine that statement's truth value. If both parts of the disjunction are true, what is the truth value of the disjunction? True. This gives us the following result:

$$(A \ v \ B) > X$$
$$(T \ v \ T) > F$$

$$T > F$$

Notice that the rest of the statement is carried down. We now have determined that our antecedent is true. Our consequent remains unchanged. It is false. If we have a true antecedent and a false consequent, the truth value of the conditional statement is false (tutti-frutti). That is the truth value for the entire statement. Usually that value is circled in order to indicate that it is the value for the statement as a whole.

$$(A \lor B) > X$$
$$(T \lor T) > F$$
$$T > F$$

$$\boxed{F}$$

You can see from this example how to proceed. You first determine the truth value of those statements within parenthesis. You then take that result and carry it out to the next operator. This is very much like math. Consider this math problem (6 - 2) + 5. In this problem, do you add both 6 and 2 to 5? No. You first get the result for 6 - 2, and then carry that result outside and add it to 5. We are doing the same thing with our statements. In the above example we do not apply A or B directly to the conditional statement. Instead, we get a value for the disjunction first and then carry that forward.

Here is another example. Again, assume that A and B are true, and that X and Y are false.

$$(B > Y) \lor \sim (Y \lor X)$$
$$(T > F) \lor \sim (F \lor F)$$

Now that we have assigned the truth values to the simple statements, we proceed to the operators. T > F gives us a false result. F v F is also false. This gives us:

$$(B > Y) \text{ v} \sim (Y \text{ v } X)$$
$$(T > F) \text{ v} \sim (F \text{ v } F)$$
$$F \text{ v} \sim F$$

At this point, we still have to apply the negation to the second part of the statement. It is important to understand that negations outside parenthesis are not carried inside the parenthesis. Instead, you determine the truth value of the statement within the parenthesis and then carry that value outside to the negation. In other words, you always work inside out. In the above example, we have determined that the disjunction inside the parenthesis is false. We carry that false value outside the parenthesis to the negation. Negating a false statement (~F) gives us a true result:

$$(B > Y) \text{ v} \sim (Y \text{ v } X)$$
$$(T > F) \text{ v} \sim (F \text{ v } F)$$
$$F \text{ v} \sim F$$
$$F \text{ v } T$$

We then have a disjunction of a false and true statement. This gives us a true result that is circled, because it is the truth value for the statement as a whole.

$$(B > Y) \text{ v} \sim (Y \text{ v } X)$$
$$(T > F) \text{ v} \sim (F \text{ v } F)$$
$$F \text{ v} \sim F$$
$$F \text{ v } T$$

$$T$$

Here's a shorter example, involving a negation, just for clarification:

$$\sim (X \equiv Y)$$
$$\sim (F \equiv F)$$
$$\sim T$$

F

We first determine the value of the biconditional. F is equivalent to F, so the biconditional is true. We then carry that truth value out to the negation. The negation reverses the truth value, so the negation above is false. The negation is the main operator, so that is the truth value for the overall statement.

Note: if you try to bring the external negation inside the parentheses, you will often get the wrong answer. On the above problem, bringing the tilde inside would result in a result of "T" for the overall statement. That's incorrect. So, remember, never bring a negation outside the parentheses inside.

Here's one more example:

$$\sim A \ v \ [B \ v \ (Y \ v \sim X)]$$
$$\sim T \ v \ [T \ v \ (F \ v \sim F)]$$
$$F \ v \ [T \ v \ (F \ v T)]$$
$$F \ v \ [T \ v T]$$
$$F \ v T$$

T

Going line by line, here is how the problem is solved:

Line One: We assign the individual variables their truth value. Again, we assume A and B are true, X and Y are false.

Line Two: We apply the two negations. These negations are directly in front of individual variables, and so only affect those variables. A is true, so ~A is false. X is false, so ~X is true.

Line Three: We now determine the truth value of the third disjunction (inside parenthesis). After applying the negation in line two, we have a F v T statement. That gives us a true result.

Line Four: We now determine the truth value of the second disjunction (inside the brackets), B v (Y v ~X), or B v (F v T). We determined on line 3 that the third disjunction is true. That disjunction represents the right side of the second disjunction. We also know B, which is the right side of the second disjunction, is true. That means we have a T v T statement. Thus, our second disjunction is true.

Line Five: We now determine the truth value of the first disjunction, the main operator, where we have ~A v [...]. We already know that ~A was F (from Line One) and inside the brackets, we determined that it was T. So, we have a F v T statement. Since at least one part is true, the disjunction is true.

PART THREE

||||||||||||||||||||||||||||||||||||||||||||||||||||||||||||||||||||||||||||||||||||||||||||||||||||||||||||||||

CALCULATING TRUTH-VALUES OF COMPLEX STATEMENTS - *WITHOUT ANY GIVEN DESIGNATED TRUTH-VALUES*

USING THE TRUTH TABLES

We have seen how to determine the truth value of a compound statement, once we know the truth values of the individual statements involved. For example, if A is true and B is false, then we know A v B is a true statement. However, that is just one particular case. What if A is false, and B is true? What if both are false? Obviously, there are a number of different possibilities. To examine all of these different possibilities, we need to use a truth table. A truth table extends the procedure for determining the truth value of a compound statement. Rather than examining the statement in one particular case, a truth table allows you to examine the statement in all possible cases.

BUILDING TRUTH TABLES

NUMBER THE POSSIBILITIES

In order to construct a truth table, you must first determine how many possible cases you have to consider. In other words, you need to determine how long the table will be. The length of a truth table depends on the number of unique variables in the statement you are examining. If a statement only has one unique variable, then there are two possibilities: the variable is either true or false. For example, there are only two possibilities for the variable C:

The above example captures both of the possibilities for C. This is important, because as noted, a truth table is supposed to allow us to examine a statement in all possible situations. Now, let us add a second variable, B. B could be true in the two cases above:

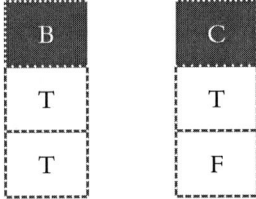

Or: B could be false in those same two cases:

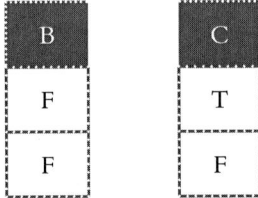

This gives us a total of four possible cases, as illustrated below:

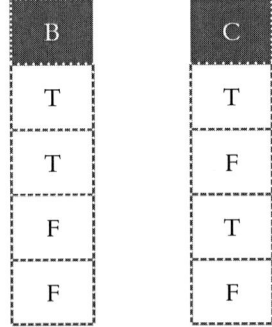

Adding a second variable doubles the number of possibilities. Why? Initially, we had two possibilities. We then added B. B might be true in both of our initial cases, or B might be false in those cases. This gives us four distinct possibilities. Now, add a third variable, A. A might be true in the four cases detailed above, or A might be false in those same four cases. This gives us a total of eight cases, as illustrated below:

A	B	C
T	T	T
T	T	F
T	F	T
T	F	F
F	T	T
F	T	F
F	F	T
F	F	F

You can see from the examples above that each time a new variable is added, the number of possibilities doubles. If we add a fourth variable, we have 16 lines to consider; if we have five variables, we have 32 lines; if we have six variables, then we have 64 lines; and if we have 10 variables, we would have 1,024 lines to consider. Obviously, statements with many unique variables will be problematic to deal with.

SETTING THE TABLE

Now that we have seen how to determine how many lines are in a truth table, we can proceed to construct a truth table. You start off by determining how many lines the table requires. As seen, the number of unique variables in the statement determines this. For example, the statement A v ~A has only one unique variable: A. It therefore requires only two lines. A v B, though, has two unique variables and requires 4 lines.

After determining the number of lines you need, you then set up the table. You start by taking the variable that occurs first in the statement. For example, in the statement A > (B • C), A occurs first and is the variable you first deal with. In the statement B > (A ≡ C), B occurs first, so you deal with it first. You do not follow alphabetical order. It is the order in the statement that matters. Take the first variable and make the first half of the lines under it true, then the second half of the lines false. For example, consider the statement B > (A • B). B occurs first. We have two variables, so the truth table has four lines. Half of four is two. So, you make the first 2 lines under B true, the second two lines false:

B
T
T
F
F

You then move to the next variable. In our example, this is A. Take the pattern of truth values you assigned to the first variable and cut it in half. Apply that to the new variable. The pattern applied to B is two Ts, two Fs. Half of two is one. So A has a one T, one F false pattern, as shown below:

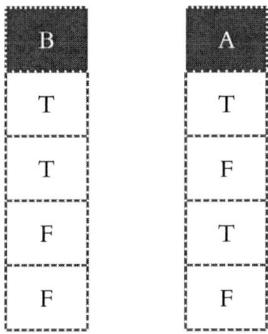

All truth tables are set up this way. To sum up, there are 3 steps:

3 STEPS TO BUILDING A TRUTH TABLE

1. Determine the number of lines needed.
2. Take the first variable and make the first half of the lines under it true, the other half false.
3. Move on to each new variable, cutting the pattern in half as you go. You know you are finished when the column to the last variable repeats the pattern, T/F.

For example, take the following statement:

$$C \text{ v } (B \cdot A)$$

This requires an eight line truth table, because it has three variables. C is the first variable, so we deal with it first. Half of eight is four. We make the first four lines under C true, the second four false. The pattern we applied to C is four Ts, four Fs. We then move to B. We cut our pattern in half and apply that to B. Half of four is two. So, B will have a two

T, two F pattern. Finally, we come to A. Again, we cut our pattern in half. Half of two is one. So, A will have a one T, one F pattern.

C	B	A
T	T	T
T	T	F
T	F	T
T	F	F
F	T	T
F	T	F
F	F	T
F	F	F

It is important to be rigorous when setting up a truth table. Our goal is to consider every possible case. If we are haphazard when setting up the table, we may not consider each possible case.

Note: the last variable you deal with in a truth table should always have the one T, one F pattern. If it does not, you have done something wrong.

⚡ SOLVING (THE) TABLE

Now that we have considered how to set up a truth table, let us actually do one. Take the the following statement:

$$A > (B \lor A)$$

How many variables are there? Two. (The fact that A occurs twice does not mean we have three unique variables.) This means our truth table has four lines. A is the first variable. Since we have four lines, that means the first two lines under A are true (half of four is two) and then the other half are false. We then work inwards to our next variable, B. We assigned A two Ts, then two Fs. We cut this pattern in half when we get to B. This means we assign B one T, then one F.

A	B	A	>	(B	v	A)
T	T					
T	F					
F	T					
F	F					

We next map out the logic of our statement in all four cases. This is exactly the same as the procedure for determining the truth value of a compound statement, except rather than assume A and B have a particular truth value, we instead consider all cases. First, we deal with the disjunction. In line one, both A and B are true. This gives us T v T and makes the disjunction true. On line two, A is true and B is false. This gives us T v F and a true disjunction. On line three, A is false and B is true. This gives us F v T and a true disjunction. On line four, both A and B are false. This gives us F v F and a false disjunction. We record our results underneath the disjunction operator.

A	B	A	>	(B	v	A)
T	T				T	
T	F				T	
F	T				T	
F	F				F	

Next, we deal with the conditional statement. A is the antecedent of the conditional statement. To determine the truth value of A, we need only look at the truth values we assigned to A when setting up the table. The consequent is the disjunction (A v B) and is represented by the results we recorded underneath the disjunction. In the illustration below, the two columns we now look at are greyed out.

A	B	A	>	(B	v	A)
T	T				T	
T	F				T	
F	T				T	
F	F				F	

On line one, this gives us T > T. That makes the conditional statement true. On line two, this gives us T > T. That makes the conditional statement true. On line three, this gives us F > T. That makes the conditional statement true. On line four, this gives us F > F. That makes the conditional statement true again. The table below records these results.

A	B	A	>	(B	v	A)
T	T		T		T	
T	F		T		T	
F	T		T		T	
F	F		T		F	

Normally, you will want to circle the column under the main operator and, in this case, that would be the horseshoe. So we circle the horshoe. This column represents the statement as a whole. Notice that on every line under the main operator, there is a true result. This indicates that the statement is a tautology. A **tautology** is a statement that is always true. The truth values of the variables in a tautology have no effect on the truth value of that statement. You can assign A and B any truth value and the tautology will be true.

We should note that there is another way of organizing truth tables. The way we build and solve these tables is not to write the truth values for the individual variables off to the side. Do not fill in the truth values for these variables in the actual statement. Instead read them from the side and only fill in the truth values for the operators. If you want, you can fill in the individual variables as they occur in the statement, rather than placing their truth values off to the side. To give you an idea of this strategy, here is the truth table for the above problem, redone in this style:

PART THREE

A	>	(B	v	A)
T	T	T	T	T
T	T	F	T	T
F	F	T	T	F
F	F	F	F	F

As you can see, the result is the same. The table is set up in the same way. The only difference is in the format. Rather than write the results for A and B to the side, you write them in the main part of the truth table. We prefer my method, because the resulting truth table is less cluttered and easier to read. You can use whichever method you prefer.

 ## INTERPRETING THE RESULTS OF THE TRUTH TABLE

We noticed that last example of A > (B v A) resulted in a column of all trues under the main operator. We told you this was thus a tautology because for any given result of a truth-table where every row of a column is true, we know that there is no situation in which that compound statement can in fact be false. This is the power of the truth tables! It helps us identify different types of statements. It can tell us whether a statement is also self-contradictory, which can be quite useful. Moreover, however, we can also use the solutions of truth tables to compare statements to determine logical equivalency or consistency.

Thus, when applying the solutions of truth tables to statements, we discover that they are useful in a) identifying statements and b) comparing statements. In the next part of this chapter, we will also learn truth tables can help us determine validity of arguments, but for now, let's stick to what it tells us about statements alone.

IDENTIFYING STATEMENTS

We already know that a column of all trues under the main operator is a tautlogy. Let us look at the following statement which represents another type of statement:

$$(A \cdot B) \cdot \sim(A \cdot B)$$

How many lines will the truth table require? Four, because we have two unique variables, A and B. We set up the truth table as before:

A	B	(A	•	B)	•	~	(A	•	B)
T	T								
T	F								
F	T								
F	F								

Now, we determine the truth value of the statement in all four cases. We start with the statements in parenthesis.

A	B	(A	•	B)	•	~	(A	•	B)
T	T		T					T	
T	F		F					F	
F	T		F					F	
F	F		F					F	

Next, the negation outside the second conjunction is applied. Since the negation is outside the parenthesis, we take the results for the statement inside the parenthesis, and reverse them.

A	B	(A	•	B)	•	~	(A	•	B)
T	T		T			F		T	
T	F		F			T		F	
F	T		F			T		F	
F	F		F			T		F	

Finally, we take the columns under the first conjunction and the negation and use them to determine the value of our main operator, which is the middle conjunction.

A	B	(A	•	B)	•	~	(A	•	B)
T	T		T		F	F		T	
T	F		F		F	T		F	
F	T		F		F	T		F	
F	F		F		F	T		F	

In the table above, the column under the main operator (our result) is circled. The two columns that determined the results for the main operator are colored grey. In this statement, every line under the main operator is false. This is a **self-contradictory** statement. A **self-contradictory statement** is a statement that is always false. The truth values of the individual variables in the statement have no effect on a self-contradictory statement. We can assign A and B any truth values we want, and the statement will still be false.

Let us take another example:

$$A > (\sim B \bullet A)$$

There are two variables, so our truth table will have four lines. It will be set up as illustrated below:

A	B	A	>	(~	B	•	A)
T	T						
T	F						

F	T					
F	F					

We must next deal with the negation. This negation is directly on B. Therefore, to get a result for the negation, we reverse the truth values under the B column.

A	B	A	>	(~	B	•	A)
T	T			F			
T	F			T			
F	T			F			
F	F			T			

Next, we take the result of our negation and the A column (the two columns colored grey below) and use those to get the results for the conjunction.

A	B	A	>	(~	B	•	A)
T	T			F		F	
T	F			T		T	
F	T			F		F	
F	F			T		F	

Finally, we determine the result for our conditional statement. A is the antecedent, (~B • A) is the consequent.

A	B	A	>	(~	B	•	A)
T	T		F	F		F	
T	F		T	T		T	
F	T		T	F		F	
F	F		T	T		F	

The column under the conditional statement is circled, because that is the main operator. The two columns in grey are the antecedent and consequent of the conditional statement. These columns determine the results under the main operator. There are both true and false results under the main operator. This is an example of a contingent statement. A **contingent statement** is one when there is at least one true result and at least one false result. It is called contingent because the statement's true value is contingent or dependent on the truth values of the variables, Make A and B true, you get one result. Make them both false, and you get a different result.

COMPARING STATEMENTS

Another useful use of the truth tables is their use of comparing statements. The key here is that you already know how to do construct the tables and so we do not need to show how to do that. Instead we just have to know how to intrepret the results. There is one caveat, however. When comparing statements, you must take the columns of the variables in the first statement and transfer them over to the second statement with which you want to compare. Thus, you only need to build one table, that is, using the first statement, and using the results, transfer the truth values to the second statement. What do we mean.

Let's take the results of two previous examples and put them side by side:

A	B	A	>	(~	B	•	A)
T	T		F			F	
T	F		T			T	
F	T		T			F	
F	F		T			F	

(A	•	B)	•	~	(A	•	B)
	T		F	F			
	F		F	T			
	F		F	T			
	F		F	T			

So, what you want to do is when solving the second statement, you want to use the truth values of variables A and B from the first statement, the problem on the left. Notice, we get the two columns under each of the main operators for each of the statements.

When you interpret the results, you want to compare each row with the corresponding row of the other statement. So, row 1 on the left is a F, and row one on the right is a F. This means the truth values are identical or the same. But row 2 on the left is a T and on the right it is a F. This makes the rows contradictory, or opposite. Interpret each row accordingly.

When comparing statements and comparing the results under each of the corresponding main operators, use this chart to identify the relationship the statments have with one another:

Comparing Statements Chart

Relationship	Main Operator Column
logically equivalent	same truth value on each row
contradictory	opposite truth value on each row
consistent	there is at least one row upon which both at true
inconsistent	there is no row upon which both are true

Notice that logically equivalent and contradictory are emboldened. This is because when you interpret the results of a the truth tables when comparing statements, always seek to identify whether the two statements are either logically equivalent or contradictory **first**. Only after you check for these two relationships then do you want to check for consistency or inconsistency.

PART FOUR

||||||||||||||||||||||||||||||||||||||||||||||||||||||||||||||||||||||||||||||||||||||||||||||||||||||||||||||||||||||||||||||||||||||||

APPLYING TRUTH-TABLES TO ARGUMENTS

 ## TRUTH TABLES FOR ARGUMENTS

So far we have seen how to use truth tables to examine statements. We are now going to consider how to use truth tables to determine the validity or invalidity of arguments. As defined in Chapter One of the textbook, an argument is a group of statements that express an inference. The key here is the first part of this definition: an argument is a group of statements. As we have already seen, statements can be mapped out on a truth table. Given that an argument is made up of statements, that means it can be mapped out on a truth table as well. The main differences are that we will be dealing with several statements, rather than just one, and we will be examining the logic of the argument as a whole, rather than examining the individual statements.

You set up a truth table for an argument just as you would for a statement. You determine the number of lines needed by counting the number of unique variables in the argument. You then take the first variable that occurs in the argument, and make half the lines true and half the lines false under that variable. You then work inwards to the next variable. After setting up the truth table, you then map out each statement in the argument.

You then read the results of your truth table. You are not examining the individual statements, though. You are searching for evidence that the argument is invalid. You will recall that when doing counterexamples, in order to show an argument invalid, you needed to have true premises and a false conclusion. Only invalid arguments can have this form. This is also what you are looking for in your truth table: true premises and a false conclusion. If you find this, the argument is invalid. If you do not find this situation, the argument must be valid. Why? Because a truth table examines every possible case. If the truth table fails to show a case where the argument has true premises and a false conclusion, then that case does not exist. The argument is therefore valid.

Essentially, when you construct a truth table for an argument, you are searching for a defect: you are searching for invalidity. If you find a defect, then the argument is invalid. If you fail to find a defect, you know there is no defect, because you examined all possible cases. In this way, a truth table is superior to a counterexample, because a counterexample can only show invalidity. A truth table can show both validity and invalidity.

TABLING THE DISCUSSION

This description may seem puzzling, so let us consider an example. Take the following argument:

$$A > B$$
$$\underline{B \qquad\;}$$
$$A$$

(The bar above A is a conclusion indicator. The statement below the bar is the conclusion.)

We set this up like any other truth table. We separate our premises with a single forward-slash, and separate the conclusion from the premises with a double forward-slash.

A	B	A	>	B	/	B	//	A
T	T							
T	F							
F	T							
F	F							

We then proceed to fill in each of the statements that make up our argument. The illustration below shows the results.

A	B	A	>	B	/	B	//	A
T	T		T			T		T
T	F		F			F		T
F	T		T			T		F
F	F		T			F		F

Next, we examine the result, looking to see if there is a line where the premises are true, and the conclusion is false. On the above table, we can see that line 3 in fact has true premises and a false conclusion. This means the argument is **invalid**. Normally, you circle this line to show the invalidity.

A	B	A	>	B	/	B	//	A
T	T		T			T		T
T	F		F			F		T
F	T		T			T		F
F	F		T			F		F

PART FOUR

Another example:

$$A > B$$
$$\underline{A}$$
$$B$$

We set this up like any other truth table:

A	B	A	>	B	/	A	//	B
T	T							
T	F							
F	T							
F	F							

We then fill in the individual statements:

A	B	A	>	B	/	A	//	B
T	T		T			T		T
T	F		F			T		F
F	T		T			F		T
F	F		T			F		F

We then examine the results. There is no line on the above truth table where the premises are true and the conclusion is false. Since we have looked at every possible case, this argument is therefore valid. There is no line to circle here, because there is no one line that shows validity. What reveals validity is the absence of invalidity from the table as a whole. You cannot circle an absence. Rather, we simply note the absence and answer that the argument is **valid**.

Note: Do not make the mistake of thinking that because line one in the table above has true premises and a true conclusion, that this shows the argument is valid. No single line in a truth table can prove an argument is valid. It is the truth table as a whole that shows validity. Earlier we said that in searching for invalidity, you are searching for a defect in the argument. What shows that the argument is not defective? That there are no defective cases. So, it is the absence of a defect (the absence of invalidity) that makes an argument **valid**.

Another example:

A > B

C > B

A > C

We set this up like any other eight-line truth table:

A	B	C	A	>	B	/	C	>	B	//	A	>	C
T	T	T											
T	T	F											
T	F	T											
T	F	F											
F	T	T											
F	T	F											
F	F	T											
F	F	F											

Next, we fill in the premises and the conclusion.

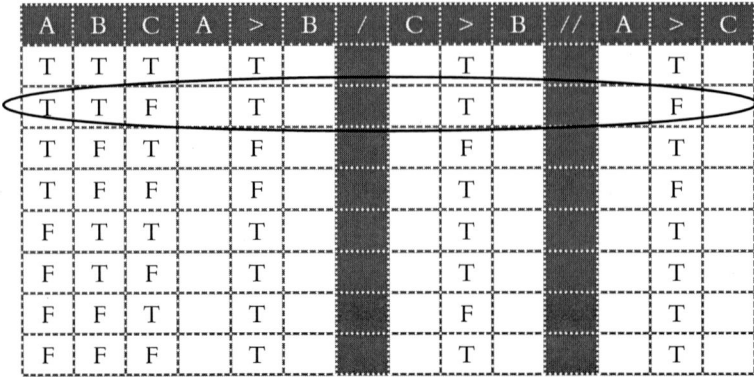

A	B	C	A	>	B	/	C	>	B	//	A	>	C
T	T	T		T				T				T	
T	T	F		T				T				F	
T	F	T		F				F				T	
T	F	F		F				T				F	
F	T	T		T				T				T	
F	T	F		T				T				T	
F	F	T		T				F				T	
F	F	F		T				T				T	

Line 2 above has true premises and a false conclusion, so the argument is **invalid**.

One more example:

$$A > (B \text{ v } C)$$
$$C > B$$
$$\underline{B > A \qquad}$$
$$C > A$$

A	B	C	A	>	(B	v	C)	/	C	>	B	/	B	>	A	//	C	=	A
T	T	T																	
T	T	F																	
T	F	T																	
T	F	F																	
F	T	T																	
F	T	F																	
F	F	T																	
F	F	F																	

A	B	C	A	>	(B	v	C)	/	C	>	B	/	B	>	A	//	C	>	A
T	T	T		T		T				T				T				T	
T	T	F		T		T				T				T				T	
T	F	T		T		T				F				T				T	
T	F	F		F		F				T				T				T	
F	T	T		T		T				T				F				F	
F	T	F		T		T				T				F				T	
F	F	T		T		T				F				T				F	
F	F	F		T		F				T				T				T	

The above table shows the results for the argument. Only the grey shaded columns are relevant in our search for invalidity. The other columns are not under the main operators of the statements in the argument. They therefore do not factor in when determining validity. Examining the relevant columns reveals that the premises are never all true when the conclusion is false. This argument is therefore **valid**.

CHAPTER EIGHT

||||||||||||||||||||||||||||||||||||||||||||||||||||||||||||||||||||||||||||||||||||||||||||||||||||||||||||||||||||||||||||||

CALCULUS OF
NATURAL DEDUCTION

⚡ LEARNING OUTCOMES

- Learn the rules of inference.
- Work backwards when constructing a deduction. Never make a move unless you know why you are making it.
- Be sure all the moves you make in a deduction are justified by one of the rules of inference.
- Be sure to do the reading and the homework.

PART ONE

||||||||||||||||||||||||||||||||||||||||||||||||||||||||||||||||||||||||||||||||||||||||||||||||||||||||||||||||||||||||||||

RULES OF INFERENCE 1

ARGUMENT FORMS REDUX

The valid argument forms we have studied can be used to show the validity of a deductive argument. For example, imagine we have the following argument:

P > ~Q
P
<u>Q v S</u>
S

We want to prove that the premises listed will in fact yield S as a conclusion. Is there any way we can show this, without using a truth table? Yes, there is. Look at the first two premises in the argument.

P > ~Q
P

If P is sufficient for ~Q, and P is true, what can we infer? ~Q. This is an example of a modus ponens argument. By using modus ponens on the first two premises, we can add ~Q as a premise to our argument. As we add ~Q, we will also note how we obtained it.

P > ~Q
P
~Q (MP)
<u>Q v S</u>
S

But Q v S is also a premise. What can we now infer? If we have two choices (Q v S) and one choice is contradicted (~Q), then the other choice (S) must be true. S is the conclusion we want. This is a disjunctive syllogism. So, by using MP and DS, we can show that the premises do in fact lead to the conclusion.

P > ~Q
P
~Q (MP)
Q v S
S (DS)

Another example:

P > Q
~R
Q > R
~P

Can we show that the conclusion follows from the premises? Yes. Look at premise 1 and 3 (see in bold):

P > Q
~R
Q > R
~P

If we have P > Q and Q > R, what can we infer? According to hypothetical syllogism, we can infer P > R. So, we can add that as a premise.

P > Q
~R
Q > R
P > R (HS)
~P

PART ONE

But look at the two premises highlighted in bold above. If P > R and ~R are true, what can we infer? By modus tollens, we can infer ~P, which is the conclusion.

P > Q
~R
Q > R
<u>P > R (HS)</u>
~P (MT)

DEDUCTIONS OR PROOFS

The examples above are informal versions of what is known as a **deduction**, or a proof. A deduction is a way of showing a deductive argument to be valid. It can only show validity. If we wish to show invalidity, then we must use a counterexample or a truth table. This limitation may make you wonder about the usefulness of deductions. After all, a truth table can show both validity and invalidity. But while a truth table can show you that an argument is valid, it cannot show you why it is valid. A deduction can, because it reveals the reasoning that the argument is based upon. It demonstrates how one can get from the premises to the conclusion. This is the purpose of a deduction: to show how one can go from point A (the premises) to point B (the conclusion.)

A **deduction** works by showing how the premises lead, step by step, to the conclusion. Each step in the proof must be documented, and must be in accordance with the rules governing the procedure. The first four rules we will consider are part of the Rules of Inference. The first four rules of inference are all based on valid argument forms that we can show using truth tables.

FIRST 4 RULES OF INFERENCE

MODUS PONENS (MP)

P > Q

P

Q

MODUS TOLLENS (MT)

P > Q

~Q

~P

HYPOTHETICAL SYLLOGISM (HS)

P > Q

Q > R

P > R

DISJUNCTIVE SYLLOGISM (DS)

P v Q

~P

Q

These rules are used to justify the steps within a proof. Consider the following argument.

1. P > Q
2. ~Q
3. P v R   /R

This is how an argument is displayed in a deduction. Each premise is numbered. After the final premise, the conclusion will be written. The single slash line in front of the conclusion is the conclusion indicator. The conclusion cannot be used in the deduction: it is listed simply to show you the target you are aiming for. The goal here is to show that the conclusion can be obtained from the premises. You are showing how to get from point A (the premises) to point B (the conclusion.)

Go backwards

In doing a deduction, the best strategy is always to try to work backwards. At this stage, you do not actually add anything to your proof. Instead, you look to see where the conclusion is located in the premises and try to figure out what you need to obtain it. You then look for that. For example, in the argument above to we want to get R. R is located in premise 3: P v R. That leaves us with the following situation:

P v R

?_____

R

The question mark represents the missing piece of the puzzle that will enable us to get R from the statement P v R. Looking at the rules of inference, notice that DS will enable us to break apart a disjunction and get one part of the disjunction by itself. To do a DS on P v R, we need to eliminate P as a choice. After all, P v R tells us that at least one choice is true. If P is eliminated, then R will have to be true. What eliminates P as a possible choice? ~P. So, the question mark can now be replaced by ~P.

P v R

~P_____

R

Now look at the rest of the premises. Does ~P occur anywhere? No, it does not. However, P does occur in line #1, as part of the statement P > Q. That means we are faced with the following situation:

P > Q

?_____

~P

Looking over my rules, is there a rule that enables us to get a negated antecedent as the conclusion? Yes, MT allows this. That means the ? needs to be replaced by ~Q.

P > Q
~Q
‾‾‾‾‾
~P

Looking in the argument, we can see that ~Q already occurs. This means we can stop working backwards, and now actually begin to work the proof.

To clarify, everything we have done so far has been preparatory work, normally done in our head or perhaps scribbled as notes. We have not actually done any of the proof. To summarize this stage, the idea is to locate the conclusion in the premises. Figure out what you need to obtain the conclusion from the statement it occurs in. If you do not have what you need, then begin to look for that in the premises. For example, we looked for R in the premises. We realized that in order to get R, we needed ~P. Since ~P did not occur as a premise, we then needed to figure how to get ~P. Keep working the problem backwards until you get to a point where you have the statement you need. For example, we realized that to get ~P, we required ~Q. Since ~Q occurs as a premise, we do not need anything else to get it. Now we can work forward. You do this by using your premises to obtain the lines you need.

1. P > Q
2. ~Q
3. P v R   /R
4. ~P   1, 2, MT

In the argument above, our first move is to obtain ~P. We know that we need ~P in order to get the conclusion, because we have already

PART ONE

planned out the deduction by working backwards. After adding a new premise to the argument, we then note how and why we obtained it. We used lines 1 and 2, and the MT rule to get ~P. Although the initial lines do not require annotation (because they are part of the initial argument), any addition we make to a deduction has to be annotated, to explain where the new line comes from. We need to do this to show that each new step in the argument is based on valid reasoning. If all the steps in the argument are valid, what do we then know about the argument as a whole? That it is valid. Annotation, then, serves to prove that argument as a whole is valid by assuring each step is valid.

We can proceed with our argument. Since we have ~P on line 4 and P v R on line 3, we now have a DS. The conclusion of that DS will be R, which is also the conclusion of our overall argument. That completes our proof:

1. P > Q
2. ~Q
3. P v R   /R
4. ~P   1, 2, MT
5. R   3, 4, DS

Another example:
1. A > B
2. B > C
3. A   /C

Again, we start by working backwards. We are looking for C. C occurs in the second premise. This means we have the following situation:

B > C

?_____

C

Is there a way to break apart a conditional statement and obtain the consequent as the conclusion? Yes, there is. MP allows us to do this. To do MP, our missing premise needs to be the antecedent: B.

B > C
B_____
C

Does B occur anywhere else in the argument? Yes, in the first premise. That gives us this situation:

A > B
?_____
B

Again, we want to break apart the conditional statement and get the consequent as the conclusion. That is again MP. That means the missing premise must be A.

A > B
?_____
B

Does A occur in the argument? Yes, it occurs as premise 3. So, we have no more need to work backwards, since we do not have to get A. It is given to us as a premise. Now we can construct the proof.

1. A > B
2. B > C
3. A   /C
4. B   1, 3, MP

The first move we make is to obtain B. We use MP on lines 1 and 3 to do so. (Note that in annotating our moves, the line numbers are listed in numerical order. In other words, line 1 is listed before line 3. You always follow this format.) Next, we obtain the conclusion, also by using MP.

1. A > B
2. B > C
3. A   /C
4. B   1, 3, MP
5. C   2, 4, MP

ANOTHER WAY

You may have noticed that there was another way to work this problem. Consider premises 1 and 2:

A > B
B > C

These two premises set up a hypothetical syllogism. We can therefore create a new conditional statement as our conclusion:

A > B
B > C
A > C

If we have A > C as a premise, we could then use the premise 3, A, to obtain our conclusion. This is the resulting proof.

1. A > B
2. B > C
3. A   C
4. A > C 1, 2, HS
5. C   3, 4, MP

PART TWO

||||||||||||||||||||||||||||||||||||||||||||||||||||||||||||||||||||||||||||||||||||||||||||||||||||||||||||||||||

USING THE RULES

TOOLS AND RULES

At this point, each of our four initial rules has been used in an example and so we want to revisit each one. The way to think about these rules is that each of them is a logical tool. Each has its own unique function, just as actual tools do. Hammers and wrenches have different uses; so, too, do our rules. We are going to sum up those uses. You may want to copy this section for review purposes.

THE RULES & THEIR USES

MODUS PONENS (MP)

P > Q

P‾‾‾‾‾

Q

MP, known as affirming the antecedent, breaks apart a conditional statement and allows you to obtain the consequent by affirming the antecedent.

MODUS TOLLENS (MT)

P > Q

~Q‾‾‾‾

~P

MT, known as denying the consequent, breaks apart a conditional statement and allows you to negate the antecedent by negating the consequent.

HYPOTHETICAL SYLLOGISM (HS)

P > Q

Q > R

P > R

HS allows you to construct a new conditional statement, out of two other conditional statements.

DISJUNCTIVE SYLLOGISM (DS)

P v Q

~P

Q

DS breaks apart a disjunction and allows you to obtain the right side disjunct by negating the disjunct on the left side.

Both MP and MT have the same basic function. They break apart conditional statements. This is important, for we cannot use the rules of inference on parts of larger statements. For example, if we have the statements P > ~Q and Q v S, we cannot do a DS on Q v S. The statement P > ~Q does not contradict Q, because the fact P > ~Q is true does not tell us that ~Q by itself is definitely true. The only way to do a DS on Q v S is if Q is contradicted. To contradict Q, we need ~Q. That requires that we know ~Q is true. To know this, we have to obtain ~Q by itself: We have to break apart the conditional statement. Similarly, if we have the statements P > (Q > R) and R > S, we cannot do a hypothetical syllogism and get Q > S. The reason for this is that Q > R is part of a larger statement. We cannot use part of the statement by itself. In order to use Q > R, we have to first break it out of the conditional statement it belongs to.

So, you can see why it is necessary to break apart statements. Both MP and MT allow us to break up conditional statements. However, they do so in very different ways. MP allows us to break apart a conditional statement so that we get the consequent as the conclusion. Whenever you need to consequent of a conditional statement by itself, MP is the tool to use.

On the other hand, MT allows us to obtain the antecedent of a conditional statement. However, the antecedent is negated by the use of MT. So, if you need to break apart a conditional statement to get the antecedent in a negated form, you use MT. Also, if you need a variable or a statement in a negated form, and it does not occur as a negation in your premises, you should look to see if MT applies.

Our third rule, HS, is the only rule we have at this point that allows us to make a new statement. HS allows us to create a new conditional statement out of two others. Therefore, whenever you need to create a new conditional statement, you should use HS.

Finally, DS enables us to break apart disjunctions. (Do not confuse this rule with MP and MT. DS breaks apart disjunctions, not conditionals. Watch the operators!) Anytime we need to obtain part of a disjunction by itself, we should use DS.

THE RIGHT TOOL FOR THE RIGHT JOB

Keeping the uses of these rules in mind when doing a deduction is helpful, because you will often be able to figure out which rule to apply by determining what sort of tool you need in a given situation. Let us look at another deduction.

1. P > (R > S)
2. P > (S > T)
3. Q v P
4. Q > X
5. ~X   /R > T

Looking at this argument, we note that the conclusion does not occur in the premises. Since it does not, that means we need to make the conclusion. The conclusion is a conditional statement. Which rule allows us to construct a new conditional statement? HS. Do we have the statements necessary for constructing an HS? Look at the first two premises.

P > (**R > S**)
P > (**S > T**)

The two consequents of the above conditional statements set up the HS we need. We have emboldened them to illustrate this. If R > S is true, and S > T is true, then by HS, R > T. The problem is that we cannot do an HS yet, because R > S and S > T are both part of larger statements. To use R > S and S > T, we first must break apart the conditional statements these statements belong to. Take R > S first. We want to get that statement. It occurs in P > (R > S). That gives us this situation:

P > (R > S)
?_____
R > S

We need to break apart the conditional statement and get the consequent. What rule enables us to do this? MP. So the ? needs to be replaced by the antecedent, P.

P > (R > S)
P_____
R > S

Now, let us turn to the other statement we need for the conclusion, S > T. It is part of P > (S > T). That gives us this:

P > (S > T)
?_____
S > T

Again, we want to get the consequent of a conditional statement as the conclusion. That means we need to use MP to break apart the conditional statement. To do MP, we need to replace the ? with the antecedent, which is P. So, we need P for both of these steps.

P > (S > T)
P_____
S > T

P, however, does not occur as a premise by itself. It does occur as part of premise 1, premise 2, and premise 3. We need to obtain P from one of these premises. we can eliminate premises 1 and 2 from consideration. The reason we want P is to use it on premises 1 and 2. So, we are not likely to get P from there. That leaves premises 3, and gives us the following situation:

Q v P
?_____
P

We need to break apart a disjunction and get one part of the disjunction as my conclusion. What rule enables us to break apart a disjunction? DS. To do a DS, one of your choices must be contradicted. We want P, so that means We need to contradict Q. The ? therefore needs to be replaced by ~Q.

Q v P
~Q_____
P

~Q does not occur as a premise. Moreover, it does not occur as part of a premise, either. However, Q does occur as part of the fourth premise, Q > X. This gives us the following:

Q > X
? _____
~Q

Is there a rule that allows you to break apart a conditional statement, and as your conclusion, take the antecedent in a negated form? Yes, MT. So, we need to use MT here. To do an MT, our ? needs to be replaced by the negation of the consequent: ~X.

Q > X
~X _____
~Q

Does ~X occur as a premise in our argument? Yes, it is the fifth premise. We are therefore now ready to move forward in the deduction.

1. P > (R > S)
2. P > (S > T)
3. Q v P
4. Q > X
5. ~X   /R > T

Our first step is to take premises 4 and 5 and use them to do an MT. (They are highlighted blue in the example below.) This gives us ~Q.

1. P > (R > S)
2. P > (S > T)
3. Q v P
4. Q > X
5. ~X   /R > T
6. ~Q   4, 5, MT

Next, we take ~Q and use it in a DS with premise 3. This gives us P.

1. P > (R > S)
2. P > (S > T)
3. Q v P
4. Q > X
5. ~X   /R > T
6. ~Q   4, 5, MT
7. P   3, 6, DS

Next, we use P on premise 1 and do MP. This gives us R >S.

1. P > (R > S)
2. P > (S > T)
3. Q v P
4. Q > X
5. ~X   /R > T
6. ~Q   4, 5, MT
7. P   3, 6, DS
8. R > S 1, 7, MP

We then use P again. (You can use a premise over as many times as you need to in a deduction.) This time, we use P on premise 2, again doing MP. This gives us S > T.

1. P > (R > S)
2. P > (S > T)
3. Q v P
4. Q > X
5. ~X   /R > T
6. ~Q   4, 5, MT
7. P   3, 6, DS
8. R > S 1, 7, MP
9. S > T   2, 7, MP

Finally, we take lines 8 and 9 and use them in a HS. This gives us R > T, which is our conclusion.

1. P > (R > S)
2. P > (S > T)
3. Q v P
4. Q > X
5. ~X   /R > T
6. ~Q   4, 5, MT
7. P   3, 6, DS
8. R > S   1, 7, MP
9. S > T   2, 7, MP
10. R > T   8, 9, HS

Note: It is tempting to think of a deduction as an abstract manipulation of symbols. But that fails to recognize what a deduction actually is: a model of our reasoning process. I'll illustrate this with the following example. Imagine we tell you the following:

IF YOU CHEAT, YOU'LL BE CAUGHT, AND IF WE CATCH YOU CHEATING, YOU'LL FAIL THE CLASS. YOU DON'T WANT TO FAIL.

What do you now know to avoid doing? Cheating. You worked this answer out in your head. The reasoning process that took place was very quick, but it took the form of the following deduction:

1. C > Y
2. Y > F
3. ~F   / ~C
4. ~Y   2, 3, MT
5. ~C   1, 4 MT

Where C ≡ you cheat, Y ≡ you'll be caught, & F ≡ you'll fail the class.

The thing to keep in mind is that deductions are in fact capturing the way our minds work. This is not simply an abstract game: it allows us to model our reasoning process with great clarity.

PART THREE

|||||||||||||||||||||||||||||||||||||||||||||||||||||||||||||||||||||||||||||||||||||||||||||||||||||||||||||||||||||||||||

MORE RULES OF INFERENCE

 4 NEW RULES

We are now going to consider four additional rules of inference. Just as with the four rules discussed earlier, these rules are used in the construction of a proof. The new rules are listed below. We will then discuss each one, and then summarize the function of each rule.

SECOND 4 RULES OF INFERENCE

Constructive Dilemma (CD)

(P > Q) • (R > S)

P v R
‾‾‾‾‾
Q v S

CD, breaks apart a conjunction joining two conditional statements and allows you to obtain the consequent of each of those conditional statements by affirming the antecedents.

Simplification (Simp)

P • Q
‾‾‾‾‾
P

Simp breaks apart a conjunction and allows you to obtain only the left side of the conjunction by bringing the left side down by itself.

Conjunction (Conj)

P

Q
‾‾‾‾‾
P • Q

Conj allows you to bring two premises together by joining them as a conjunction.

Addition (Add)

P
P v Q

Add allows you to generate a new disjunction by adding a wedge between the premise you want to bring down and any other statement you wish to create.

CONSTRUCTIVE DILEMMA

The first of our new rules is CD, a common argument form. CD enables us to construct new disjunctions. If a deduction requires a disjunction that does not occur in the premises, then CD may be the way to obtain that disjunction. Generally, if a deduction has a number of conditional statements as premises, or a conjunction of two conditional statements, you should look to see if CD is a move you want to make.

SIMPLIFY!

Simplification breaks apart a conjunction. You will recall that a conjunction claims that both parts are true. For example, the statement "The Braves and the Red Sox will play in the World Series" claims that it is true both teams will be in the World Series. Therefore, if a conjunction is true, what do we know about the individual parts of the conjunction? That they must both be true. This is what simplification is claiming: since the conjunction is true, each part is true. One caveat: you may only simplify the left side of a conjunction - not the right side. The following are all examples of simplification:

~P • R
~P

(M v G) • W
M v G

(S > M) • E
S > M

[B • (H v F)] • X
B • (H v F)

Note that, unlike the other argument forms we have looked at so far, simplification only requires one premise: the conjunction. This means you can simplify anytime you have a conjunction. No additional premises are required. When annotating a simplification step in a deduction, you only cite one line as justification, because this argument form has only one premise.

Simplification allows you to break apart conjunctions. Imagine you have the following statements:

P • Q
P > R

You need to get R. MP will allow you to get R from P > R, but you do not have P as a premise. Thus, you cannot use MP. You do have P • Q, however. If both P and Q are true, it follows that P must be true. So, you use simplification to break apart the conjunction. That gives you P by itself:

P • Q
P > R
P (simp)

Once you have P, you can use it and P > R, and do MP to get R.

Simplification is one of the easiest rules to apply, because it does not require a second premise. Therefore, whenever you see a conjunction in a deduction, you should keep in mind that the statement can broken up whenever you want. That does not mean you always simplify conjunctions. It just means you should be aware of simplification as an option.

CONJUNCTION

Our next rule also deals with conjunctions. Where simplification breaks apart conjunctions, conjunction lets you make new conjunctions. The conjunction rule says that if two things are individually true, then they are both true. If I is true, and W is true, then the conjunction of I • W has to be true. The following are all examples of conjunction:

~X
Y
~X • Y

T v C
G
(T v C) • G

M
U
U • M

~(S v C)
W
~(S v C) • W

As the third example demonstrates, the order of the individual statements in your premises does not matter. In creating the conjunction, you can list the two parts in any order you like. For example:

P

Q

P • Q

P

Q

Q • P

Conjunction is useful whenever you need a conjunction that does not occur in your deduction. For example, if the conclusion of an argument is P • Q, but that statement does not occur anywhere in the premises, then you have to make the conclusion using conjunction. That tells you that you need to get P and Q individually, and then use conjunction to put them together. Or, imagine you have the following statements:

P

Q

(P • Q) > R

Say you need to get R. Using MP on (P • Q) > R will give you R. But to do MP, you need to have P • Q. As the statements stand, you do not have this. However, you can use conjunction to put P and Q together. That will set up MP, and enable you to get R:

P

Q

(P • Q) > R

P • Q (Conj)

Remember any time you need to create a conjunction, conjunction is the rule to use. Also, conjunction can be used to set up CD. If you have two conditional statements by themselves, you can use conjunction to put the two statements together. Look at this example:

A > B
C > D
A v C

We have two conditional statements, and a disjunction. The disjunction is made up of the two antecedents from the conditional statements. But CD cannot be performed, because our conditional statements are not part of a conjunction. The way to deal with this is to use conjunction to put the two conditional statements together:

A > B
C > D
<u>A v C</u>
(A > B) • (C > D)   (CD)

This then allows CD to be used. Anytime you have a number of conditional statements in your argument, and there also is a disjunction in the argument, you should see if setting up a CD by using conjunction will help you.

ADDITION

Our final new rule is addition. This rule is the one that students most often misapply. It is not a difficult rule to understand, but because it seems to be "magic," students often fail to grasp how it works.

Addition is based on the logic of the disjunction. A disjunction says that at least one part is true. Imagine Q is true. What do you then know about the statement Q v S? Is at least one part true? Yes, because Q is true. Therefore, Q v S must be true, regardless of the truth value of S. This will only work with disjunctions. Therefore, addition is restricted to the disjunction operator. The result of any addition must have a disjunction as its main operator. To help remember this, keep in mind that addition is like your big brother: it exists to give you a wedgie. The following are all examples of addition:

<u>T</u>
T v ~B

<u>H • G</u>
(H • G) v A

<u>B</u>
B v (W > ~C)

<u>F</u>
F v (U ≡ T)

As you can see in the above examples, you can add compound statements as well as simple variables. The only restriction is that whatever you add must be linked via a disjunction to a statement you already know is true. Also, addition, like simplification, is an argument form with only one premise. When annotating addition moves, you therefore need to only cite one line.

Addition's most obvious use is to enable you to manufacture disjunctions. CD also allows this, but CD requires two premises. Addition allows you to create any disjunction you want, as long as you have half of the disjunction already. Take the following statements:

P
(P v Q) > R

Imagine you want R. Doing MP on (P v Q) > R will give you R, but you need P v Q to do this. Since you know P is true, addition will allow you to create the disjunction you need. Simply add Q to P to get P v Q:

P
(P v Q) > R
P v Q (add)

This will then allow you to do MP to get R.

Addition also will allow you to add variables and statements to your argument that are not found in any of your premises. For example, imagine the conclusion of an argument is P v T. Looking at the premises, you realize that T does not occur anywhere in them. This tells you that you have to use addition, because that is the only way to add a new variable to your argument. This is one of the few definite rules in constructing deductions, so it is a good idea to remember this.

Note: do not confuse addition with conjunction. Because conjunction sticks together two individual statements to form a conjunction, it is easy to see it as "adding" things together. But the conclusion of conjunction always has a conjunction as its main operator. Addition, on the other hand, gives you a conclusion with a disjunction as its main operator. (Remember that addition has to give you a wedgie!)

PART THREE

PART FOUR

|||||||||||||||||||||||||||||||||||||||||||||||||||||||||||||||||||||||||||||||||||||||||||||||||||||||||||||||||||||||||||||||||||||||||||||

APPLICATION OF ALL EIGHT RULES

 ## APPLICATION OF ALL EIGHT RULES

Let us now look at some examples, to see the rules at work. Consider the following argument:

1. (X v Y) > Z
2. (Z v T) > W
3. X _____ / W

Working backwards, we see that W occurs in premise 2 as the consequent. That gives us this situation:

(Z v T) > W
?_
W

W is the consequent of the conditional statement. What rule breaks apart conditional statements, and gives us the consequent as the conclusion? MP. To do MP, though, we need the antecedent from the conditional statement. The ? needs to be replaced by Z v T.

(Z v T) > W
Z v T
W

We are now looking for Z v T. That statement does not occur anywhere else in the premises. We are not going to get it from premise

2, because we are trying to use Z v T on premise 2. That means we have to make Z v T. There are two ways to make a disjunction: CD and add. CD is not applicable here, so add is the rule to use. To create Z v T using add requires that we have Z. Does Z occur anywhere in the argument? Yes, premise 1. That gives us the following:

(X v Y) > Z
?
Z

Again, we want the consequent of a conditional statement. We need to use MP. But that requires that we have X v Y.

(X v Y) > Z
X v Y
Z

Does X v Y occur anywhere else in the argument? No. This is a disjunction, and we need to make it. Add is the best possibility. To get X v Y via add, we need X. Do we have X? Yes, X occurs as premise 3. We can now work forward.

1. (X v Y) > Z
2. (Z v T) > W
3. X   / W
4. X v Y   3, Add

First, we add Y to X. Remember, add is an argument with only one premise, so we only cite one line number. Now, we can use MP to get Z.

1. (X v Y) > Z
2. (Z v T) > W

3. X _____ / W
4. X v Y   3, Add
5. Z   1, 4, MP

Now, we want to get W. That requires that we use MP on line 2. But to do an MP requires us to add T to Z.

1. (X v Y) > Z
2. (Z v T) > W
3. X _____ / W
4. X v Y   3, Add
5. Z   1, 4, MP
6. Z v T   5, Add

Now, we do MP to get the conclusion.

1. (X v Y) > Z
2. (Z v T) > W
3. X _____ / W
4. X v Y   3, Add
5. Z   1, 4, MP
6. Z v T   5, Add
7. W   2, 6, MP

Another example:

1. X > (Y v Z)
2. Y > W
3. Z > K
4. X _____ / W v K

W v K does not occur anywhere in the premises. This means we need to make this disjunction. That requires either CD or add. Looking at the premises, you will notice that we have several conditional statements. You also notice that the first premise has a disjunction as a consequent. That suggests a possible CD. Closer examination reveals that the consequents of premises 2 and 3 are the variables we want in the disjunction that makes up our conclusion. That means we will get the conclusion via CD, and that we need to use conjunction to join premises 2 and 3 together:

1. X > (Y v Z)
2. Y > W
3. Z > K
4. X   /W v K
5. (Y > W) • (Z > K)   2, 3, Conj

To do a CD on line 5, we need a disjunction. There is one in premise 1. It is Y v Z. Y is the antecedent of one of the conditional statements in line 5; Z is the other antecedent. So, that disjunction will set up the CD. We need to break that disjunction out of premise 1. That gives us this:

X > (Y v Z)
?
Y v Z

To break apart a conditional statement and get the consequent, we need to use MP. To do an MP on line 1, we also need X, which is the antecedent. So, the ? is replaced by X:

X > (Y v Z)
X
Y v Z

X occurs as premise 4. That means we can go ahead and do the MP.

1. X > (Y v Z)
2. Y > W
3. Z > K
4. X   /W v K
5. (Y > W) • (Z > K)   2, 3, Conj
6. Y v Z   1, 4, MP

This, in turn, allows us to get W v K via CD.

1. X > (Y v Z)
2. Y > W
3. Z > K
4. X   /W v K
5. (Y > W) • (Z > K)   2, 3, Conj
6. Y v Z   1, 4, MP
7. W v K   5, 6, CD

Another example:

1. X > Y
2. (~X v W) > K
3. ~Y • Z   /K v T

The conclusion is K v T. T does not occur in the premises. That means we will have to get it via addition. That means we first have to get K, so we can add T to K. K occurs in premise 2. It is the consequent. So, we need to use MP to get K:

(~X v W) > K
~X v W
K

As illustrated above, in order to get K, we need to first get ~X v W. That does not occur anywhere else in the argument, though. Moreover, ~X is not found anywhere else in the argument, either. However, there is a way to make a negation. MT will allow you to create a negation. If we do MT on premise 1, that will give us ~X:

X > Y
<u>~Y</u>
~X

Once we have ~X, we can use add to create ~X v W. But as the illustration above shows, to get ~X requires that we have ~Y. ~Y occurs as part of a conjunction in premise 3. That means we can simplify the conjunction, and get ~Y by itself. We can now proceed with the deduction.

1. X > Y
2. (~X v W) > K
<u>3. ~Y • Z   /K v T</u>
4. ~Y   3, Simp

You will recall that simplification has only one premise, so we need to only cite one line in our justification. Having obtained ~Y, we can now do MT on line 1.

1. X > Y
2. (~X v W) > K
<u>3. ~Y • Z   /K v T</u>
4. ~Y   3, Simp
5. ~X   1, 4, MT

Now, we do an addition to get ~X v W. This is to set up an MP on line 2.

1. X > Y
2. (~X v W) > K
3. ~Y • Z   /K v T
4. ~Y   3, Simp
5. ~X   1, 4, MT
6. ~X v W   5, Add

Now, we can do the MP.

1. X > Y
2. (~X v W) > K
3. ~Y • Z   /K v T
4. ~Y   3, Simp
5. ~X   1, 4, MT
6. ~X v W   5, Add
7. K   2, 6, MP

We wanted to get K so we could add T to it. That is the final step.

1. X > Y
2. (~X v W) > K
3. ~Y • Z   /K v T
4. ~Y   3, Simp
5. ~X   1, 4, MT
6. ~X v W   5, Add
7. K   2, 6, MP
8. K v T   7, Add

ADDENDUM

1.1 SENTENCES, PROPOSITIONS AND STATEMENTS

Required Reading: Textbook Section 1.1

Everyone knows from English class what a sentence is. A **sentence** is string of words with a subject and a predicate, expressing a complete thought. It is a string of words put together in accordance with the grammatical rules of a language.

Sentences can be used for different purposes such as making statements, asking questions, giving orders, cussing and exclaiming. We are interested in sentences used to make statements because we are interested in arguments, and arguments are composed only from statements.

A statement is a sentence used to make an assertion. This means that a statement is capable of being true or false. Thus, a statement is distinguished from a question, order or an exclamation since these are never true nor false.

It should be clear to you that statements must be distinguished from questions, orders, exclamations, requests since these other linguistic items are neither true nor false. For example, *Salem is the capitol of Oregon* is a statement since it is capable of being true or false. But a question such as *What's your name?* or a command such as *Shut the door* is neither true nor false.

Finally, sometimes a sentence constructed as a question will be a disguised statement. These are called **rhetorical questions** since they are not really questions but rhetorical devices for making a statement forcefully. For example, a person who angrily asks, *How long are we* *going let the courts coddle criminals?* likely is stating that we should not let the courts coddle criminals any longer.

We need to consider propositions.

A proposition is what a sentence expresses. It is a meaning or interpretation of a sentence.

A sentence that is incoherent fails to express a proposition. It's a meaningless sentence. For example, if you say *Love is the square root of gravity*, you have uttered a grammatically proper sentence but you haven't expressed a proposition. What you've said is meaningless given the usual meaning of the words used.

Furthermore, most sentences have more than one meaning. Thus, the same sentence can express different propositions. For example, when you say *Liberty Valance was shot* you can mean that Liberty Valance was tired or that he was shot with a gun or that he was photographed, etc.

Likewise, different sentences can express the same proposition. Thus, *It is raining, Il pleut, God is crying, The rain doth fall* may serve to express the proposition that it is raining.

Normally, the context will tell others which proposition you mean or which statement you are trying to make. But unless you make clear exactly what proposition you mean, your utterance remains ambiguous and you have not succeeded in making a statement.

Thus, in order to make a statement, you have to use a proper sentence, and make clear exactly which proposition you mean to express.

Finally, you need to distinguish two categories of statements--simple and complex statements.

A simple statement is a statement that contains no other statements as logical components.

A complex statement contains embedded statements as logical components.

The following statements are simple since they have no embedded statements as logical components:

My name is Aram.
All humans are mortal.
There is life after death.
I believe that Bill lives in Marin or he lives in Sonoma.

Note: Any statement that asserts a belief, desire, hope, wish or other "propositional attitude" is a simple statement since any embedded sentential component it contains is not a logical component. Study the class text or ask your instructor if you don't clearly understand this point.

The following statements are complex since they have embedded sentences as logical components. These embedded components are highlighted in red.

It's not true that blondes have more fun.
I love parties and I hate being bored.
Either Bill lives in Marin or he lives in Sonoma.
If I pass this course, then I will graduate.

The first denies or negates its one embedded component--*Blondes have more fun*. It is called a **negation**.

The second statement joins together its two components--*I love parties*; *I hate being bored*. It is called a **conjunction**.

The third presents has two embedded components--*Bill lives in Marin, Bill lives in Sonoma.* This statement presents its components as alternatives. It is called a **disjunction**.

The fourth statement has two components *I pass this course, I will graduate.* It asserts a conditional relation between the components. It is called a **conditional**.

These are the four basic types of logically complex statements that we will be concerned with in this course. In learning about logically complex statements, you are taking your first step in learning the logical structure of language. And this is the backbone of all good reasoning.

Summary of Central Points:

1. **Sentences** are strings of words put together according to the grammatical rules of a language. Sentences are used to perform various tasks such as stating, questioning and ordering.
2. A **proposition** is the meaning of a sentence. A proposition is what a sentence expresses.
3. The same sentence can express different propositions. Different sentences can express the same proposition.
4. Statements are distinguished from questions, orders and exclamations. Statements are true or false. Questions, orders, explanations are neither true nor false.
5. Arguments are composed of statements
6. Complex statements contain embedded statements as logical components. Simple statements do not.
7. Statements stating propositional attitudes such as beliefs, hopes, desires, fears are simple statements.
8. The 4 types of complex statements are negations, conjunctions, disjunctions and conditionals.

Skills to Be Learned:

1. Know how to distinguish statements from questions, exclamations and other linguistic functions.
2. Learn to recognize rhetorical questions and understand the intended statements behind them.
3. Learn to be sensitive to ambiguous sentences that express more than one proposition.
4. Learn to distinguish simple from complex statements.
5. Learn to recognize the four types of complex statements and their embedded components.

Homework Sample 1.1
Sentences, Propositions and Statements

Provide two separate and distinct propositions for each sentence and describe the contexts that would clearly demonstrate each propositions.

Example: It's really hot in here.

Proposition 1: The temperature in here is uncomfortably high.
Context 1: Two students in a classroom with the heating controls stuck on high.

Proposition 2: The patrons of this establishment are very attractive.
Context 2: Two people discussing the clientele at the local dance club.

1. I enjoy looking at stars.

Proposition 1:
Context 1:

Proposition 2:
Context 2:

2. I love you.

Proposition 1:
Context 1:

Proposition 2:
Context 2::

3. There are three rings

Proposition 1:
Context 1:

Proposition 2:
Context 2::

4. I didn't do it.

Proposition 1:
Context 1:

Proposition 2:
Context 2:

5. You are a mirror.

Proposition 1:
Context 1:

Proposition 2:
Context 2:

1.2 - 1.6 COMPLEX STATEMENTS

Required Reading: Textbook Sections 1.2, 1.3, 1.4, 1.5 and 1.6

The topic of this lesson is the logical structure and truth of complex statements.

Two important reasons why we study the logical structure of statements are:

We want to know exactly what a statement means

We want to know what conditions make a statement true or false.

To be able to determine the logical structure of statements requires that you develop a keen analytical eye that is sensitive to logical detail. This lesson will help you to develop that skill. Many of the lessons, homework and practice exercises at the beginning of this course aim to sharpen your analytical eye.

From Lesson 1.1, you should know that there are four types of complex statements:

Negation: Washington did **NOT** sleep here.

Conjunction: Adam was the first man **AND** Eve was the first woman.

Disjunction: EITHER life is beautiful **OR** life is tragic.

Conditional: IF one puts sugar into water, **THEN** the sugar will dissolve.

What makes these statements **complex** is that they contain other statements as logical components.

To determine whether a complex statement is true or false, you often need first to determine the **truth–value** (i.e. the truth or falsity) of its components. This in turn requires that you be able to grasp its logical structure to identify those components.

This lesson describes some tools for revealing and displaying the logical structure of the four kinds of complex statements, and briefly states the conditions that make them true or false. Consult your text for more details on these topics.

NEGATION

The logical structure of negations is relatively easy to grasp. A negation denies its embedded component statement. We make the logical structure of negations clear by rewriting the statement in standard form with the logical term "not" at the beginning. The following examples should make this clear.

NEGATION	STANDARD FORM
He can't be the last of the Mohicans	not (He can be the last of the Mohicans)
Dead men tell no tales	not (Dead men tell tales)
He doesn't want pie or cake.	not (He wants pie or he wants cake)

To save ink and paper, and to grasp logical structure without being encumbered by lots of words, we sometimes use logical shorthand. So, letting a tilde be the shorthand symbol for negation, and letting letters stand for embedded <u>simple</u> components, the logical structures of the above statements are abbreviated as:

not (He can be the last of the Mohicans) ~**M**

not (Dead men tell tales) ~**D**

not (He wants pie or he wants cake) ~(**P** or **C**)

Truth Conditions for Negation:

The truth values for negations for negation are relatively easy to grasp.

Negations always have the opposite truth-values of their components. Thus, a negation is false when what it denies is true, and a negation is true when what it denies is false.

Abbreviated in our logical shorthand, we can say that for any statement **P**, **P** is true when and only when ~**P** is false and ~**P** is true when and only when **P** is false.

CONJUNCTION

As the word suggests, a conjunction conjoins or brings together two or more statements. Although everyday statements use words such as "but," "while," "yet," "though" to conjoin statements, the standard logical term for conjunctions is the word "and."

Here are some conjunctive statements and their standard forms. We use an ampersand to stand for "and."

CONJUCTION	STANDARD FORM
Adams and Polk were presidents.	Adams was president **&** Polk was president
Paul is tall, while Joe is not.	Paul is tall **&** not (Joe is tall)
We have dogs, cats but no birds.	We have dogs & we have cats & not(we have birds)

Using parentheses as punctuation marks to remove ambiguity, and abbreviating the embedded <u>simple</u> components with appropriate letters, the logical structure of the above conjunctions is abbreviated as:

Adams and Polk were presidents. **A & P**

Paul is tall, while Joe is not. **P & ~J**

We have dogs, cats but no birds. **(D & C) & ~B**

Truth Conditions for Conjunction:

The truth-values for conjunction are also relatively easy to understand. Conjunctions are false when one or more of their components (conjuncts) are false. They are true only if all of their conjuncts are true.

Abbreviated in our logical shorthand, we can say that for any statements **P** and **Q**, **P & Q** is true when and only when both **P** and **Q** are true, and it is false when and only when either **P** or **Q** or both are false.

Note that in cases where everyday statements use "but," "though," and other contrast conjunctions, the standard form which uses "and" may not fully capture the meaning of the original statement.

DISJUNCTION

Disjunctions state their components, called **disjuncts**, as alternatives. The standard form for disjunctions requires you that write out the components clearly separated by the "or"

DISJUNCTION	STANDARD FORM
We will go to Paris or London.	We will go to Paris or we will go to London
He's either for us or against us.	Either he's for us or he's against us.
He will pick Door 1, Door 2, or Door 3 or he won't pick anything.	He will pick Door 1 or he will pick Door 2 or will pick Door 3 or not(he will pick anything)

The conventional notation for "or" is a small "v". It is also conventional to use parentheses to separate disjunctions (and conjunctions) into groups of two disjuncts each. Using some appropriate letters for simple components, the logical structure of the above disjunctions is portrayed as follows:

We will go to Paris or London. **P v L**

He's either for us or against us. **F v A**

He will pick Door 1, Door 2, or Door 3 or he won't pick anything. **((D1 v D2) vD3) v ~P)**

Truth Conditions for Disjunction:

In this course, unless explicitly indicated, we will always treat disjunctions in what is called the **inclusive** sense. This means that a disjunction is true when one or more components are true, and false only when all the components are false.

Abbreviated in our logical shorthand, we can say that for any statements **P** and **Q**, **P v Q** is true when and only when only **P** is true, when only **Q** is true or when both **P** and **Q** are true. It is false when and only when both **P** and **Q** are false.

The implications of this will become clear after you've worked with disjunctions a bit more. Just remember that the statement *We have either pie or ice cream* will be taken as true when we have either or both pie and ice cream and false only when we have neither.

The inclusive sense of "or" should be contrasted with the **exclusive** sense which is used in everyday language to mean "either one or the other but not both."

 ## CONDITIONALS

Becoming familiar with conditionals is more difficult than with the other three kinds of complex statements. The standard form for the conditional is the **If-Then** statement, with the If clause coming first and the Then clause following. The component statement in the If clause is called the **antecedent**, and the component in the Then clause is called the **consequent**.

But conditionals are stated in many ways. Often the conditional relation is hidden and you must translate it into the standard form. We introduce the topic in this lesson, and devote the next section to conditionals alone.

Here are some examples of standard form conditionals. Where possible, try to say whether the conditional is true or false, and why you think so. The shorthand abbreviation for the if-then conditional connective is a horizontal arrow "--> ". Using some appropriate letters for the standard form conditionals and their logical structure are:

STANDARD FORM CONDITIONALS

If you put sugar into water, then the sugar will dissolve.	**S --> D**
If you put sugar into water, then the sugar will explode.	**S --> E**
If you don't love yourself, you can't love others.	**~Y --> ~O**
If the moon is made of brie, then it has high fat content.	**M --> H**

Truth Conditions for Conditionals:

Logicians have not been able to give a simple or universally accepted answer to what makes conditionals true or false. In the first two statements above, the answer seems straightforward.

If you do put a little sugar in enough water, under ordinary conditions the sugar will dissolve. Thus, if both the antecedent and the consequent of a conditional are true, and they are relevant to each other, then the conditional as a whole is true.

On the other hand, if you put ordinary sugar in water, it will not explode. Thus, if the antecedent is true, and the consequent is false, the conditional as a whole is false.

The truth of the last two statements is more problematic. The third is speculative and open to interpretation. But its truth or falsehood will depend on whether your views on love can find someway to make the consequent true whenever the antecedent is true.

The antecedent and consequent of the fourth statement are both false. Although it seems strange and initially false to many, we think the fourth statement is true. This is because we know that brie has high fat content, so that whatever is made of brie, actual or imagined, would have high fat content. What do you think?

In some systems of formal logic, a conditional is taken as false when its antecedent is true and its consequent is false. It is taken as true in the three other cases. Conditionals interpreted this way are called **material conditionals**. They are often inaccurate as a way of interpreting everyday language conditionals. See your text for more details.

The logical structure of statements can be very complex since one statement can include all four types of logical connectives. For example, this statement is fairly complicated, and a bit ambiguous.

If you make over $50,000 and have no dependents, then if you are not over 65 or carry medical insurance and you need medical care, then you are not eligible for Medicare.

Using our logical shorthand, and with a little practice, given the most reasonable interpretation, you might portray its logical structure as:

$$(M \ \& \ D) \ \text{-->} \ [(\sim O \ v \ C) \ \& \ N] \ \text{-->} \ \sim E$$

However, the above portrayal contains one little error. Can you see what it is? Remember, each of the letters must stand for **simple** components--statements that are not complex.

Summary of Central Points:

1. Negations have the opposite truth-values of their components.
2. Conjunctions are true if only if all their conjuncts are true.
3. Disjunctions are false if and only if all their disjuncts are false. They are true when one or more disjuncts are true. This is the inclusive sense of "or".
4. In this course, we will always understand disjunction in the inclusive sense unless otherwise specified.
5. A Conditional if interpreted as a "material conditional" is false when its antecedent is true and its consequent is false. It is true in the three other cases where the antecedent is false or the consequent is true.
6. In everyday contexts, you will not usually interpret conditionals as material conditionals, but rather rely on your knowledge and intuition to determine a conditional's truth-value.

Skills to Learn:

1. Know how to recognize the logical structure of compound statements.
2. Be able to recognize conditional statements and to translate various conditional statements to standard form.
3. Know how to determine the truth-value of compound statements.

SECTION 1.1

Homework Sample 1.2
Distinguishing Simple from Complex Statements.

A. (a) Count the sentences in the passages below? (b) Count the statements?

1. Why all this fuss about the gender pay gap? First, this inequality is correlated with hours worked. Second, inequality is correlated with difficulty and risk. Third, economic inequality is correlated with experience and education. Fourth? Simple. There is no justification for accommodation or restriction based on genital structure.

a)   b)

2. Isn't it obvious? Think about it. Gasoline prices will not go down. Under the new administration we will get additional oil from once protected parts of the country, but the amount will be too small to have any effect on the overall supply. Coal production is going to be raised, but it will not offset the ever-increasing amount of gasoline that is consumed by cars, trucks, and airplanes. In addition, the new administration will more than likely reduce the pressure on the automakers to increase development of electric cars.

a)   b)

B. (a) Which of the following statements are simple and which are complex? (b) Use complete sentences to write out the simple components of each complex statement.

Example: She wants to get the plum colored one and the grey one, but not the white one.

a) Complex

b) She wants to get the plum colored one. She wants to get the grey colored one. She wants to get the white colored one.

1. Either tomorrow is another day, or it's not.

a)

b)

2. If the speed of light is 186,000 miles per second, then it is not variable.

a)

b)

3. I hope that we have Macaroni & Cheese for dinner.

a)

b)

4. Last night I dreamt of a Pegasus and a red pizza.

a)

b)

5. You know that if we go today, then we'll miss the sale.

a)

b)

Homework Sample 1.3 Negation

Clarify the negations in the following sentences. If you think double negations are used colloquially (as slang) then indicate that and write the sentence as a negation.

> Hint: If there are an odd number of negations write "it is not the case that" in front of the statement after you have removed all negations. If there is an even number of negations remove all negations and write it out

Example: Your daughter is not making her education loan payments on time.

It is not the case that your daughter is making her education loan payments on time.

1. Today is not the last day of the month.

2. No one wants to get attacked by a bear.

3. The song cannot be played on a cheap guitar.

4. You can't be the winner without there being a loser

5. I can't get no satisfaction.

6. Bill did not mean to displease his mother.

Sample Homework 1.4 Conjunctions

(a) Rewrite each of the sentences below as a compound statement of simple statements (or negations) connected by "and". **(b) Briefly describe how the resulting conjunction(s) may fail to capture the meaning of the original.**

Example: I put apples, peaches and cinnamon in the pie.

a) I put apples in the pie. I put peaches in the pie. I put cinnamon in the pie.

b) In the original it sounds like a process that involves mixing those ingredients. In the rewrites it sounds like I did one, and then I did the next, and then I did the next.

1. I am going to eat some Macaroni & Cheese today.

a)

b)

2. John married Sylvia, although he should have married Sonya.

a)

b)

3. Success takes talent and persistence.

a)

b)

4. David is competing neither at the local nor state level, but at the national level itself.

a)

b)

5. I like my coffee bitter and murky.

a)

b)

6. Santa gave Dasher, Dancer, Prancer, Vixen, Comet, Cupid, Donner, but not Blitzen and Rudolph, a heartfelt thank you.

a)

b)

Homework Sample 1.5
Disjunction (Inclusive and Exclusive Senses)

A. Indicate whether the following disjunctions are likely being used in the exclusive sense (E), or the non-exclusive or inclusive sense (I). If you aren't able to say which sense is likely, briefly describe why. (Hint: Exclusive means it is not possible to do, be or have both)

Example: You are either for us or against us.

This is likely meant in the exclusive sense, where the speaker would be indicating that it is not possible to be both.

1. A human being is either a male or a female.

2. One can take Critical Thinking or the Critical Thinking Challenge Exam to satisfy the Critical Thinking requirement.

3. Famous people are either nice or wealthy.

4. We can now either take BART to West Oakland or Daly City.

5. It was either lack of sleep or a drug induced stupor that caused the accident.

6. Either Mary murdered him or Jane did.

1.5 B. Demonstrate the logical structure of the following statements. Use capital letters to abbreviate simple statements. Use parentheses to eliminate ambiguity. Make sure to define your letters.

Example: He liked her, but she didn't like him or his dog.
H & ~(S v D)
H = He liked her.
S = She liked him.
D = She liked his dog.

1. Either adjustments are needed in equalization or in pitch.

2. You are either with us or you are alone, and there's no way you're with us.

3. You are either a scoundrel or you aren't telling me the truth, and neither God nor the Devil can help you.

4. You must either take algebra and geometry or trigonometry and calculus or statistics and logic.

5. Either you can sing that song and lull us all or you will make money or you will enjoy yourself and continue your decadent existence.

C. To the best of your knowledge, which of the following statements are true and which are false. If you are unable to determine, then suggest possible answers and justify them.

1. It is either day or night.

2. Brazil is either in West Africa or in Latin America.

3. Of these three bands, either the Beatles were famous or both the Rolling Stones and the Critical Thinkers were famous.

4. Either tomorrow is not the day after today, or it is.

5. Fall comes either after summer or it comes before winter, but not both.

1.7 NECESSARY AND SUFFICIENT CONDITIONS (CONDITIONAL RELATIONS)

Required Reading: Textbook Section 1.7

This lesson aims to get you started on learning the use of conditional statements, and understanding the logic of conditional relations.

The first thing to note is that conditionals are stated in a wide variety of ways. Some of these ways are found on LES or in Section 1.6 of your textbook. You should study this section carefully and become familiar with various ways of stating conditionals. The following discussion should serve only as a summary or supplement to your study of that section.

As you know from the last lesson, the standard form conditional is an If-Then statement that has the if-clause preceding the then-clause.

The condition stated in the if-clause is the **antecedent** and the condition contained in the then-clause is called the **consequent**.

IF (antecedent) THEN (consequent)

Quite often in everyday talk the "then" is omitted or the clauses are stated in reverse. The first two conditionals below have *you are in Berkeley* as their antecedents, and *you are in California* as their consequents. The third has *you are not in California* and *you are not in Berkeley* as its antecedent and consequent.

If you are in Berkeley, you are in California.
You are in California if you are in Berkeley.
If you are not in California, you are not in Berkeley.

NECESSARY CONDITIONS

To understand the logic of conditionals, let's take a simple example. Suppose you want to analyze or clarify the concept of bachelorhood.

Now there are certain conditions that are necessary for being a bachelor. For example, one necessary condition is that one be unmarried. Another is that one be a male. Yet others are that one be an adult and human. (By our understanding of the term, neither cats nor children are bachelors.)

To say that these are necessary conditions for bachelorhood means that whatever doesn't have these properties is not a bachelor. And to state these conditional relations, you use conditional statements. The following are true statements all correctly describing necessary conditions for being a bachelor.

> If you're not a male, you're not a bachelor.
> If you're not an adult, you're not a bachelor.
> If you are a bachelor, then you are a male.
> If you are a bachelor, then you are unmarried.
> If you are a bachelor, then you are an unmarried, adult, human male.
> Being an unmarried, adult, human male is a necessary condition for being a bachelor.

Note that a standard form conditional is an assertion that its consequent is a necessary condition for its antecedent. So, where **P** and **Q** are statements describing conditions,

> If P then Q means that Q is a necessary condition for P.

SUFFICIENT CONDITIONS

In our analysis of bachelorhood, we also want to know what conditions are sufficient for being a bachelor. That is, we want to know a condition or set of properties that makes something a bachelor. For example, being a male is a necessary condition for being a bachelor but it is not sufficient since you can be a male and not be a bachelor.

However, being an unmarried, adult, human male is sufficient for being a bachelor. To say that this is sufficient for being a bachelor means that whatever has these properties must be a bachelor. The following standard form conditional states this:

If something is an unmarried, adult, male human, then it is a bachelor.

From the above, observe that a standard form conditional is an assertion that its antecedent is a sufficient condition for its consequent. So, where **P** and **Q** are statements describing conditions,

If P then Q means that P is a sufficient condition for Q.

The following are true standard form conditionals all correctly asserting their antecedents as sufficient conditions for their consequents.

If you're a bachelor, then you are unmarried.
If you're a bachelor, you are an adult male.
If you're a mother, then you are a female.
If one is in Berkeley, then one is in California.
If you decapitate a live person, you will kill that person.

NECESSARY AND SUFFICIENT CONDITIONS

Putting the above points together, we see that the relation between standard form conditionals and conditional relations is as follows: Where **P** and **Q** are statements describing conditions,

> **If P then Q** means **Q is a necessary condition for P**
> **If P then Q** means **P is a sufficient condition for Q**
> **Q is a necessary condition for P** means **P is a sufficient condition for Q**

Logicians describe the above by saying that "necessary" and "sufficient" are **correlative terms**. This means that these terms are defined or understood in reference to each other. Accordingly, the following rule always holds:

P is sufficient for Q when and only when **Q is necessary for P**

Note that some conditions may be both necessary and sufficient for something. In our analysis of bachelorhood, we found a set of conditions that was both necessary and sufficient for being a bachelor. Thus, assuming we're talking only about humans the following statements are true:

> If you're an unmarried, adult, male, then you're a bachelor.

> If you're a bachelor, you're an unmarried, adult male.

These two conditionals provide what is called a **necessary and sufficient condition definition** of the term "bachelor." They stipulate the conditions without which something can't be a bachelor and with which it must be a bachelor. This is sometimes called a **necessary and sufficient analysis** of the concept bachelor.

SECTION 1.7

A widely accepted expression for stating that conditions are both necessary and sufficient is **if and only if**, commonly abbreviated as **iff**. That is, for any condition **P** that is necessary and sufficient for **Q**, we can write:

P if and only if Q (abbreviated **P iff Q**)

And our necessary and sufficient definition of "bachelor" above becomes:

You're a bachelor if and only if you're an unmarried, adult male.

Unfortunately, ordinary language is so open-textured or vague that it is difficult to provide both necessary and sufficient conditions for the use of most terms.

 HIDDEN CONDITIONALS

In everyday speech, not all conditional relations are stated as standard form conditionals. Depending on whether you wish to stress the necessity or sufficiency, the temporal, causal or conceptual aspects of the conditions related, you may choose a variety of different ways of stating conditional relations. Study your text to become familiar with these ways.

Some statements of conditional relations don't even employ the terms "if" and "then". These are often called **hidden conditionals**, and it is important for you to learn to recognize them. Furthermore, it is often helpful to translate a hidden conditional into standard form so that you can better judge its truth-value. Unfortunately, some translations may sound strange or may distort the intended meaning of the original statement.

SOME THINGS TO REMEMBER ABOUT CONDITIONALS

To summarize what we've said and to make some additional points about conditionals, we consider one final example--the conceptual relation between the terms "husband" and "married." We know that all husbands are married. Thus, the following are true and equivalent ways of stating this truth.

> If you're a husband, then you're married.
> If you're not married, then you're not a husband.
> Being a husband is sufficient for being married.
> Being married is necessary for being a husband.

The first two statements above are **contrapositives**.

To get a statement's contrapositive, you negate <u>and</u> exchange its antecedent and consequent. Accordingly,

If P then Q is the contrapositive of **If not Q, then not P**.

Contrapositives of conditionals are always **logically equivalent**, i.e., they state the same proposition or have the same truth-values. (See the next lesson for more a more precise statement logical equivalence)

Note that merely exchanging the antecedent and consequent of a conditional produces its **converse**, which is not logically equivalent to the original Thus,

> *If you're a husband, then you're married* is not equivalent to *If you're married, then you're a husband* since the first statement is true and the second false.

Also, merely negating the antecedent and consequent of a conditional results in a statement that is not logically equivalent to the original. Thus,

If you're a husband, then you're married is not equivalent to *If you're not a husband, then you're not married* since the first is true and the second false.

In general then,

If P then Q is <u>not</u> equivalent to **If Q then P**
If P then Q is <u>not</u> equivalent to **If not P then not Q**, but
If P then Q <u>is</u> equivalent to **If not Q then not P**.

Here are some hidden conditionals employing the terms "only" and "unless" that are equivalent to the above truth that *If you're a husband, then you're married.*

You're a husband only if you are married.
Only ones who are married are husbands.
You're not a husband unless you're married.
Unless you're married, you're not a husband.

The terms "only" or "only if" "or "only when" point directly to necessary conditions. These terms may be roughly translated as "then," which enables you to know what condition goes in the consequent. So, you would mentally read the first two statements above as

"You're a husband (THEN) you are married"
"(THEN) ones who are married are husbands"

You can then rewrite the sentences in proper English with the "if" put in front of the related condition. In both cases, the result is "If you're a husband, then you are married," which is logically equivalent to the original statement.

The term "unless" may be translated as "if not." Thus, you would mentally read the last two sentences above as

"You're not a husband (IF NOT) you're married.

"(IF NOT) you're married, you're not a husband."

Rewriting these in proper English results in "If you're not married, you're not a husband," which is again correct. Using this **If-not** rule, introduces a lot negatives, so you can obtain the contrapositive of this result to get "If you're a husband, then you're married."

Finally, don't be discouraged if the subject of conditionals is confusing to you. With practice, it will become less confusing. Contact your instructor for help. When you come to understand conditional relations, you will have taken a large step in learning the logic needed for good critical thought.

Summary of Central Points:

1. Q is a necessary condition for P means *If P then Q.*
2. P is a sufficient condition for Q also means *If P then Q.*
3. Q is a necessary condition for P means that *If not-Q, then not-P.*
4. *If P then Q* is logically equivalent to *If not-Q then not-P.* Statements related in this way are called **contrapositives**.
5. *If P then Q* is <u>not</u> logically equivalent to *If not-P then not-Q.*
6. *If P then Q* is not logically equivalent to *If Q then P.* Statements related in this way are called **converses**.
7. "Only" and "Only if" mean "then" and point to necessary conditions that go in the then–clause of a conditional.
8. Use the **if-not** rule for «unless» to obtain standard form translations of conditionals that employ it.

Skills to Learn:

1. Be able to recognize logically equivalent conditional statements.

2. Learn to understand how conditional statements assert necessary and sufficient conditions.

3. Learn to translate hidden conditionals into standard form conditionals.

4. Learn how difficult it is to stipulate necessary and sufficient conditions for the use of terms.

Sample Homework 1.7 Necessary and Sufficient Conditions (Conditional Relations)

A. Provide a **necessary condition** for each of the following events or states of affairs.

Example: Petting a dog
If you are petting a dog then you are touching something.

1. Being a Father
If you are a father then you . . .

A necessary condition for being a father is . . .
2. swimming
If you are swimming then you . . .

A necessary condition for swimming is . .
3. Birth
If you are born then you . . .

A necessary condition for being born is . .
4. Being late
If you are late then you . . .

A necessary condition for being late is . .
5. Eating a cookie
If you eat a cookie, then you

A necessary condition for eating a cookie is . .
6. Being a US Citizen
If you are a US Citizen then you

A necessary condition for being a US Citizen is . .
7. Being an adult

If you are an adult then you

A necessary condition for being an adult is . .

B. Provide a **sufficient condition** for each of the previous events or states of affairs.

Example: Petting a dog
If you pet a brown dog, then you are petting a dog.
Petting a brown dog is a sufficient condition for petting a dog.

1. Being a Father
If you_____
then you are a father.

_____

is a sufficient condition for being a father.

2. Swimming
If you _____then
you are swimming.

_____

is a sufficient condition for swimming.

3. Birth
If you _____
then you are born.
_____ is a sufficient
condition for being born.

4. Being late

If you _____

then you are late.

_____

is a sufficient condition for being late.

5. Eating a cookie

If you _____

then you eat a cookie.

_____

is a sufficient condition for eating a cookie.

6. Being a US Citizen

If you _____ then

you are a US Citizen.

_____

is a sufficient condition for being a US Citizen.

7. Being an adult

If you _____ then

you are an adult.

_____

is a sufficient condition for being an adult.

C. Provide a **necessary and sufficient** condition for the following. You may use disjunctions and conjunctions of conditions.

1. Being a sister

2. Reading a book

D. Describe a context in which

1. Using a gun would be a sufficient condition for killing someone.

E. Describe the conditions that are sufficient for .

1. starting a fire

F. Describe all of the conditions that are necessary for

1. making an omelet

||||||||||||||||||||||||||||||||||||||||||||||||||||||||||||||||||||||||||||||||||||||||||||||||||||||||

2.1 - 2.2 PREMISES AND CONCLUSIONS & DEDUCTIVE AND INDUCTIVE

Reading Assignment: Textbook Sections 2.1 and 2.2

This lesson introduces some terms to help you to understand the logical structure of arguments. We will then distinguish between deductive and inductive arguments.

ARGUMENTS

In the logician's sense of the word, the term argument refers to a collection of statements that support a conclusion.

More formally, an **argument** is a sequence of statements in which statements called **premises** are given as reasons or evidence for the truth of a statement called the **conclusion**.

People use arguments to try to convince others that various claims are true. So, whenever you support your beliefs, rather than merely state these beliefs, you have produced an argument.

An argument in our sense differs from arguments in the everyday sense. In the everyday sense, people argue when they angrily make charges against each other, or vent their anger in a dispute. But these are quarrels, and they don't involve arguments in our sense unless the disputants give reasons for their claims.

INFERENCE INDICATORS

Here, for example, is a string of unsupported claims that would not constitute an argument in our sense.

> *People who perform abortions are immoral. Abortion should be outlawed in every state. We should lock up people who perform abortions. Any legislator who favors abortion should be impeached.*

Here is a second example that clearly is an argument since premises are offered for a conclusion.

> **Since** the foetus is a human being, and ***since** abortion kills the foetus and since killing a human being is murder,* ***it follows that*** abortion is murder.

The word "since" in this passage means "for the reason that". It signals the premises of an argument. The expression "it follows that" signals the conclusion. By using these words, the arguer indicates that if you accept his premises as true then you should also accept his conclusion as true.

Words like "since" and "it follows that" are called "inference indicators."

An **inference indicator** is a word or phrase used to signal an inference from the premises to the conclusion of an argument.

You have a list of some common inference indicators in your text. You should become supersensitive to these words. Although often misused, they are logical terms that help you determine the structure of an argument.

To help sensitize you to their use, you should circle them when you see them in all the materials of this class. You should also learn to use them whenever you provide arguments to support your views.

The first argument is a generalization from a sample of swans to the whole population. The second argument argues from what has happened in the past as evidence for what will happen in the future.

Arguments that argue from a sample to the whole or from the past to the present or future will be inductive since their premises cannot guarantee their conclusions.

In both of the above arguments, the arguer jumps to a conclusion. The evidence is not taken as a guarantee that conclusion is true, but rather that it makes the conclusion more likely to be true.

These arguments are inductive.

> *In the past, Jones has always become upset when the Warriors lost. So, we expect that he will be upset over the Warriors' next loss.*

> *All the swans that we have ever seen are white. So, it's likely that all swans are white.*

Consider some other examples:

Induction and deduction are sometimes distinguished as arguments that make inferences from particular statements to general statements and general statements to particular ones. This is incorrect. Induction and deduction are distinguished by what sort of guarantee is intended between an argument's premises and its conclusion.

There are two distinct classes of arguments--deductive arguments and inductive arguments. These argument types represent two ways of reasoning by which people support their claims.

DEDUCTIVE AND INDUCTIVE ARGUMENTS

Since people often misuse these terms, we will define them before we consider some examples. According to your text:

An argument may be taken as **deductive** if the truth of its premises is intended to guarantee the truth of its conclusion.

An argument may be taken as **inductive** if the truth of its premises is intended to make likely, but not guarantee, the truth of its conclusion.

Here's an example of a deductive argument:

Since all Democrats are big spenders and Clinton is a Democrat, ***we must conclude that*** *Clinton is a big spender.*

Note that in this argument, by using the expression "we must conclude that" the arguer intends that if the premises are true, you can be guaranteed that the conclusion has to be true. You can't accept his premises as true and reject his conclusion as false.

In contrast, here's an example of an inductive argument:

Since ***most*** *Democrats are big spenders and Clinton is a democrat,* ***it is probable that*** *Clinton is a big spender.*

Clearly, in this second argument, the arguer does not intend that his premises guarantee his conclusion. He intends that given his premises, his conclusion is likely to be true.

There is an element of uncertainty in his argument since he believes that most and not all Democrats are big spenders.

This uncertainty is the mark of inductive arguments. Indeed, the term induction is used in informal logic to cover reasoning processes under conditions of risk and uncertainty.

You will be spending the next few weeks studying deductive arguments. These are much simpler to evaluate than inductive arguments. After we discuss the analysis and evaluation of deductive arguments, we'll consider inductive ones.

ARGUMENTS AND OTHER FORMS OF DISCOURSE

Of course, language is used for purposes other than argumentation. For example, if I'm merely describing a situation or reporting on events that occur or if I'm clarifying a point, I am not arguing. I'm providing a narrative or a report or an exposition.

But when I'm trying to convince someone that something happened or trying to get him to believe that a statement is true, then I'm arguing.

Also, when I am trying to make my listener or reader understand why something happened or to make clear why a statement is true, this would be an explanation. And there are techniques for evaluating narratives, reports or explanations that assess how well they perform their intended functions.

You will study how to evaluate arguments. With a little thought and practice, the techniques for arguments can be extended to cover explanations.

Unfortunately, there is no hard and fast procedure for determining when you have an argument and when you have an explanation.

Both explanations and arguments use logical words like "since" and "because" to signal inferences.

Usually, you can tell from the context whether people are trying to convince you of something or alternatively when they are trying to explain something to you. But sometimes, this won't be clear. When that happens, be prepared to evaluate it as an argument or as an explanation.

Before concluding, let's consider some examples to drive the points concerning arguments home.

Example 1:

As Val opened Chris's aged and rotted coffin, he thought he saw an almost imperceptible rise and fall of the corpse's chest. He glanced up to see the door slowly shut behind him, leaving him no route of escape. As he turned back to the coffin, out of the corner of his eye, he detected movement. He could not scream, for his heart had slammed into his throat in terror. He realized that the badly decomposed head had turned to observe him.

Now, clearly this is not an argument but mostly a description or narrative of what happened to Val. Note, however, the use of the word "for" in this sentence. We could easily see this as indicating an explanation of why Val could not scream. It's explaining that he could not scream because he was too terrified. The last sentence also seems to be an explanation of what terrified him.

The next two examples are not arguments despite their use of the words "since" and "because".

Example 2:

Alice had not had a bite to eat since she had followed the white rabbit into the hole.

Example 3:

> *Yes, you're right. I hate you. And I hate you because you are cruel and insensitive.*

In Example 2, "since" is used in a temporal sense, indicating a lapse of time. It is just a straightforward claim and not an argument.

Example 3 seems like an explanation. The writer is not trying to convince the hearer that she hates him. That is already known. The word "because" is indicating an explanation of why she hates him. Contrast this with the following argument:

Example 4:

> *Yes, you can be sure that she hates him. That must be true since she hates anyone who is cruel and insensitive and that's exactly what he is. What more need I say to convince you?*

Example 4 seems like an attempt to provide reasons for accepting the claim that she hates him. The arguer is trying to convince his hearer of the point. This is not likely to be an explanation. The uses of "you can be sure that" and "that must be true" indicate a deductive argument.

Example 5:

> *Jones is blushing and he looks uncomfortable. He's probably embarrassed.*

Example 5 contains no inference indicator words, but it's probably an argument. The first two claims look like the kind of evidence one might use to support the third claim. Blushing and looking uncomfortable can be signs of embarrassment. And since the last claim is qualified by probably, I see this as an inductive inference to that conclusion. So, the argument clearly stated would be:

Jones is blushing and he's uncomfortable. So, it's likely that he's embarrassed.

Example 6:

How could you leave me for Mervin? He's not half the man I am since he's soft and flabby, and all he likes to do is read books. Furthermore, he's socially awkward since he can't carry on a decent conversation and he can't be comfortable with anyone other than his mother.

Example 6 is also an argument, but it's a little more complicated. Note that the first sentence is a question, but it is a rhetorical question--that is, it's meant as a statement. The statement, which is also the conclusion, is: You should not leave me for Mervin. The rest of the passage attempts to argue for this conclusion.

Let's examine the structure of the argument. We'll number each of the claims, and provide a description of how the arguer gets to his conclusion. This is the sort of thing you will be doing in future lessons.

1 [You should not leave me for Mervin]. 2 [He's not half the man I am] since 3 [he's soft and flabby,] and 4 [all he likes to do is read books.] Furthermore, 5 [he's socially awkward] since 6 [he can't carry on a decent conversation] and 7 [he can't be comfortable with anyone other than his mother.]

If you pay attention to the inference indicators, you can easily see that the arguer uses 3 and 4 to argue for 2, and he uses 6 and 7 to argue for 5. The main conclusion, which is 1, follows from 2 and 5. Can you see this? A diagram can make it easier to see. Here is one:

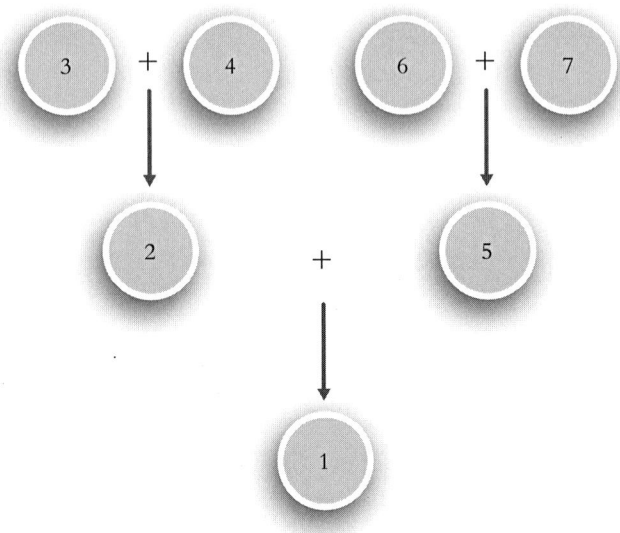

The above diagram is called a "tree diagram." You should learn to diagram arguments in this way as soon as possible. These diagrams provide a concise and clear way to portray argument structure and thus make it easier for you to reconstruct and evaluate arguments.

Summary of Central Points:

1. An argument is a sequence of statements in which premises are offered in support of a conclusion.
2. The inferences that make up arguments are often signaled by certain words or phrases called "inference indicators." You should become supersensitive to the use of these words since they help determine the logical structure of arguments.
3. It is often difficult to distinguish arguments from explanations since both use inference indicator words. If in doubt, treat an explanation logically as an argument.
4. We distinguish between deductive and inductive arguments in accordance with what we take as the intentions of the arguer

and not as inferences from particular claims to the general and general claims to the particular.

DEDUCTIVE ARGUMENTS: Arguments where the arguer intends the truth of the premises to guarantee the truth of the conclusion

INDUCTIVE ARGUMENTS: Arguments where the arguer intends the truth of the premises to make likely, but not guarantee, the truth of the conclusion.

5. Unless specified, we will be working with deductive arguments. We will treat inductive arguments later in the semester.

Skills to Learn:

1. Learn to distinguish between argumentative and other forms of discourse.
2. Learn to identify the main conclusion of an argument.
3. Learn to identify the premises of an argument.
4. Start learning to identify arguments with more than one step.

Sample Homework 2.1
Identifying Arguments, Premises, Conclusions

A. (a) For each of the following passages, if there is an argument then **UNDERLINE** each inference indicator, explaining its purpose if it's not indicating a premise or conclusion of an argument. (b) In any argument, put its claims in **[SQUARE BRACKETS]** and **use numbers to identify the premises and conclusion** as done in the example below.

Example: We can conclude that the Democratic candidate will not win the presidential election since he hasn't built up any support in the western states and no one can win without that kind of support.

We can conclude that 1[the Democratic candidate will not win the presidential election] since 2[he hasn't built up any support in the western states] and 3[no one can win without that kind of support.]

This is an argument with 1 as the conclusion and 2 and 3 as premises.

1. Since if you flip the switch, then the light will go on. And since if the light goes on then the generator is working. It follows that if you flip the switch then the generator is working.

2. Of course scientists often put forth conflicting theories. We can test these theories by seeing if their predictions come true.

3. We can conclude that they are going to get married. Because they love each other and want to have children together. And because they are perfect for each other.

B. The following passages contain statements that one might construe as arguments. Supply inference indicators for each claim in order to indicate how, if possible, the statements could be formed into an argument.

Example: All men are mortal. Socrates is a men. Socrates is mortal.

Since all men are mortal. And <u>since</u> Socrates is a men. <u>It follows that</u> Socrates is mortal.

1. Socialism does not provide adequate incentives. Adequate incentives are needed for a prosperous economy. Socialism is doomed to failure.

2. My keys are either at home or at my office. My keys are not at the office. My keys are at home.

3. 81 is not a prime number. 81 is divisible by 3.

C. Which of the following passages contain arguments? (a) **UNDER-LINE** all inference indicators. (b) If a passage contains an argument, **identify its premises and conclusion** as in the example for Exercise 2.1 A above. (c) If a passage has no arguments, try to state what purposes it serves, giving reasons for the purposes you attribute to each passage.

Example: All men are mortal. Socrates is a men. Socrates is mortal.

<u>Since</u> 1[all men are mortal.] And <u>since</u> 2[Socrates is a men.] <u>It follows that</u> 3[Socrates is mortal.]

Claims 1 and 2 are premises. Claim 3 is the conclusion.

1. An argument may be taken as deductive if the truth of its premises is intended to guarantee the truth of its conclusion.

2. The solitary confinement is a cruel and unusual punishment. The Constitution prohibits cruel and unusual punishments. Hence, solitary confinement should be declared unconstitutional.

3. She is either using her messaging app or talking on the iPhone. She is not talking on her iPhone. So we can conclude that she is using her messaging app.

4. Only a mentally ill person would kill someone. So, anyone who kills someone is automatically mentally ill.

5. The Roman Empire would have fallen even without Christianity. After all, there were many public health and environmental problems. Rome had not mastered the process for the succession of new leaders. And, its highest class became intricately involved with perverted behaviors, losing moral strength. These factors in combination would have been enough to make any empire fall.

Sample Homework 2.2 Recognizing Arguments and Distinguishing Deductive from Inductive Arguments

UNDERLINE inference indicators, [SQUARE BRACKET] and number the claims and **IDENTIFY THE PREMISES AND CONCLUSIONS** for the following arguments. **Determine whether the arguments are deductive or inductive.**

Example: We can conclude that the Democratic candidate will not win the presidential election since he hasn't built up any support in the western states and no one can win without that kind of support.

<u>We can conclude that</u> 1[the Democratic candidate will not win the presidential election] <u>since</u> 2[he hasn't built up any support in the western states] and 3[no one can win without that kind of support.]

Claims 2 and 3 are premises. Claim 1 is the conclusion.

Deductive

1. Since all clowns are from Tennessee. And Sam is a clown. It is likely that Sam is from Tennessee.

2. If this school were at the South Pole, then I'd be at the South Pole. But, I'm not at the South Pole. Therefore, this school is not at the South Pole.

3. The goal in using guarding terms is to find a middle way: We should weaken our premises sufficiently to avoid criticism, but not weaken

them so much that they no longer provide strong enough evidence for the conclusion..

4. In the past, the Bureau of Land Management has negotiated with ranchers. But whenever there has been an agreement between the Bureau of Land Management. and ranchers, the Bureau of Land Management has violated it. So, we can expect that they will violate any agreement that comes from the current proposals of the U.S. Department of Interior. It follows, therefore, that we must not agree to their current proposed agreement.

5. There are only three possible places where Jimmy Hoffa could be buried--Boston, Paris or Ojai. We know that it would have been difficult getting his body to Paris given the rigor of custom officials. The very insular natives inhabiting Ojai at that time would have made it nearly impossible for burying a body to go unnoticed there. So, it's likely that Hoffa is buried in Boston.

||||||||||||||||||||||||||||||||||||||||||||||||||||||||||||||||||||||||||||||||||||||||||||||||||||||||||||||||||||||||

2.3 ASSESSMENT: VALIDITY AND SOUNDNESS

Reading Assignment: Textbook Section 2.3

This lesson concerns two properties that are used to assess deductive arguments validity and soundness.

We have distinguished between deductive and inductive arguments. This distinction is based on the intentions of the arguer. If you take an argument as intended to guarantee the truth of its conclusion, you will evaluate it by deductive standards. Alternatively, if you take the argument as intended to make its conclusion likely, you will evaluate it as inductive.

In everyday contexts, you have to use good judgment in deciding when a person is arguing, rather than explaining or narrating. You will also have to use good judgment in interpreting arguments as deductive or inductive. Making these judgments is often difficult.

However, we will make your task a little easier. For the next few weeks, we will focus exclusively on deductive argumentation. Unless otherwise specified, our discussions, lectures and exercises will deal with deductive arguments.

⚡ VALIDITY

The first thing you need to know about deductive arguments is that we evaluate them on the basis of two related properties--validity and soundness. We'll first explain these properties to you and then go on to consider some examples.

According to the definition in your text, a deductive argument is **valid** if and only if it is logically impossible for all of its premises to be true and its conclusion to be false.

Any argument that doesn't have this property we call **invalid**.

Now that an argument is valid means that if you were to take the premises of as true, then you would be logically forced to accept the conclusion as true. That's what people mean when they say that the conclusion logically follows from the premises. Consider the following valid argument:

All elephants are poets.
All poets are thin.
Hence, all elephants are thin.

If you were to accept as true that all elephants are poets and that all poets are thin, then you would have to accept on logical grounds that all elephants are thin. This conclusion follows from those premises. That's just good deducing.

However, no one would accept the conclusion that all elephants are thin. Nor would you accept the premise that all elephants are poets. So this example should tell you that validity is not all that's required to make a deductive argument convincing. Good reasoning is not enough. You also need true premises. And this leads to the concept of a sound argument.

 ## SOUNDNESS

According to your text, a deductive argument is **sound** if and only if

1) it is valid and
2) all its premises are true.

SECTION 2.3

So, the problem with our elephant argument above is not one of validity but one of soundness. The argument was valid, and if its premises were true, we would have to accept the conclusion that all elephants are thin. But the premises were not true. The argument was not sound.

However, if you argued that all elephants are mammals and all mammals are warm-blooded, so all elephants are warm-blooded, you would have a sound argument. This argument is sound because it is valid, and because all its premises are true.

Note that all sound arguments are valid since validity is part of the definition of soundness. But not all valid arguments are sound since a valid argument can have false premises and thus could not be sound.

Remember also that it's not your actual belief in the truth of the premises and conclusion that matters with validity. To determine validity, you suppose for the sake of argument that the premises are true and then decide whether you would be forced logically to accept the conclusion as true.

When you have determined that the argument is valid, then you have to decide whether you believe that the premises are indeed true. That is, you must decide whether the argument is sound.

Let's take another simple example. Suppose I argue that all philosophy professors are intelligent and that all intelligent people are sensitive, and that therefore, all philosophy professors are sensitive.

Now assuming we could agree on the meanings of the terms here, you would have to agree that my argument is valid. That is, you would have to agree that the conclusion would have to be true if the premises were true.

But, you might judge my premises to be false or questionable and for that reason refuse to accept my argument as sound. You might probably ask for some proof that my premises are true before you would accept my conclusion.

We often agree on the validity of arguments but disagree on their soundness since we disagree on the truth of their premises.

Before we consider some other examples, note that arguments with false premises and false conclusions can be valid. So can arguments with false premises and true conclusions. The only possibility not allowed by definition to be valid is an argument whose premises could all be true and its conclusion be false.

Note also that we are using the terms "valid" and "sound" as technical terms. They refer only to properties of deductive arguments.

Arguments aren't true or false. That's bad English. Statements are true or false, and premises are true or false.

And in our sense, regardless of the common usage, statements aren't valid or sound. Only deductive arguments or inferences are valid or sound.

Let's consider some more examples to clarify these points. When you are asked to evaluate a deductive argument, you go into a two step process. You need to determine whether it's valid or invalid. Then, if you determine that it is valid, you need to decide whether its premises are true.

Example 1: An Invalid Argument
What an upset! The Giants lost the game. If they had won, the would have gotten the pennant. So, now they wont get it.

Step 1: Is the argument valid. No, it's not. The premises could be true and the conclusion false in the following situation:

> *It's the fourth game of the pennant series. The Giants have won three games. The Giants have lost the fourth game. If they had won the fourth, they would have gotten the pennant. But it doesn't follow that they wont get it since they can win the fifth game. A team wins the pennant by winning 4 out of seven games.*

Step 2: The argument isn't sound since it isn't valid.

Example 2: An Invalid Argument with All True Premises and True Conclusion

> *Some people are liars. Some liars are crooks. Therefore, some people are crooks.*

Although all the statements in this argument are no doubt true, the argument is not sound since it's not valid. The conclusion does not follow from the premises. If it had said that all people are liars and all liars are crooks, therefore all people are crooks, there would be a valid argument.

Example 2 is similar to arguing in the following obviously invalid way:

> *Some fire engines are red things. Some red things are strawberries. Therefore, some fire engines are strawberries.*

Example 3: A Valid Argument with False Premises and a True Conclusion

> *All alligators are Presidents of the United States. Bill Clinton is an alligator. Therefore, Bill Clinton is President of the United States.*

It's clear that the premises of this argument are false. Hence, the argument is unsound. But the argument is valid. If the premises were true, the conclusion would have to be true as well. It's obviously a bad argument for a true conclusion.

Well continue to discuss validity in the next lesson by introducing another way of defining it.

Summary of Central Points:

1. In this course, validity and soundness are technical concepts. They are properties used to evaluate deductive arguments.
2. Thus, only deductive arguments can be valid or sound. In our terminology, premises and conclusions and other statements are true, false or questionable. They are never valid or sound. Inductive arguments are neither valid nor sound.
3. Our first definition of validity is the "informal" definition.

    DEFINITION: A deductive argument is valid if and only if it's logically impossible for its premises to be true and its conclusion to be false. You should compare this definition with the "formal" definition of validity found in the next lesson.
4. To say that an argument is valid is merely to recognize that if its premises were true, then its conclusion would have to be true. The premises and conclusion of a valid argument need not in fact be true.
5. An argument with false premises and a true conclusion, or with false premises and a false conclusion may still be valid. An argument with all true premises and a false conclusion can never be valid.
6. A valid argument with all true premises is sound. Thus, a sound argument has to be valid, but a valid argument need not be sound since it may contain false premises.

7. Soundness is a mark of success in deductive argumentation. If an argument is sound, then its conclusion must be true, and you are forced to accept it.

Skills to Learn:

1. Learn to recognize argument validity and invalidity.
2. Learn to find counterexamples for invalid arguments. This requires imagining circumstances where the premises could be true and the conclusion could be false.
3. Learn to distinguish between validity and soundness. Don't think that an argument is invalid merely because it has false premises or a false conclusion.

Sample Homework 2.3
Distinguishing Valid from Invalid Inferences.

Example:

A. Make up an example of each of the following:

1. A valid argument with all false premises and a true conclusion.
   All whales are fishes
   <u>All fishes are mammals</u>
   All whales are mammals

2. A valid argument with all false premises and a false conclusion.
   All spiders have four legs
   <u>All four legged creatures have wings</u>
   All spiders have wings.

3. A valid argument with all true premises and a true conclusion.
   All whales are mammals
   <u>All mammals have lungs</u>
   All mammals have lungs

4. An invalid argument with all true premises and a true conclusion.
   If I owned all the gold in Fort Knox, then I would be wealthy.
   <u>I don't own all the gold in Fort Knox</u>
   I am not wealthy.

A. Make up an example of each of the following:
1. A valid argument with all false premises and a true conclusion.

2. A valid argument with all false premises and a false conclusion.

3. A valid argument with all true premises and a true conclusion.

4. An invalid argument with all true premises and a true conclusion.

B. Try to determine which of the following arguments are invalid. That is, try to describe possible circumstances where it would be logically possible for the premises to be true and the conclusion to be false.

Example: The day after February 28th is February 29th. Today is February 28th. Therefore, tomorrow is February 29th.
This argument is invalid as stated because although in leap years the day after February 28th is February 29th, in non-leap years the day after February 28th is March 1st.

1. I am on a plane to Paris. Therefore I will not be stopping in New York.

2. Smoking causes cancer. You smoke. Therefore you will get cancer.

3. Some mammals are swimmers. Some swimmers are fish. Therefore, some mammals are fish.

4. All the players on the team are great players. Therefore it is a great team.

5. Ida sometimes says things that are untrue. Hence, Ida is a liar. So, you shouldn't trust Ida.

C. For each of the following: **Portray the argument's structure – underline, bracket, number, list premises and conclusions. Evaluate the validity and soundness of each argument.** If you believe it is unsound, explain your answer by saying whether the argument is valid or invalid, and by explaining why you believe any of its premises is false. If you believe that its soundness is questionable explain why its premises need further clarification and support. [Hint:

An argument is considered sound if it is valid (there is no way the premises could be true, and the conclusion not follow}and all of the premises actually are true.]

Example:

The day after Monday is Tuesday. We know that today is the day after Monday. Hence, today is Tuesday.

1(The day after Monday is Tuesday.] <u>We know that</u> 2[today is the day after Monday.] <u>Hence</u>, 3[today is Tuesday.]

1 and 2 are premises. 3 is the conclusion.

This argument is valid as stated. If we logically accept the premises we must accept the conclusion. This argument is sound because it is valid and both of the premises are true.

1. Since all men are mortal and Arnold Schwarzenegger is a man, it follows that Arnold Schwarzenegger is mortal.

2. Since no one can say what the future will hold, and no one can be the messiah unless he can do this, it follows that there are no messiahs. The Bible says that Jesus is the messiah. Hence, sometimes what the Bible says is untrue.

3. Modesto is north of Santa Barbara. Santa Barbara is south of Bakersfield. Therefore, if you travel in a straight line from Santa Barbara to Modesto, you will have to pass through Bakersfield.

4. You should not pay for cryonic suspension. If and when you're revived, you'll be lonely. You can't afford it. And even if you can afford it then when you're revived, you'll have no money and, potentially, no transferable skills.

2.7 - 2.8 FORMAL VALIDITY

Reading Assignment: Textbook Sections 2.7 and 2.8

The topic of this lesson is formal logic. More specifically, we'll cover some elementary sentential or propositional logic.

This study will make you more sharply attuned to the logical structure of English. It will help to sharpen your analytical eye.

Equally important, this study should help you to grasp the logical structure of deductive arguments in order to determine whether or not they are valid.

To this end, in this lesson we will introduce you to statement and argument forms, and to substitution instances of argument forms. Relying on these concepts, we will provide the formal definition of validity in the next lesson.

⚡ LOGICAL SYMBOLS

In sentential logic, we use small letters to stand for variables whose values are simple sentences or statements. Just like in algebra where you have variables that range over numbers, in logic we have variables that range over simple statements.

Much of what you do here will be a little easier because well use the symbols that we have already introduced to you to stand for logical connectives. That is, a tilde stands for "not", an ampersand for "and," a small " v" for inclusive "or" and an arrow for "if-then." Thus, you have:

Negation: **~p** Conjunction: **p & q** Disjunction: **p v q** Conditional: **p àq**

SPECIFIC FORMS FOR STATEMENTS

In Lesson 1.2, you were asked to look for simple components of complex statements and to depict the logical structure of complex statements. Here we are doing roughly the same thing. We try to get what is called a statement's specific form, namely the form that fully exhibits the detailed logical structure of the statement.

To say that the specific form fully exhibits the statement's logical structure means that you must make sure that any of the four logical connectives that are in the statement must be portrayed in the statement's specific form.

Finding the specific forms of statements is one of the best ways to learn how to pay attention to logical structure, to learn how to get precise about language. We're momentarily ignoring the content of ordinary English statements and focusing on their logical form. This forces you to recognize the presence and function of the above four logical connectives.

From your study of Chapter 1 or your text, you already have a rough idea about how to determine the logical form of complex statements. So, a good way to help refine your logical sense is to jump in and do some examples. We'll start with simple statements, then complex ones, and then consider some argument forms.

Simple statements are easy to portray. Since they have no logical complexity, you just replace them with a letter, using a different letter for each different simple statement.

Logicians usually employ letters at the end of the alphabet from **p** on as variable letters. They use letters at the beginning of the alphabet as constants.

But you can use whatever letters you want that may suggest statement content, if that helps you to remember the original statement.

So, for example, we have the following **simple statements** and their specific forms in propositional logic:

Martha slept here.	**m**
Adam was made from Eve's rib.	**a**
Doug believes in the Buddha.	**b**
I know the Kama Sutra by heart.	**k**

Negations of simple statements are also fairly easy to portray. Give the component a letter and put a tilde in front. Thus, the logical structure of these negations is simply:

Martha did not sleep here.	**~m**
Doug doesn't believe in the Buddha.	**~b**

Conjunctions and **disjunctions** with simple components are also fairly straightforward. For example, letting **g** replace *Otto is a German,* **s** replace *Otto is a squealer,* and **h, y** and **b** respectively replace *he's going to Harvard, he's going to Yale, he's going to Berkeley,* the formulas for the following conjunctions and disjunctions are:

Otto is a German and a squealer.	**g & s**
He's going to either Harvard or Yale or Berkeley.	**(h v y) v b**

Note that parentheses are used as punctuation to eliminate ambiguity. The convention is to pair up conjuncts and disjuncts beginning on the left. So, if his alternatives above included Princeton as well, you would have a formula with two pairs of disjuncts: **(h v y) v (b v p)**

Let's see if your analytical eye is improving. Can you see that this next example is not a disjunction, but a negation whose component is a disjunction?

He's not going to either Harvard or Yale.

More formally it says *it's not the case that either he's going to Harvard or he's going to Yale.* We use parentheses as punctuation to show that scope of the negation sign covers the whole disjunction. We get the specific form as: **~(h v y)**

Similarly, the logical structure of next example is a negation of a conjunction. Note again the use of parentheses to mark the scope of the negation sign. It covers whatever is inside the parentheses.

It's not true that Otto is both a German and not a squealer **~(g & ~s)**

Conditionals are fairly easy to formalize when they are stated in standard form. The following conditional and its contrapositive are easily portrayed as follows:

If it's a mammal, it's warm-blooded.   **m** --> w

If it's not warm-blooded, it's not a mammal.   **~w** --> ~m

However, conditionals will always remain problematic until you learn to recognize hidden conditionals and learn how to translate them into standard form. Here are some hidden conditionals and a specific form for each.

Only the brave are lonely.
If you're lonely then you're brave.   **l** --> **b**

Being wealthy is necessary for happiness.
If you're happy, then you're wealthy.   **h** --> w

Unless I'm mistaken, the referee called a penalty.
If I'm not mistaken, the referee called a penalty.   **~m** --> **p**

In each case, we translate the hidden conditional into a logically equivalent standard form conditional, and then get the specific form of the latter.

And as you may expect, we often get statements whose logical structure is very complicated. Determining their specific forms enable you to determine when they are true.

Here is a slightly more complicated example taken from your text. We use the logicians convention of using **p, q, r**, as variable letters standing for the first, second, third simple components occurring in the sentence.

> *If you earn over $10,000 in taxable income, then you may file the short form only if you do not wish to claim more than $3,400 in deductions and have no dependents.*

Specific Form: **p** --> (q --> (~r & ~s))

Can you tell that the above regulation would be broken (i.e., you'd make the conditional false) when it's true that **p**, true that **q** and either **r** or **s** are true? Or in other words, its false when you earn over $10,000 and you file the short form, but either you wish to claim more than $3400 or you do have dependents.

With some practice, you should eventually be able discern the logical structure of such complicated statements without the use of letters and symbols. Thats your goal. But most of us reach that goal only after learning to work out the laborious details as were doing here.

SPECIFIC FORMS FOR ARGUMENTS

Finally, we get to specific argument forms. And this is nothing really different from what we have just been doing.

Obviously, arguments are composed from statements. And we've been portraying the specific forms of statements.

So to find an argument's specific form, you just determine the specific forms of the individual statements making up its premises and conclusion.

You will then be in a better position to judge whether or not the argument is valid. Remember that that's our main objective.

Let's look at some illustrations for getting an argument's specific form. We've underlined the inference indicators in the arguments to help you identify the premises and main conclusion.

Argument 1:

Either you will become a success or you will fail. If you fail, you will not be remembered. <u>Since</u> you won›t become a success, <u>it follows that</u> you will not be remembered.

This argument has three premises leading to the main conclusion. We've put the specific forms to the right of the premises and conclusion. The solid line separating the premises from the conclusion is read as "therefore."

ARGUMENT	SPECIFIC FORM
Either you will become a success or you will fail.	s v f
If you fail, you will not be remembered.	f --> ~r
You won't become a success.	~s
You will not be remembered.	~r

where **s** = you will become a success; **f** = you will fail; **r** = you will be remembered

Note that all the connectives are represented in the specific form at the right.

Note also that we use the same letter for each simple component everywhere that component occurs in the argument. Be very careful not to omit the negation signs for negative statements, and be careful not to use different letters for the same simple component.

Argument 2:

> *If I spend my money on guitar lessons, I can't buy my schoolbooks. And if I can't buy my schoolbooks, I can't pass my classes. If I can't pass my classes, I will flunk out of school. So, if I spend my money on guitar lessons, I will flunk out of school.*

ARGUMENT	SPECIFIC FORM
If I spend my money on guitar lessons, I can't buy schoolbooks.	s --> ~b

And if I can't buy schoolbooks, I can't pass my classes.	~b --> ~p
<u>If I can't pass my classes, I will flunk out of school.</u>	<u>~p</u> --> f
If I spend my money on guitar lessons, I will flunk out of school.	s --> f

where the s = I spend my money on guitar lessons; b = I buy school-books; p = I pass my classes; f = I will flunk out of school With a little practice, you should be able to determine the specific forms of arguments in a relatively short time.

 ## SUBSTITUTION INSTANCES OF ARGUMENT FORMS

A substitution instance of an argument form is a relatively easy concept to grasp. Rather than determining an argument's form from the argument, we can do the reverse process by getting an ordinary English argument from an argument form.

A **substitution instance** of an argument form is an argument that you get by substituting the letters in the argument form with simple English statements.

Thus, a substitution instance of an argument form is nothing other than an example of an argument that has that form. In the examples above, the arguments are substitution instances of their specific forms.

Here are some other examples to make this concept clear. We provide two argument forms and a substitution instance for each.

ARGUMENT FORM	SUBSTITUTION INSTANCE
~p --> ~q	If Jim doesn't ski, he can't go on the winter outing.
~p	And since Jim doesn't ski, it follows that he can't go on
~q	the outing.
p v q	Either we leave today or we will be late for the meeting.
~p	But we will not be leaving today. So, we will be late for the
q	meeting.

Remember that a substitution instance has only simple statements substituted for the sentential letters of its argument form.

Summary of Central Points:

1. You get the specific form of a statement by replacing its simple components with small letters and replacing its logical terms with the symbols for negation, conjunction, disjunction and the conditional. Use parentheses for punctuation.
2. You get the specific form of an argument by determining the specific form of its premises and its conclusion.
3. The symbols used for the four logical connectives are:

Negation: **~p**
Conjunction: **p & q**

Disjunction: **p v q**

Conditional: **p —> q**

4. Substitution instances are obtained from argument forms by substituting simple statements for sentential letters.

Skills to Learn:

1. Learn to recognize negations, conjunctions, disjunctions, and conditionals.
2. Learn to portray the logical structure of complex statements by using sentential letters and the symbols for the logical connectives to get a statement's specific form.
3. Learn to determine the specific forms of arguments.
4. Learn to invent several clear substitution instances of any argument form whenever you need them as demonstrations of a form's validity or invalidity.

Sample Homework 2.7
Translating Sentences into Sentential Forms

Put the following statements into symbolic form. Do not forget to use logical connectives. Define your letters

Example: Today is not the first day of the rest of your life, or the posters are wrong.

~T v P

T = Today is the first day of the rest of your life.

P = The posters are wrong.

1. Today is not Friday.

2. Both Christmas and New Year's Day fell on a Monday this year.

3. I have class on Thursdays and either I am going to fail or both my final and my midterm will be accepted by the instructor as adequate.

4. Iraq won't raise the price of oil unless Libya does so. (Hint: Use LES)

5. This piece of blue litmus paper will turn red if this piece of blue litmus paper is placed in an acidic solution. (Hint: Use LES)

6. Either he will be acquitted or if he gets a great lawyer then he will not go to jail or serve time.

7. The car runs only if there is fuel in the tank. (Hint: Use LES)

||||||||||||||||||||||||||||||||||||||||||||||||||||||||||||||||||||||||||||||||||||||||||||||||||||||||||||||||||||||||||

2.11 FORMALLY VALID ARGUMENT FORMS

Reading Assignment: Textbook Section 2.11

In this lesson we introduce the formal concept of validity and study some commonly used argument forms. This will end our preliminary study of the logical structure of language in preparation for our analysis and evaluation of everyday arguments.

So far in your study of sentential logic, you have learned how to portray the logical structure of statements by using letters for simple statements and symbols for connectives. You've also learned to portray the specific forms of arguments, which after all are just series of statements.

Your reason for determining the logical structure of arguments is to determine whether those arguments are valid. That is, you want to see whether their conclusions follow from their premises. By the informal definition of validity, you want to know that whether or not it's logically possible for the premises to be true and the conclusion false.

Now one nice thing is that we have argument forms that generate only valid arguments. These are called **valid argument forms**. If you see an argument that has one of forms, then you can immediately judge it to be valid.

Before we see how this works, we need to provide you with the formal definition of validity. This definition relies on the informal definition of validity and on the concept of substitution instance that you learned in the last lesson.

The Formal Definition of Validity: An argument is **valid** if it is a substitution instance of a valid argument form.

Although the above definition seems circular, it is not. Formal logicians have devised methods of proving independently which argument forms are valid. One of these methods is the method of truth tables found in your text. But you will not be concerned with proving which argument forms a valid.

Instead, we want you to learn to recognize valid and invalid argument forms, and recognize when an argument is an instance of those forms. This will require that you commit to memory the valid argument forms found in your text and know when an argument is a substitution instance of those forms.

Your knowledge of argument forms gives you a quick procedure for determining an argument's validity. First you determine the form of the argument. If you recognize it as an instance of a valid argument form, you can immediately judge it valid without having to imagine circumstances where the premises could be true and the conclusion false. You know immediately that if this argument's premises are true, then it is logically impossible for its conclusion to be false.

Now of course, this procedure requires that you be able to recognize whether or not an argument form is valid. So, we will briefly discuss some commonly used valid argument forms that you should commit to memory. Consult your text for more examples of each of these forms.

AFFIRMING THE ANTECEDENT (AC)

When an argument has a conditional premise, and another premise that affirms the antecedent of that conditional, you may validly infer the consequent. This form is also called **modus ponens**.

P --> Q   *If Jim is a Marxist, he believes in the common ownership of property.*

P_____   *And since Jim is indeed a Marxist, he must believe in the common*

Q   *ownership of property.*

Note that we have used capital letters in the above argument form. This is to indicate that the components of these formulas need not be simple. For example, an argument with the form below still follows the rule of affirming the antecedent.

(p v q) --> ~r

_p v q_

~r

Since this principle applies to all our argument formulas, we will continue to use capital letters.

⚡ DENYING THE CONSEQUENT (DC)

When an argument has a conditional premise, and another premise which denies the consequent of that conditional, you may validly infer the negation of the antecedent. This form is also called **modus tollens**.

P --> Q   If the Duke had drunk the arsenic laced solution,

_~Q_   then he'd be dead. But *he clearly is not dead. Hence, he*

~P   *did not drink the solution. An elementary deduction, my dear Watson!*

NOTE: Do Not Confuse the Above Valid Argument Forms with the Following

INVALID ARGUMENT FORMS!

AFFIRMING   DENYING
THE CONSEQUENT (AC)   THE ANTECEDENT(DC)

P --> Q   P --> Q
Q_____   ~P_____
P   ~Q

 ## HYPOTHETICAL SYLLOGISM (HS)

Both premises of this argument form are conditionals, and so is the conclusion. This form is also called a **conditional chain**.

P --> Q   *If I pass this class, then I will complete the major. And if I complete the*

Q --> R   *major, then I can graduate. Thus, if I pass this class, I can graduate.*

P --> R

Note that you can have more than two conditional premises in a conditional chain.

Note also that the use of hidden conditionals sometimes makes the hypothetical syllogism difficult to recognize.

Note finally that the order in which the premises are stated may also make this form difficult to identify. Consider the following arguments that employ hidden conditionals and that state the premises in a non-serial order. Can you see that these are valid conditional chains? We've abbreviated the arguments and then translated the conditionals into standard form to help you see this.

The President can trim excess spending only if he is willing to cut the White House staff. And he is not justified in raising taxes unless he trims excess spending. Thus, if he is to justify raising taxes, then he must be willing to cut the White House staff.

Abbreviation:	**t** only if **w**	Argument Form:	**t** --> w
	not **j** unless **t**		**j** --> t
	If **j** then **w**		**j** --> w

If you practice safe sex, then you must have one exclusive sex partner or use condoms. And you can be morally responsible only if you practice safe sex. Hence, you can be morally responsible only if you have one exclusive sex partner or use condoms.

Abbreviation:	If **p**, then (**e** or **u**)	Argument Form:	**p** --> (e v u)
	m only if **p**		**m** --> p
	m only if (**e** or **u**)		**m** --> (e v u)

If the above is confusing to you, DON'T BE DISCOURAGED! Some confusion is normal when you first begin to learn this logic stuff. WE'VE ALL BEEN THROUGH IT! With practice and a little time, it will become more familiar and easier for you.

Remember that in all arguments using conditional premises, you must translate hidden conditionals correctly into standard form, and then see whether the resulting argument form is valid. But since you are just learning about hidden conditionals, this process will be difficult.

HANG IN THERE! Continue to do all your assigned work and get help whenever you need it. You've got the brains and talent to master the skills needed for analytic thought--or else you'd never have come this far in your educational career!

DISJUNCTIVE SYLLOGISM (DS)

When an argument has a disjunctive premise, and another premise that denies one of the disjuncts, you may validly infer the other disjunct.

P v Q
~P
Q

I will either live with my parents for two more years or get a job to pay for my tuition. But I know that I will not live with my parents. So, I'm going out to get that job!

There are two things two note about arguments with disjunctive premises.

Your disjunction may have more than two disjuncts. Thus, you need to be careful about how many alternatives are offered, and how many are rejected to draw the conclusion. The following argument is a valid use of the disjunctive syllogism:

> *I can go either to France, Germany, England or Italy. But I certainly don't want to go to France or Germany. Hence, I will go either to England or Italy.*

Don't confuse the disjunctive syllogism with a similar looking but invalid form called **the disjunctive fallacy**. Here are the two forms. Only the first is valid since we are using "or" in the inclusive sense. This means that if you have a disjunctive premise, and you know one of the disjuncts is true, you can't infer that the other disjunct is false since both disjuncts may be true.

DISJUNCTIVE SYLLOGISM	DISJUNCTIVE FALLACY
P v Q	P v Q
~P	P
Q	~Q

Our last two valid argument forms are logical dilemmas.

⚡ CONSTRUCTIVE DILEMMA (CD)

In the constructive dilemma, if an argument has two conditional premises and a premise stating the disjunction of their antecedents, you may validly infer a disjunction of their consequents.

P --> Q	*If I want to study philosophy, I'll go to Berkeley. And if I*
R --> S	*want to study economics, I'll go to Chicago. Since I want to*
P v R	*study either philosophy or economics, it follows that I'll go*
Q v **S**	*either to Berkeley or to Chicago.*

⚡ DESTRUCTIVE DILEMMA (DD)

In the destructive dilemma, if you have two conditional premises and a disjunction of the negations of their consequents, you may validly infer a disjunction of the negation of their antecedents.

P --> Q	*If I marry Tom, I'll be able to pursue my career. If I marry*
R --> S	*Jim, I'll have to start raising a family. Well, either I won't*
~Q v ~S	*be able to pursue my career or I won't start raising a family.*
~P v ~R	*Hence, either I won't marry Tom or I won't marry Jim.*

Note one thing about the destructive dilemma. You will often find it in either of the slightly different but logically equivalent forms given above.

SOME FINAL POINTS:

Arguments may have several steps in a chain of reasoning that uses these various forms in combinations. So long as each step employs a valid form, the argument as a whole is valid. Learn to spot such chains of reasoning and determine which forms are used.

Also, everyday arguments may have unstated premises or conclusions that are incomplete versions of these forms. In such cases, you should learn to identify what statements are needed to complete the argument form.

After some practice, you will be able to make a direct translations from ordinary English into symbols to portray argument forms. But while you are learning, it may be helpful to follow the 5 step procedure in your textbook for determining argument forms.

This procedure is as follows:

1. READ THE ARGUMENT CAREFULLY
2. CIRCLE INFERENCE INDICATORS
3. UNDERLINE LOGICAL CONNECTIVES
4. DETERMINE AND LETTER THE SIMPLE COMPONENTS
5. WRITE OUT THE ARGUMENT FORM

Remember that you are not concerned at this point with argument soundness. That is, you aren't concerned with whether the premises of arguments are <u>indeed</u> true. At this point you are concerned only with validity. That is, you want to know whether the premises of an argument, <u>if they were true</u>, would force you logically to accept the conclusion as true.

Summary of Central Points:

1. Remember our first definition of validity was the "informal" definition.

   DEFINITION: A deductive argument is valid if and only if it's logically impossible for its premises to be true and its conclusion to be false.

2. The formal definition of validity relies on argument forms and on the informal definition of validity.

   DEFINITION: An argument is formally valid if and only if it is an instance of a valid argument form.

3. Thus, you have two ways of detecting validity and invalidity.

   1) You can try to imagine conditions where the premises could be true and the conclusion   false.

   2) You can see if the argument is an instance of a valid or invalid argument form.

Some Valid Argument Forms:

AA: $p \rightarrow q$	DC: $p \rightarrow q$	HS: $p \rightarrow q$	DS: $p \vee q$	CD: $(p \rightarrow q) \,\&\, (r \rightarrow s)$
p	$\sim q$	$q \rightarrow r$	$\sim p$	$p \vee r$
q	$\sim p$	$p \rightarrow r$	q	$q \vee s$

Some Invalid Argument Forms:

AC: $p \rightarrow q$	DA: $p \rightarrow q$	Disjunctive Fallacy: $p \vee q$
q	$\sim p$	p
p	$\sim q$	$\sim q$

Skills to Learn:

1. Learn to recognize valid and invalid argument forms.
2. Learn to recognize substitution instances of valid and invalid argument forms.

3. Learn to provide clear substitution instances of valid and invalid argument forms to illustrate to others the validity and invalidity of those forms.

4. Learn to fill in the missing statements needed to complete arguments so that they correspond to valid argument forms.

⚡ GENERAL POINTS TO REMEMBER:

- So far, we have taken up logical preliminaries that are required for effective argument analysis and evaluation. Although we have moved fairly quickly, a rough grasp of this subject matter will suffice. Your understanding of these materials will be sharpened through review and through use in further work.

- Help is available. Ask your instructor.

- Note that the reading assignments precede the lessons and class tutorials that deal with the subject matter of those assignments. We want you to read through a subject before we cover it. You can then review the materials in order to do your homework.

- Make sure to contact your instructor with any difficulties you are having with the course materials.

- Remember that we expect you to evaluate the course materials and their presentation for clarity and effectiveness. That is part of the course. This means that you should leave messages on CANVAS regarding materials that are unclear to you. You should leave messages providing suggestions for improvement of the lessons and suggestions for additional lessons or exercises that you believe would be helpful to you and to future students. THANKS!

Sample Homework 2.11 Formally Valid Argument Forms

A. **Fill in the missing premises** needed to make each of the following arguments valid. **Determine the form** of the resulting argument and **show it. Give the name of the form** if it is one of the formally valid argument forms. If more than one form is used, name each form in order of use.

Example: If you like chocolate and strawberries then you like dessert. Harriet likes chocolate and strawberries. Therefore, Harriet likes dessert.

1[If you like chocolate and strawberries then you like dessert.] 2[Harriet likes chocolate and strawberries.] Therefore, 3[Harriet likes dessert.]

C —> D
C
D
C = You like chocolate and strawberries★
D = You like dessert
Affirming the Antecedent
★Chocolate and strawberries is taken here to mean something like chocolate dipped strawberries and so is not taken to be a conjunction.

1. If the taxes are increased for the poor, poverty will increase; and if taxes are increased on the wealthy, the poor will lose their jobs. Therefore, either poverty will increase or the poor will lose their jobs.

2. You are not for us. Therefore, you are against us. And therefore, you will not be invited to the wedding.

3. She is either going to have to have to do the assigned reading or she's asking to fail the class. We can conclude that she does not want to fail the class. Therefore, she will be doing the assigned reading at some time in the near future.

4. If a woman is a slave to beauty, she is not free; and if a woman is a slave to fashion, he is not free. Hence, no woman is free.

B. Fill in the missing premises or conclusions needed to make the following incomplete arguments valid. Determine the form of the resulting argument, and identify the form if it is one of the argument forms named above.

Example: The spicier the taco the better the taco. And the tacos are better at Taco King!

This can be seen as a Hypothetical Syllogism since the premises can be read as hidden conditionals.

Missing conclusion: The tacos are spicier at Taco King.

Form: l-->b   Roughly, if spicier taco then better.

k-->l   if Taco King taco, then spicier.

k-->b   if Taco King taco, then better.

1. If today is the first step toward the future then we had best get started. So we had best get started.

2. Either Israel negotiates with the Palestinians or they will end up going to war with them. If they negotiate with them, someone will have to make some concessions but they will survive. If they go to war with them, they must be prepared to have innocent people die. They are not prepared to have innocent people die. The conclusion is obvious.

3. If we support the home team, we must be prepared to face the taunting of the visiting teams fans. But we are not prepared to face the taunting. So, ...

C. The following arguments are incomplete substitution instances of valid argument forms. Determine the form of the given argument and supply the statement and statement form needed to make the argument valid. Use categorical logic or sentential logic as needed.

Example: No self-respecting human beings are members of a sexist, misandrist organization. Hence, no NOW members are self-respecting human beings.
If you are a member of a sexist, misandrist organization then you are not a self-respecting human being.
<u>NOW is a of a sexist, misandrist organization.</u>
NOW members of are not self-respecting human beings.
M ~S
<u>M</u>
~S
M=You are a member of a sexist, misandrist organization.
S = You are a self respecting human being.
Affirming the Antecedent

1. If the snake encouraged them to eat the apple, then he encouraged them to sin against God. Hence, the snake encouraged them to sin against God.

2. If we eat a heavy snack in the afternoon, we will need a nap; and if we eat no snack at all, we will have hunger pains. So, it's clear that we are going need a nap or we will have hunger pains.

3. All the animals in this zoo have fur. So, no amphibians are in this zoo.

4. If we go to the rodeo, then we'll miss movie night. If we go to the horse races, then we'll miss game night. So, we are either not going to the rodeo or we aren't going to the horse races.

5. We will either go to the Dodger's game or to the Angel's game tonight. So, either we will go to Los Angeles or to Anaheim tonight.

3.1 - 3.2 UNDERSTANDING ARGUMENT STRUCTURE

Reading Assignment: Textbook Sections 3.1 and 3.2

In this lesson, we introduce terms that describe argument structure and introduce a method of portraying argument structure called "the tree diagram." Don't worry if you're not able to understand all the material in this lesson. We devote the rest of Chapter 3 to clarifying and supplementing this material.

Before you can effectively evaluate an argument, you need to understand the argument's logical structure. That is, you need to understand which statements are basic premises, which are sub-conclusions, and to know how the arguer gets from her basic premises to her main conclusion. We begin with some definitions that you will find more fully discussed in your text.

ARGUMENT CHAINS, BASIC PREMISES AND SUBCONCLUSIONS

In everyday reasoning, arguments often come in chains. That is, the arguer uses a premise to support a conclusion, and then uses that conclusion as a premise to support another conclusion and so on.

These arguments or lines of reasoning are sometimes called **argument chains**.

Each sub-argument in an argument chain is called a **step** in the argument.

Any premise in an argument that is stated without support is called a **basic premise** of the argument.

The final conclusion of any argument or argument chain is called the **main conclusion** of the argument.

A conclusion of any step other than the main conclusion is called a **sub-conclusion** or **intermediate conclusion** in the argument.

Consider the following argument to clarify these terms:

> *Since* all feminists believe in equal rights for men and women, and Joan is a feminist, *it follows that* Joan believes in equal rights for men and women. But if she believes in such equal rights, then she must believe in equal pay for equal work. *Therefore, Joan believes in equal pay for equal work.*

If you heed the underlined inference indicators in this argument, you should see that it is an argument chain with two steps. The solid line under a claim indicates that what follows is a conclusion. It is read as "therefore."

Step 1:

All feminists believe in equal rights for men and women.	**BP**
Joan is a feminist.	**BP**
Joan believes in equal rights for men and women.	**SC**

Step 2:

Joan believes in equal rights for men and women	**SC**
If she believes in such equal rights, then she must believe in equal pay for equal work.	**BP**
Joan believes in equal pay for equal work.	**MC**

The conclusion of the first step is: *Joan believes in equal rights for men and women.*

This is a sub-conclusion since it is used as a premise for the second step in the argument.

The conclusion of the second step is the main conclusion:

Joan believes in equal pay for equal work.

The other claims in the argument are unsupported and are basic premises.

ELLIPTICAL ARGUMENTS

Most arguments that you find in everyday writing and speaking are logically incomplete. Arguers fail to state premises and conclusions that are required for validity. So, the above argument might be more commonly stated as:

> <u>Since</u> all feminists believe in equal rights for men and women, Joan must believe in equal rights for men and women. *<u>Therefore</u>, she must believe in equal pay for equal work.*

In this version of the argument, the arguer takes for granted that the two missing claims are true and doesn't bother to state them.

As defined in your book, an argument that is missing a premise or conclusion needed for deductive validity or inductive strength is called an **elliptical argument**.

Inferential assumptions are unstated premises needed to make an elliptical argument valid or strong. These are also called **implicit** or missing premises.

Unstated conclusions needed to complete an elliptical argument are called **implicit conclusions**.

SECTION 3.1 - 3.2

In order to evaluate elliptical arguments properly, you need to make their logical structure clear by identifying and filling in their missing premises and conclusions. Consider the following example:

> *You're an embezzler. Therefore, you're a criminal. So, you know where you'll end up, don't you? And say Hello to the warden when you get there.*

The above argument is elliptical. But we can make a good guess at what the arguer means. Here is the reconstructed argument with the inferential assumptions and implicit main conclusion filled in.

Valid Reconstruction:

You're an embezzler.	Basic premise
<u>All embezzlers are criminals.</u>	**Inferential Assumption**
You're a criminal.	Sub-Conclusion
<u>All criminals end up in jail.</u>	**Inferential Assumption**
You will end up in jail.	**Implicit Conclusion**

Remember that an inferential assumption is nothing other than a missing premise needed to make an argument deductively valid or inductively strong.

With the inferential assumptions and implicit conclusion filled in, both steps of the above argument are valid, and thus the argument is valid.

Note that any argument that has any invalid steps is invalid.

TREE DIAGRAMS
One of the best ways we know to make argument structure clear is to portray that structure with a tree diagram. Put simply, a tree diagram is a flow-chart of an argument's reasoning.

We first list the elements of tree diagrams and then work through some examples to make our procedure clear to you.

In tree diagrams:

Numbers stand for claims stated by the arguer.

Capital letters stand for implicit claims needed to complete an elliptical argument.

A **straight downward arrow** stands for the conclusion indicator in deductive arguments. The downward arrow may be read as «therefore».

A **broken arrow** to stand for the conclusion indicator in inductive arguments. The downward broken arrow may be read as «so, it is likely that».

Let's consider an argument that we portrayed above in standard form so that you can compare it with the tree diagram portrayal. These are just slightly different ways of accomplishing the same task.

Since 1[all feminists believe in equal rights for men and women,] and 2[Joan is a feminist,] it follows that 3[Joan believes in equal rights for men and women.] But 4[if she believes in such equal rights, then she must believe in equal pay for equal work.] Therefore, 5[Joan believes in equal pay for equal work.]

This argument is logically complete in that it is valid as stated. There are no missing claims needed to make it valid. So, its structure is easy to portray.

We bracket and number the claims--**always in the order that the claims appear in the argument.**

Conditional statements such as 4 receive one number. Do not break them up by giving a number to the antecedent and a number to the consequent. The same applies to disjunctions. Give them one number and don't number the separate disjuncts.

The inference indicators are not part of the argument's claims. The downward arrows represent them. By following the inference indicators, the tree diagram of the argument's structure is:

Diagram:

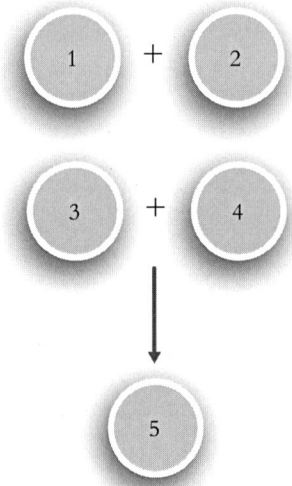

In both steps of the above diagram, we've used a plus sign and under-lining to add or link the premises. This is done to indicate that both premises are used together, not separately, to support the conclusion.

It's easy to spot the basic premises, sub-conclusions and main con-clusion of an argument in a tree diagram.

You can see that 1, 2 and 4 are basic premises since they have no arrow leading to them, and hence are unsupported.

3 has an arrow leading to it, and it is also a premise in the next step of the argument. So, it's a sub-conclusion.

5 is the main conclusion of the argument, which always comes at the bottom of the diagram.

Unfortunately, everyday arguments aren't like the ones you find in logic books. They're elliptical and their inference indicators are often omitted. In such arguments, it is helpful to provide a separate index of claims with the tree diagram.

An **index of claims** simply lists the numbered explicit claims made by the arguer and the lettered implicit claims that you have added to complete the argument. Here›s our example from above to make this clear.

1[You're an embezzler.] Therefore, 2[you're a criminal.] So, you know where you'll end up, don't you? Say hello to the warden when you get there.

Index of claims: **Diagram:** <u>1 + A</u>

1 You›re an embezzler.

2 You're a criminal.   <u>2 + B</u>

A All embezzlers are criminals.

B All criminals end up in jail.   C

C You'll end up in jail.

333

It's important that you understand the above example. Study it carefully. It was diagrammed previously in standard form. So its logical structure should be familiar to you.

Notice that we've bracketed and numbered only the statements that are part of the argument. The last two sentences of the passage are not numbered since they don't make claims found in the argument.

Note that we've used capital letters to stand for implicit claims. A and B stand for missing premises, and C stands for the implicit main conclusion.

Implicit claims come at the end of your index--after you've listed the explicit ones.

In the above argument, we've bracketed and numbered the passage, and presented both the index and diagram all in one step.

In practice, you should break up this procedure--especially with complicated arguments.
That is, you should:

1. Read the whole argument, circle indicators and find the main conclusion.
2. Bracket and number the claims in the order stated.
3. Create an index of the explicit claims that you've numbered.
4. Diagram the argument as stated.
5. Compare it with the original passage to make sure that you've got the structure right and that the diagram makes sense to you.
6. Go back over each step and fill in whatever missing claims are needed to make the argument valid.

Here's a more complicated example from your textbook that we'll use to illustrate this stepwise procedure. After you've gained some practice in diagramming arguments, you will be able to combine some of these steps.

The missiles will not hit their targets <u>since</u> their flight paths were calculated by Tech students and Tech students haven>t had sufficient mathematics to calculate accurate flight paths. Now if the missiles don>t hit their targets, the government will cancel our contracts before the year is out. And if the government cancels our contracts, we will have to lay off 2,000 workers by Christmas. <u>Hence,</u> we will be laying off 2,000 workers by the end of the year.

STEP 1: Read the passage looking for inference indicators and the main conclusion, trying to understand the argument as a whole. We've underlined the inference indicators and identified the main conclusion by angle brackets.

STEP 2: We bracket and number the claims in the order stated.

1[The missiles will not hit their targets] <u>since</u> 2[their flight paths were calculated by Tech students] and 3[Tech students haven>t had sufficient mathematics to calculate accurate flight paths.] Now 4[if the missiles don>t hit their targets, the government will cancel our contracts before the year is out.] And 5[if the government cancels our contracts, we will have to lay off 2,000 workers by Christmas.] <u>Hence,</u> 6<we will be laying off 2,000 workers by the end of the year.>

STEP 3: We create an index of the explicit claims.

Index of Explicit Claims:

1. The missiles will not hit their targets.
2. Their flight paths were calculated by Tech students.
3. Tech students haven't had sufficient mathematics to calculate accurate flight paths.
4. If the missiles don't hit their targets, the government will cancel our contracts before the year is out.
5. If the government cancels our contracts, we will have to lay off 2,000 workers by Christmas.
6. We will be laying off 2,000 workers by the end of the year.

STEP 4: We diagram the argument as stated.

Diagram:

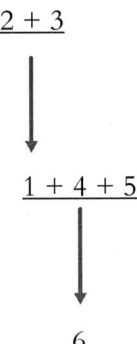

$$\underline{2 + 3}$$

$$\downarrow$$

$$\underline{1 + 4 + 5}$$

$$\downarrow$$

$$6$$

STEP 5: We read the diagram by replacing the numbers with the argument claims and reading each arrow as "therefore". You can see that this diagram accurately portrays the argument as stated.

STEP 6: We supply the missing claims needed for validity in each step and add these to the diagram and to the index of claims.

The first step assumes that if they don't have sufficient mathematics, then Tech students can't calculate accurate flight paths. It also assumes that if the missiles' flight paths aren't accurately calculated, then the missiles will not hit their targets.

The second step is informally valid. To make it formally valid we need the trivial assumption that Christmas is before the end of the year. In such cases, it's optional to add trivially true assumptions. We'll add it here for completeness.

Also, although not necessary, you can make the arguer's line of reasoning clearer by inserting implicit subconclusions used to get to the main conclusion. We've added B and D in the diagram below to illustrate this. Ask your instructor if you don't understand this process.

Here is the completed reconstruction of the argument.

1[The missiles will not hit their targets] <u>since</u> 2[their flight paths were calculated by Tech students] and 3[Tech students haven›t had sufficient mathematics to calculate accurate flight paths.] Now 4[if the missiles don›t hit their targets, the government will cancel our contracts before the year is out.] And 5[if the government cancels our contracts, we will have to lay off 2,000 workers by Christmas.] <u>Hence,</u> 6[we will be laying off 2,000 workers by the end of the year.]

VALID RECONSTRUCTION:
Index of Claims:

1. The missiles will not hit their targets.
2. Their flight paths were calculated by Tech students
3. Tech students haven't had sufficient mathematics to calculate accurate flight paths.
4. If the missiles don't hit their targets, the government will cancel our contracts before the year is out.

5. If the government cancels our contracts, we will have to lay off 2,000 workers by Christmas.

6. We will be laying off 2,000 workers by the end of the year.

A. If they don't have sufficient mathematics to calculate accurate flight paths, Tech students will not calculate accurate flight paths.

B. The flight paths of the missiles were not accurately calculated.

C. If their flight paths were not accurately calculated, the missiles will not hit their targets.

D. The government will cancel our contracts before the year is out.

E. Christmas comes before the end of the year.

Diagram:

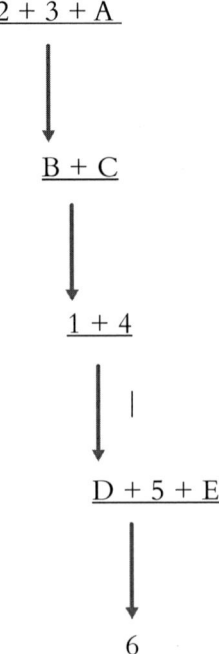

$\underline{2 + 3 + A}$

↓

$\underline{B + C}$

↓

$\underline{1 + 4}$

↓

$\underline{D + 5 + E}$

↓

6

Remember that the above diagram is a very picky and detailed reconstruction of the argument. If you choose to leave out the implicit steps and the trivial assumption E, the following diagram based on the above lettering would be adequate.

Diagram:

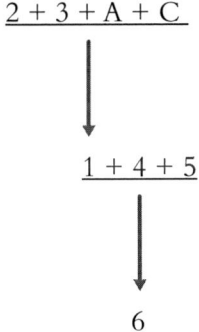

$$\underline{2 + 3 + A + C}$$
$$\downarrow$$
$$\underline{1 + 4 + 5}$$
$$\downarrow$$
$$6$$

These procedures for reconstructing arguments are not easy. And since you are just beginning to learn to read logically, they can be very difficult. You will have to see and do lots of argument reconstruction before it begins to get easier. Study Chapter 3 carefully to understand the procedures for reconstructing arguments. Ask questions about what you don't understand.

YOU WILL NEED HELP. So, make sure to ask for it. Consult with your instructor or use CANVAS to ask questions and to generate discussion on these materials.

Summary of Central Points:

1. Arguments are composed of premises offered in support of a conclusion.
2. The conclusion of one argument can be a premise for another argument to create an argument chain or chain of reasoning.

3. A **basic premise** is an unsupported premise in an argument. A premise that is supported in an argument chain is called a **subconclusion** or **intermediate conclusion**.

4. Each inference in an argument chain is called a **step** in the argument. The conclusion of the last step of an argument is the **main conclusion**.

5. Every step in a deductive argument must be valid if the argument is valid.

6. Arguments that are missing premises required for validity or whose conclusions are not explicitly stated are called **elliptical arguments**. An argument is not elliptical when it is valid as stated.

7. An **inferential assumption** is a missing or unstated premise that is needed to make a step in an argument valid. Inferential assumptions are needed to complete elliptical arguments.

8. When bracketing and numbering claims, don't break up conditionals or disjunctions by giving their components separate numbers. Each conditional or disjunction gets only one number.

9. Ask questions, consult with your instructor, and use CANVAS to get help with anything you don't understand.

Skills to Learn:

1. Learn to identify argument structure--the main conclusion, basic premises and subconclusions.

2. Learn to recognize arguments that are valid as stated.

3. Learn to recognize arguments that are invalid because they are elliptical and arguments that are invalid because of logical errors (e.g., affirming consequent, denying antecedent).

4. Learn the procedures for diagramming arguments.

5. Learn to supply inferential assumptions needed for argument validity.

NOTE:YOU SHOULD **USE TREE DIAGRAMS** WHEN YOU ARE ASKED TO PORTRAY ARGUMENT STRUCTURE. (Hint: Whenever you use tree diagrams you will need an index of claims.)

Sample Homework 3.1 Recognizing Argument Structure

The following passages contain argument chains. (a) **Portray the argument as stated** – underline, bracket, number, tree diagram. (b) **Identify the basic premises, subconclusions and the main conclusion.**

Example: Either science misjudged the health benefits of margarine and unhealthy trans fats or butter really is better for you. Science has not misjudged the health benefits of margarine and unhealthy trans fats. 3. Butter really is better for you.

1[Either science misjudged the health benefits of margarine and unhealthy trans fats or butter really is better for you.] 2[Science has not misjudged the health benefits of margarine and unhealthy trans fats.] Therefore 3[butter really is better for you.]

1. Either science misjudged the health benefits of margarine and unhealthy trans fats or butter really is better for you.

2. Science has not misjudged the health benefits of margarine and unhealthy trans fats.

3. Butter really is better for you.

1 + 2

↓

3

1. The digital currency market would collapse if everyone agreed that it is a Ponzi scheme intended to make early adopters rich. So, if investors were smart, they would immediately divest themselves of all digital currency. The investors are not smart. Therefore, they will not divest themselves of all digital currency.

2. Hard work is not valued seriously enough And hard work takes time. Therefore, you shouldn't rush through your work. And therefore, you shouldn't waste time when there is work to be done.

3. Since the EU has met with the Premier at the recent conferences, discussions on foreign policy have begun. Consequently, the channels of communication are open. With increased communication, citizens will feel reassured that agreement is possible. Agreement would result in better conditions for all of those involved. Hence, things will shortly be improving.

Sample Homework 3.2 Completing Elliptical Arguments

A. **Diagram the following arguments** (underline, bracket, number, tree diagram) and **supply the inferential assumptions** (missing premises) needed to make them valid. (Hint: Whenever you use tree diagrams you will need an index of claims.)

Example: Since all feminists believe in equal rights, Joan must believe in equal rights for men and women. Therefore, she must believe in equal pay for equal work. Equity based ideology is based on improving just women's wages. So Joan must not support equity based ideologies.

Since 1[all feminists believe in equal rights,] 2[Joan must believe in equal rights for men and women.] Therefore, 3[Joan believes in equal pay for equal work.] 4[Equity based ideology is based on improving just women's wages.] So J5[Joan must not support equity based ideologies.]

1. All feminists believe in equal rights
2. Joan must believe in equal rights for men and women.
3. Joan believes in equal pay for equal work.
4. Equity based ideology is based on improving just women's wages
5. Joan must not support equity based ideologies.
6. If all feminists believe in equal rights then Joan must believe in equal rights for men and women.
7. If Joan believes in equal rights for men and women then she must believe in equal pay for equal work.
8. If Joan believes in equal pay for equal work and equity based ideologies are based on improving just women's wages then Joan must not support equity based ideologies.

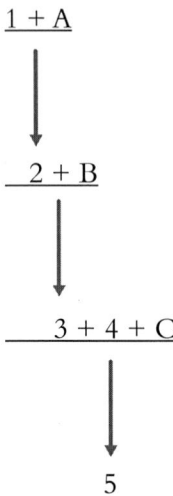

1. Martha was not the leader of the doomed expedition. Therefore, Theodore must have been. So, Homer is now a widower.

2. The plane went down 10 miles off the coast of Malaysia. Therefore, it must gone down in the Malacca Straight.

3. The Maduro regime and its associates in Venzuela have robbed the country of billions of dollars. It stole the election against Radonsky through fraud. Therefore, the U.S. will no longer support this regime.

4. America was originally settled by Puritans sailing over from England. Hence, most of today's Americans are descended from Puritans. And hence, there must be a high rate of puritan belief in the country today.

5. All successful Cabinet departments must have a workable strategy, adequate power, and popular support. It follows that some of the current administration's Cabinet departments are not successful.

B. The following passages are to be taken as arguments whose conclusions are unstated. **Fill in the missing conclusions** so that each argument is valid.

Example: If you learn to crawl you can learn to walk. If you learn to walk you can learn to jog. If you learn to jog you can learn to run. If you learn to run you can run a marathon. So . . .

Missing Conclusion: If you learn to crawl you can run a marathon.

1. No fat creatures run well and some greyhounds run well. So, . . .

2. If the U.S. were interested in justice for male college students, then Title IX would never be abused by American universities and colleges. But we know it was. The conclusion is obvious.

3. If the in crisis Middle East is not settled soon, then either the United States will have to intervene or the Soviet Union will extend its influence in that area. But we know that the Middle East crisis will not be settled soon and we know that the United States will not intervene. The conclusion is obvious.

C. The following passages contain elliptical chains of argumentation. **Supply the missing premises and conclusions** so that you produce a non-elliptical, valid argument chain. **Portray the argument's structure** (underline, bracket, number, tree diagram). (Hint: Whenever you use tree diagrams you will need an index of claims.)

Example: If the day after Friday is Saturday then today is Saturday. So . . .

1[If the day after Friday is Saturday then today is Saturday.] <u>So</u> . . .

If the day after Friday is Saturday then today is Saturday

The day after Friday is Saturday.

Today is Saturday

$$\frac{1 + A}{}$$

B

1. If we post the revenge porn now, then we will continue to be tempted to do it more and more in the future. So, we will not post the revenge porn. And if we are not tempted to do more of it, then we do not need to save these pictures. So, . . .

2. Since butterflies do not use words, it follows that they do not have abstract ideas. From that it follows that they cannot use reason. Since

what can't use reason isn't capable of morality, the conclusion to be drawn is clear . . .

3. Abortion is not the killing of an innocent human being, and since it is not the killing of an innocent human it is not murder. So, you can see how that makes abortion a woman's choice, can't you? But if that's true, then it doesn't make abortion against the will of God and contrary to civilized behavior. It follows that we must allow abortions to take place.

3.3 PORTRAYING ARGUMENT STRUCTURE (TREE DIAGRAMS)

Reading Assignment: N/A

The more arguments you see tree diagrammed, the more familiar you become with this important technique. In this lesson, we will diagram several arguments and comment on what is done. You should study these examples and commentary carefully as illustrations of what you must learn to do. Contact your instructor about anything you don't understand.

We're taking some of these examples from your text so that you will be able to anticipate what we're doing. You can take out some paper and do a quick diagram of each argument before you see our version. Since there is a little room for variation in diagramming, make sure you understand if and why your diagram differs from ours.

We'll start with two relatively simple examples and then move to some of greater complexity.

Argument 1:

Well, Big John, if we take the high road, them injuns is gonna get us. And if we don't take the high road, the robbers is gonna get us. So, it looks like either them injuns or them robbers is gonna get us.

Whether or not an argument is simple, you must read the whole passage carefully before you begin bracketing and numbering. Look for and circle all inference indicators and bracket the main conclusion. If you don't understand the overall structure of the argument, you are more likely to make mistakes in diagramming it.

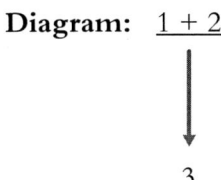

Here is the argument bracketed, numbered, with inference indicators underlined. Notice how unessential material and inference indicators are left outside the brackets.

> Well, Big John, 1[if we take the high road, them injuns is gonna get us.] And 2[if we don't take the high road, the robbers is gonna get us.] <u>So</u>, it looks like 3[either them injuns or them robbers is gonna get us.]

Since this is a simple, one-step argument, we'll omit the index of claims. The diagram of the argument as stated is:

Diagram: 1 + 2

3

To be formally valid as an instance of the **constructive dilemma**, this argument needs the missing premise that *either we take the high road or we don't take the high road*. But since this statement is always true, this argument is informally valid as stated. That is, it's not possible for its premises to be true and its conclusion false. The above diagram is acceptable without the addition of the necessarily true missing premise.

Note: You may not understand this stuff about formal vs. informal validity just used in the last example. You may have forgotten our previous discussion or perhaps you didn't fully understand it then. If so, then you should send a query through CANVAS asking about it. Or bring up the subject in your discussion sessions. It's just this kind of issue on which you can generate discussion and get help in learning. We're eager to help you.

SECTION 3.3

Argument 2:

> *If Zapata had thrown in with the government, he would not have been executed by the Juaristas. Thus, if Zapata had thrown in with the government, he would not have become a martyr and a symbol of freedom in his country.*

This argument draws its conclusion from a single premise. A careful reading shows it to be an incomplete hypothetical syllogism. As stated, the argument's diagram is:

Diagram:

It needs another conditional premise to be valid. Here is an index of claims and a diagram validly reconstructing the argument.

Index of claims:

1 If Zapata had thrown in with the government, he would not have been executed by the Juaristas.

2 If Zapata had thrown in with the government, he would not have become a martyr and a symbol of freedom in his country.

A If Zapata hadn't been executed by the Juaristas, he would not have become a martyr and a symbol of freedom in his country.

Diagram: <u>1 + A</u>

2

Argument 3:

One cannot love another if one does not love oneself. It is clear that Hamlet does not love himself since he despises himself for not having avenged his father's death. It follows that Hamlet cannot love Ophelia.

A careful reading shows that this is a two-step argument whose main conclusion is that Hamlet cannot love Ophelia. We bracket and number the claims and underline the inference indicators, and diagram the argument as stated.

1[One cannot love another if one does not love oneself.] It is clear that 2[Hamlet does not love himself] <u>since</u> 3[he despises himself for not having avenged his father's death.] <u>It follows that</u> 4[Hamlet cannot love Ophelia.]

Diagram:

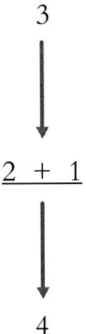

3

<u>2 + 1</u>

4

Notice that the arguer makes claim 1 at the beginning. But logically, this claim must be used with 2 to get to the main conclusion. He uses the second sentence to support 2. If you read the diagram by replacing the numbers with the claims, you see that it makes sense. You may not accept the truth of the claims, but the argument as stated is certainly understandable.

The second step is valid as stated, but the first step is missing a premise. We add a conditional assumption to turn the first step into an instance of Affirming the Antecedent. Here is the valid reconstruction of the argument.

Index of Claims:

1. One cannot love another if one does not love oneself.

2. Hamlet does not love himself

3. He despises himself for not having avenged his father's death.

4. Hamlet cannot love Ophelia.

A If Hamlet despises himself for not having avenged his father's death, then he does not love himself.

Diagram: 3 + A

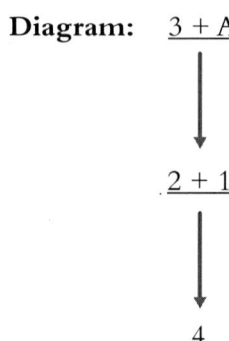

2 + 1

4

Here is a slightly more complicated example. You need to get into the arguer's mind by reading the passage carefully and trying to understand his reasoning. We've underlined the indicators and angle bracketed the main conclusion.

Argument 4:

God is all good. *Therefore*, he will not allow evil to exist. God is all-powerful. *Therefore*, what he will not allow to exist cannot exist. *Therefore*, evil cannot exist. *Therefore*, evil does not exist.

As we see it, the arguer supports the claim that God will not allow evil to exist. He also supports the claim that what God will not allow to exist cannot exist. Then he uses these two subconclusions to support the claim that evil cannot exist, which he uses to support his main conclusion. Here is the argument diagrammed as stated:

1[God is all-good.] Therefore, 2[he will not allow evil to exist.] 3[God is all-powerful.] Therefore, 4[what he will not allow to exist cannot exist.] Therefore, 5[evil cannot exist.] Therefore, 6[evil does not exist.]

Diagram:

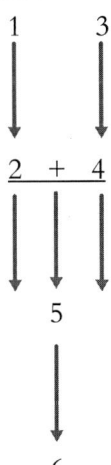

It's clear that the first two steps of this argument are missing premises need for validity. The second two steps may be valid as stated since the premises needed for formal validity seem to be necessarily true. We'll put all the premises in, however, so that we can see exactly what the arguer is thinking when he makes those inferences. Here is a valid reconstruction of the argument. See if you agree.

Index of claims:

1. God is all good.
2. He will not allow evil to exist.
3. God is all-powerful.
4. What he will not allow to exist cannot exist.
5. Evil cannot exist.
6. Evil does not exist.
    A. If God is all good, then He will not allow evil to exist.
    B. If God is all-powerful, then what he won't allow to exist cannot exist.
    C. If God won't allow evil to exist, and whatever He won't allow to exist can't exist, then evil can't exist.
    D. What cannot exist does not exist.

Diagram:

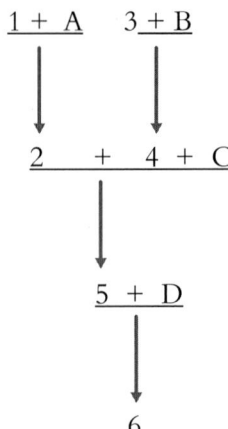

Once again, C and D in the last two steps appear to be necessarily true. So, you can omit them from the diagram if you choose.

Here is an argument that is made more complicated because a premise that is needed later in the argument is stated at the beginning. With such added complexity, it is important that you read and understand the whole argument before you bracket and number. We've underlined the indicator and bracketed the main conclusion.

Argument 5:

Either the rights of the fetus sometimes outweigh the mother's rights or we must admit that our case against abortion is weak. But the fetus is not a legal agent. And if it is not a legal agent, then its rights never outweigh those of the mother's. <u>Hence,</u> *<we have to admit that our case against abortion is weak. >*

We now bracket and number all the claims, provide an index, and diagram the argument as stated. Can you see that the argument is valid as stated?

Index of Claims:

1. Either the rights of the fetus sometimes outweigh the mother's rights or we must admit that our case against abortion is weak.
2. The fetus is not a legal agent.
3. If the fetus is not a legal agent, then its rights never outweigh those of the mother's.
4. We have to admit that our case against abortion is weak.

Diagram:

$$\underline{1 + 2 + 3}$$

$$\downarrow$$

4

It may be unclear to those untutored in logic that this argument is valid. That is, if you accept its premises, you have to accept its conclusion. So, to show the arguer's line of reasoning, you can include the implicit step he uses to get to the main conclusion. Here is the filled out index and diagram. Follow the diagram carefully to make sure you understand what's been done.

1. Either the rights of the fetus sometimes outweigh the mother's rights or we must admit that our case against abortion is weak.
2. The fetus is not a legal agent.
3. If the fetus is not a legal agent, then its rights never outweigh those of the mother's.
4. We have to admit that our case against abortion is weak.
   A. The rights of the fetus never outweigh the mother's rights.

Diagram: **2 + 3**

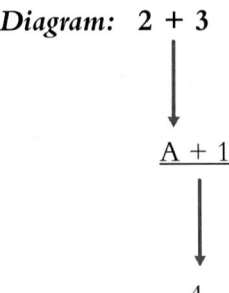

The above diagram shows that the arguer used claims 2 and 3 to get to A--a step which he did mentally and left unsaid. Matters are also confused since 1 is stated first, but is logically linked to A to get to the main conclusion.

You will find many arguments where much of the reasoning is done mentally and not explicitly stated. An arguer may perform several steps mentally and just simply state his premises without explicitly stating the assumptions and implicit subconclusions needed to get to the main conclusion. Professors who are familiar with their subject are especially guilty of this "mental argumentation" by leaving several logically separable steps in their reasoning unstated. They can make you feel stupid when you really aren't. This is often a sign of bad teaching.

In such cases, you may need to work out their reasoning to make sure that you understand what the hell they're talking about, and to make sure that they haven't screwed up. If he's available, always ask the arguer to clarify his hidden, implicit steps when you can't follow his path to the main conclusion. He too may not understand how he got there, and he may need your help.

Central Points:
You're just beginning to learn to read and respond to discourse with a keen, analytical eye. So, remember:

1. Read the whole argument, circle indicators and find the main conclusion.
2. Bracket and number the claims in the order stated.
3. Create an index of the explicit claims that you've numbered.
4. Diagram the argument as stated.
5. Compare it with the original passage to make sure that you've got the structure right and that the diagram makes sense to you.
6. Go back over each step and fill in whatever missing claims are needed to make the argument valid.
7. Ask about anything that you don't understand about this very demanding subject.

Skills to Learn:
Learn to do the above steps well, and you're half way home to achieving a good, and valuable, critical mind.

SECTION 3.3

3.4 - 3.7 THE 7 STEPS OF ARGUMENT RECONSTRUCTION—OVERVIEW

Reading Assignment: Textbook Sections 3.4, 3.5, 3.6 and 3.7

The last lesson illustrated the tree diagramming methods that we use to portray argument structure. This reconstruction and portrayal of argument structure is what we call a **valid reconstruction** of a deductive argument.

To create a valid reconstruction of a deductive argument, you identify its basic premises, sub-conclusions and main conclusion, and you fill in all the inferential assumptions needed to make each step of the argument valid. This reconstruction prepares the argument for evaluation.

This lesson presents a discussion of some the steps you take to produce a valid reconstruction. All seven steps are listed in your textbook, and most of Chapter 3 explains them. Read that chapter carefully for more details.

Please note that these steps provide the basis for a **fine-grained** or **in-depth** analysis of argumentative discourse. You might have to do such an analysis if you're a lawyer examining a legal argument, a business executive examining a proposal or a scholar analyzing and criticizing a position. In general, you may not have to do thorough, in-depth analyses of discourse, but rather focus on parts of arguments or on their weaknesses.

This course aims to prepare you for whatever analytical task you may be asked to perform in daily life, in school or at work. Hence, we want you to learn the full analytic and evaluative process.

The steps for reconstructing arguments are:

1. Identify the Main Conclusion
2. Identify Basic Premises and Sub-conclusions
3. Clarify the Key Terms
4. Simplify and Paraphrase
5. Determine Whether to Use Deductive Standards
6. Supply Missing Conclusions
7. Supply Inferential Assumptions

These steps aren't always distinguished in practice. You may need to clarify some of the key terms before you can even find the main conclusion. Or you may find inferential assumptions before you fill in the missing conclusions. So, you may have to bounce around these steps rather than slavishly following them in the order presented. In this lesson, we recognize this and will discuss a step as it's needed in reconstructing an argument, rather than in the serial order given above.

Also, you don't have to worry about 5, whether to use deductive standards, since we are dealing only with deductive arguments at this point. Induction is covered in Part II.

SECTION 3.4 - 3.7

STEPS 1 & 2: PORTRAYING THE ARGUMENT AS STATED

Finding the main conclusion and identifying the basic premises and sub-conclusions should be familiar to you. This is just the business of portraying the argument as stated that you've been doing in tree diagramming. There is nothing new here.

You have to read the argument carefully, trying to understand the argument as a whole. You circle the inference indicators. You find the main conclusion. And by bracketing, numbering and portraying the argument as stated, you identify the basic premises and sub-conclusions--which is the second step.

Consider the following example. Try to anticipate the process by numbering the claims and diagramming the argument as stated before you proceed. We've underlined the inference indicators to get you started.

Argument 1:

> In the fury that sometimes surrounds school prayer, it is sometimes forgotten that prayer is an essential part of religion. _Thus_, to permit school prayer is virtually the same as endorsing religion. What can be said, then, for religion? Not much, I'm afraid. Indeed, religion is dangerous. It has spawned numerous wars throughout history. Today it continues to sow the seeds of discontent and destruction in Northern Ireland, in Eastern Europe, in the Far East, in the Middle East and in the United States. Furthermore, _since_ it divides people by emphasizing their differences rather than their similarities, religion breeds intolerance of people of opposed views. Is there any doubt, _therefore_, that the responsible citizen should oppose school prayer?

The first thing to notice about this passage is that it contains material that is unessential to the argument. It also contains rhetorical questions. Indeed, in the last sentence, the main conclusion is put as a question. This requires that you go to step 4, simplifying and paraphrasing, before you can even do step 1.

Accordingly, you should understand the last sentence to mean that the responsible citizen should oppose school prayer. Or you could take it simply to mean that school prayer should not be permitted.

The first sentence refers to "the fury that sometimes surrounds school prayer." This may provide some background material, but it seems unessential to the argument. Leave it out of the bracketed claims.

The arguer asks and answers a question: "What can be said, then, for religion? Not much, I'm afraid." This rhetorical device is his way of stating that not much can be said in favor of religion. Since his intention is so clear, you should rewrite this as a single statement and give it a number.

Here is the rewritten passage, bracketed and numbered, with the paraphrased statements in bold-face, and the main conclusion in angle-brackets.

> In the fury that sometimes surrounds school prayer, it is sometimes forgotten that 1[prayer is an essential part of religion.] Thus, 2[to permit school prayer is virtually the same as endorsing religion.] 3[**Not much can be said in favor of religion.**] Indeed, 4[religion is dangerous.] 5[It has spawned numerous wars throughout history.] 6[Today it continues to sow the seeds of discontent and destruction in Northern Ireland, in Eastern Europe, in the Far East, in the Middle East and in the United States.] Furthermore, since 7[it divides people by emphasizing their differences rather than their similarities,] 8[religion breeds intolerance of people of opposed views.] Therefore, 9<**the responsible citizen should oppose school prayer.**>

Reading the argument as a whole, we see that the arguer supports the sub-conclusion that permitting school prayer virtually endorses religion. He then makes the unsupported claim that not much can be said for religion. He next supports the sub-conclusions that religion is dangerous and that it breeds intolerance. Finally, he uses his basic premise and sub-conclusions to draw the main conclusion.

Here is an index of claims and a diagram of the argument as stated, which completes Steps 1 and 2.

Index of claims:

1. Prayer is an essential part of religion.
2. To permit school prayer is virtually the same as endorsing religion.
3. Not much can be said in favor of religion.
4. Religion is dangerous.
5. Religion has spawned numerous wars throughout history.
6. Today religion continues to sow the seeds of discontent and destruction in Northern Ireland, in Eastern Europe, in the Far East, in the Middle East and in the United States.
7. Religion divides people by emphasizing their differences rather than their similarities.
8. Religion breeds intolerance of people of opposed views.
9. The responsible citizen should oppose school prayer.

Diagram of Argument as Stated:

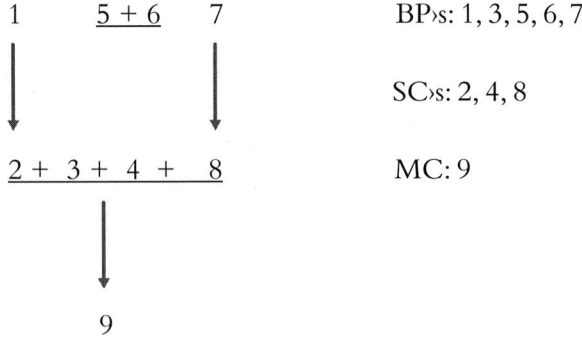

The above version merely includes rewriting of some rhetorical devices. It does not include missing premises or conclusions. Thus, it still remains the argument pretty much as stated.

In cases where an argument is so unclear that you must do extensive rewriting, make sure to include the original passage so that your audience can judge whether your version captures what the arguer intended. You may have to defend the accuracy of your interpretation.

 ## STEP 3: CLARIFYING KEY TERMS

You have no doubt noticed that much of the language of Argument 1 may need clarification. Expressions such as "school prayer," essential part of," "virtually the same as," "dangerous," and "intolerance" are important to the argument and should be clarified before you can assess its claims.

However, you will provide further clarification of key terms during the argument evaluation process covered in the next unit. At this stage, you need only understand the use of terms as they bear on your understanding of the argument's structure.

So, if you literally don't know the meaning of some terms, you should consult a dictionary or ask someone who knows. Otherwise, continue with the reconstruction process, and note which terms will need clarification in the evaluative process.

However, since you are going to the trouble of understanding the argument in order to reconstruct it, a good practice is to write down, below your diagram, the terms that may need attention when you get to the evaluation process. Jot down some questions that may occur to you in your interpretation of the arguer's language. We've done this in the section below.

 ## STEP 6: MAKING THE LINE OF REASONING CLEAR

As we read the above diagram of Argument 1, the inferences to the three sub-conclusions seem relatively clear. The last step to the main conclusion, however, is a bit abrupt. We may be puzzled by how the arguer gets to the main conclusion from all those claims.

Although the diagram correctly portrays the argument, and you are not logically required to fill in any implicit steps, you may want to show the arguer's line of reasoning to the main conclusion. Filling in implicit steps can make it easier evaluate the argument. This is the purpose of Step 6, which asks you to fill in missing conclusions.

To fill in missing sub-conclusions, you take part of the arguer's stated information and state the implicit sub-conclusion that can be drawn from that information. Let's do this for the last step of Argument 1.

We notice that he begins by arguing for Sub-conclusion 2, that permitting school prayer is virtually the same as endorsing religion. He then presents negative claims against religion in his effort to convince the responsible citizen not to endorse school prayer. To tie these threads together, we surmise that his reasoning is that the negative aspects of religion show that the responsible citizen should oppose anything that endorses religion.

This is easier to follow in a diagram. So, we provide another diagram that portrays this implicit step. We also include some notes on terms that will need further clarification. The numbers remain the same as above.

Remember, if you don't understand this process, ask you instructor about it or leave a message in CANVAS. Refer to the index of claims, and read the diagram to yourself. Compare it to the previous diagram. This version should make the arguer's reasoning to the main conclusion clearer with the implicit conclusion filled in.

Index of claims:

1. Prayer is an essential part of religion.
2. To permit school prayer is virtually the same as endorsing religion.
3. Not much can be said in favor of religion.
4. Religion is dangerous.
5. Religion has spawned numerous wars throughout history.
6. Today religion continues to sow the seeds of discontent and destruction in Northern Ireland, in Eastern Europe, in the Far East, in the Middle East and in the United States.
7. Religion divides people by emphasizing their differences rather than their similarities.
8. Religion breeds intolerance of people of opposed views.
9. The responsible citizen should oppose school prayer.

E The responsible citizen should oppose whatever endorses religion.

Diagram:

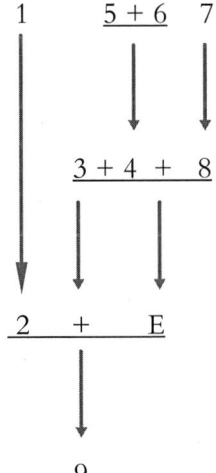

Problematic terms:

Religion: Does this mean "organized" religion (e.g., Catholic) or any personal theistic or transcendental doctrines a person might hold?

Essential part of religion: This means a necessary condition for religion. Can't you have religions without prayer?

Permit school prayer: How is this done? Organized, enforced teacher led prayer time? A non-enforced few minutes of silent meditation?

Virtually the same: What's the difference between "virtually the same" and "the same"?

Endorse religion: How does one endorse something? Explicitly by speaking in favor of it? Tacitly by not opposing it? Do you endorse everything you permit to happen?

Dangerous: Can doctrines be dangerous? In what way? Is it religious beliefs or acts in the name of those beliefs that are destructive or dangerous? Aren't many beliefs and free speech dangerous in this sense?

In the above diagram, you might ask why we labeled the implicit conclusion E? Answer: Because we've done this example before and we know that the previous steps in the argument require inferential assumptions A–D. You're welcome to fill them in before we discuss Step 7, Filling in Missing Premises, in the next lesson.

A CAUTIONARY NOTE ON ARGUMENT RECONSTRUCTION

In reconstructing arguments, you can see that we often paraphrase, simplify, fill in premises and conclusions, and in general supply or rewrite information not found in the original argument. It is extremely important that this reconstruction preserve, to the greatest possible extent, the intentions of the arguer. Do not saddle the arguer with claims and words that he did not mean. Always make amply clear what you've provided in comparison to what the arguer offered.

If an argument is so unclearly presented that you must do extensive interpretation and reconstruction, make very clear from the beginning, that your analysis and evaluation is contingent on further clarification from the arguer.

Finally, in all your efforts to analyze and evaluate arguments, never distort, deliberately misinterpret, exaggerate, ridicule or otherwise create a weaker argument than the original. Do your analysis and evaluation in a way that is most favorable to the argument so that you can then proceed to criticize it at its strongest. To do otherwise is to be guilty of the "straw man fallacy"--a very, very bad no-no.

Summary of Central Points:

1. The 7 Basic Steps for Reconstructing Arguments are:
    1. Identify the Main Conclusion
    2. Identify Basic Premises and Sub-conclusions
    3. Clarify the Key Terms
    4. Simplify and Paraphrase
    5. Determine Whether to Use Deductive Standards
    6. Supply Missing Conclusions
    7. Supply Inferential Assumptions
2. Step 1 and Step 2 of reconstructing arguments simply require that you produce a diagram of the argument as stated.
3. Steps 3 and 4 require that you understand the arguer's language enough to portray the argument's structure. Scribble some questions and notes to remind you of clarification still needed.
4. In clarifying, simplifying and paraphrasing an argument, stick as close to the arguer's intentions as possible.

SECTION 3.4 - 3.7

5. Don't create a straw man. Use the "principle of charity," which forbids you to deliberately misinterpret, distort and weaken the arguer's claims.

6. Don't worry about Step 5 yet. Unless otherwise stated, assume the argument is deductive. Inductive arguments will be covered later.

7. In Step 6, missing conclusions are filled in to make clear the arguer's line of reasoning to this conclusions.

8. In Step 7, inferential assumptions are filled in to make each step of a deductive argument valid. This is discussed in the next lesson.

Skills to Learn:

1. Learn to provide valid reconstructions of arguments.
2. Learn to identify and clarify problematic language.
3. Learn to summarize detailed arguments of editorial, journal article or book length by simplifying and then diagramming the main points of an argument. This is covered in Chapter 3.

Recommended Study:

The best way to learn how to analyze or reconstruct arguments is by doing it. Also, the more examples of reconstruction you see done, the more familiar you will become with the process. You have examples in your book, selected answers to text exercises that cover these skills. You should also ask your instructors to help you. So, your best course of study is: 1) Study your text; 2) Do the selected exercises from your text and study the answers; 3) Ask your instructor (or anyone who can) to help you with what you don't understand; 4) Learn from your mistakes.

Sample Homework 3.4 & 3.5A Identifying Main Conclusions & Portraying Argument Structure

3.4 Some of the following passages contain arguments. Bracket and number the claims in each passage. Underline inference indicator words and circle the main conclusion of each passage that contains an argument. (Hint: Whenever you use tree diagrams you will need an index of claims.)

3.5 A Identifying premises and sub-conclusions of short arguments

Portray the structure of the arguments (Since you've already done the bracketing and numbering, just add a tree diagram and an index of claims).

Example: Either the rights of the fetus sometimes outweigh the mother's rights or we must admit that our case against abortion is weak. But the fetus is not a legal agent. And if it is not a legal agent, then its rights never outweigh those of the mother's. Hence, we have to admit that our case against abortion is weak.

1[Either the rights of the fetus sometimes outweigh the mother's rights or we must admit that our case against abortion is weak.] But 2[the fetus is not a legal agent.] And 3[if it is not a legal agent, then its rights never outweigh those of the mother's.] Hence, 4[we have to admit that our case against abortion is weak.]

Index of Claims:

1. Either the rights of the fetus sometimes outweigh the mother's rights or we must admit that our case against abortion is weak.
2. The fetus is not a legal agent.

3. If the fetus is not a legal agent, then its rights never outweigh those of the mother's.

4. We have to admit that our case against abortion is weak.

Diagram:

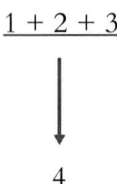

$$\underline{1 + 2 + 3}$$

$$\downarrow$$

4

1. Malta is located in the Mediterranean Sea, south of Sicily. The country consists of three islands: Malta, Comino and Gozo, and Malta is the largest island. Historically, Malta was important strategically for the domination of the Mediterranean.

2. *Lorem Ipsum* is the old standby. This is because it contains full paragraphs of Greek words that mirror actual patterns of text. And since using one sentence over and over will give you a false impression of how the text will really look on the page. And since doing this will create "rivers" of white through the paragraphs due to the repetition of the same number of characters and spaces.

3. Since, in the USA corrupt officials don't go to trial. And since in the USA when you hire enough expensive lawyers you will never go to jail. Corruption in the United States exceeds corruption in China in magnitude.

4. Turkey should not be a member of NATO. The mutual defense agreement between the members of NATO would bind the U.S. to assist Turkey. The President of Turkey stood in front of the Turkish embassy directing his armed security to beat Kurdish protestors including many women while the press recorded him watching with glee as the beatings took place. This criminal should have immediately been arrested for criminal conspiracy, assault and attempted murder. He belongs in jail and the country of Turkey needs to apologize for his actions.

Sample Homework 3.5B Portraying the Structure

Portray the structure (underline, bracket, number, tree diagram) of the arguments found in the following passages. (Hint: Whenever you use tree diagrams you will need an index of claims.)

1. Arabic numbers did not come from Arab countries. Arabic numbers originated in India. The Indians had what are now known as Arabic numerals when they were invaded in 700 BC by the Arabs. The Arabs took that numeric system back with them, where it was 'discovered' by western civilizations many years later.

2. Historically, iron was more precious than gold back. This is because iron only came from meteorites. And in turn meteorites only came from heaven.

3. One would also have to assume that if there are intelligent ET's out there that they are humanoid in nature. For there to be convergent evolution, said aliens would have to have evolved in similar environments or eco system and experience the same random mutation as us. Further, so far none of the earth like planets found are 100% like earth. In the next millennia, the human being as we know it, will

not look like it does today due to gene editing, robotics, radiation etc. Interstellar travel more than likely will be launched from Mars or the Moon. Researchers have stated that Mars humans will be different, genetically and physically from earth humans. Therefore, future humans are the aliens.

4. The Jesuit Order has historically always had a strange relationship with the Church of Rome. Remember, the Order was expulsed from the Church for almost a century, and that was not that long ago. Jesuits were always concerned more with power than they were about faith. I am an alumni of a Jesuit university. You should not attend a Jesuit University.

5. Conservatism is not necessarily pro-Christian. If the founding fathers had been pro-Christian, they would not have separated church and state in the first amendment. Conservatism lets people practice their religion freely but does not allow them to impose it on others. If some religion has a problem with that, then they need to take a walk.